# FINANCIAL
# FREEDOM
# AFLOAT

## HOW TO POCKET
## A PAYCHECK IN PARADISE

# CHARLES TULLER

**ILLUSTRATIONS BY MIMI REHOR**

Seaworthy Publications, Inc.

PORT WASHINGTON, WISCONSIN

*Designed and composed by John Reinhardt Book Design*

Printed in the United States of America.

**Library of Congress Cataloging in Publication Data**

Tuller, Charles, 1963–
    Financial freedom afloat : how to pocket a paycheck in paradise / by Charles Tuller.
      p. cm.
    Includes bibliographical references and index.
    ISBN 1-892399-06-7 (alk. paper)
    1. Finance, Personal. 2. Ocean travel. I. Title.

HG179.T825 2000
332.024–dc21
                                    00-020907
                                         CIP

**Seaworthy Publications, Inc.**
507 Sunrise Drive
Port Washington, Wisconsin 53074
Phone: (262) 268-9250
Fax: (262) 268-9208
e-mail: publisher@seaworthy.com
Web site: http://www.seaworthy.com

This book is dedicated to Maggie Purnell, my wife and sailing partner. Without her help and support the book never would have been written.

Thank you.

# AUTHORS NOTE

All the characters and events in *Financial Freedom aFloat* are based on real people and actual events. However, in the interests of privacy I have occasionally elected to change names and modify minor details in a story. Also, to maintain narrative flow and conciseness I have sometimes compressed or changed the timing of events and once in a while amalgamated two or more characters. To anyone who sees themselves in a narrative, but recognizes minor inconsistencies, I ask pardon for these artistic licenses.

Also, while I have endeavored to be as accurate and objective as possible, any errors or omissions that may have crept in are mine and not to be associated with any of the characters referred to herein."

# ACKNOWLEDGEMENTS

As I was writing *Financial Freedom aFloat* I was often struck by a peculiar sensation. Frequently, I felt not so much like an author, or creator, but rather like a go-between or messenger. I was, I often felt, simply taking the experiences and knowledge of others and repackaging them in a compact form. With that in mind, I would like to thank all the cruising sailors that Maggie and I have met over the years who have shared their experiences, wit, and wisdom with us.

Particularly, I would like to thank Steve and Cathy, Brian and Anne, Russell, Monty and Betsy, and Suzy. Also, Captain Fatty, Thatcher, Vicki, and the crowd at Coral Bay; Forrest and Suzy, Richard, Junior, Joel, and the crowd at Dinner Key; Trevor, Aimee, Michelle, and the crowd in Alcantara; and all the other cruisers, too numerous to mention, who have shown us by their examples just how much is possible. I hope some of you recognize yourselves in this book, and realize that, without you, I would have had nothing to write about.

For the illustrations, grateful thanks to Mimi. For looking over the rough draft, and providing encouragement, thanks to Mindi. To my father, Larry Tuller, a big thank you for proofreading the entire manucript and suggesting many necessary revisions. And last but not least, a big thank you to the people at Seaworthy, who have not only encouraged me throughout this whole project, but have patiently worked with me to create something that will, hopefully, be of value to the cruising community.

Charles Tuller

# CONTENTS

# What Is "Financial Freedom aFloat?"

On first glance the title "Financial Freedom aFloat" may seem self-explanatory. One might think it simply means having enough money to go cruising. However, as it is used in this book, *financial freedom* means the freedom, as a cruising sailor, to know that you can support yourself and your cruising lifestyle, where and how you want. It means freedom from monetary anxieties—pinching pennies or sticking to rigid budgets. It means the freedom to make a cruise more than just a short-term break from shoreside life. It means you can cruise as long as *you* want. Finally, it means the freedom to explore local cultures and get to know the people you meet. You're not just a tourist passing through. So how does one achieve this freedom?

The key to financial freedom, whether afloat or ashore, lies in a combination of two things. On the one hand, it requires keeping expenses down. On the other hand, it means generating an income sufficient to cover expenses. There are already many books on the market that give advice on how to cut costs while cruising. This book is not one of them. It will not address budgeting for cruising, what kind of boats and equipment are best to keep costs down, or how to save money underway.

What this book *will* do is detail the many options that are available for making money underway, either by supplementing an existing income or by paying for the cruise as you go along. Too often would-be cruisers are afraid to take the plunge. The concern and fear of not having enough money to make ends meet keeps many potential cruisers landlocked. This book aims to show that it *can* be done.

Geared toward the long-term cruising sailor, pursuing sailing as a lifestyle, this book focuses not just on sailing as an end in itself; it addresses many of the lifestyle issues that the cruising sailor must deal with. It is not just about how to scrape together cash when it's needed, but rather how to integrate a constructive approach to working and maintaining a cruising life. The book will be of use to cruisers, of all income levels, who wish to get more out of their cruising dream.

Written on three levels, this book, first, is intended as an idea book — a book to inspire dreams. Each chapter is filled with true-life anecdotes and case histories of sailors who have made work and a cruising life, work for them.

Also, each chapter contains detailed, step-by-step instructions on finding work, determining what training is needed and getting it, marketing yourself, and finding the best job. Included are summaries of the good and bad points of working in various fields. If you're interested in a particular line of work, these instructions will give you the information needed to take the next step.

Finally, each chapter is paired with an Appendix at the back of the book. These Appendices provide lists of detailed information and resources for each type of work. They include addresses and contact numbers of organizations that provide training, job placement services, in-depth books, and useful Web sites.

It is my hope that this book will provide the motivation, information, and tools needed for anyone who has ever dreamed of a cruising lifestyle, but thought that financial concerns stood in the way. The book is also for anyone who is cruising now, but is looking for more fulfillment, more security, or more freedom.

# CHAPTER ONE

# WORKING AND CRUISING: A HAPPY MARRIAGE!

Why work while cruising? For most people the idea of working, of "getting a job and making money," is at odds with going sailing. Isn't the whole idea of cruising to get away from the workaday world? If anything, working while cruising is only contemplated by cruisers on a limited budget, who often regard work as something of a last resort. "We'll keep sailing until we're broke, then we'll find something," is pretty much the attitude. This was the case for many years with my wife, Maggie, and myself. After we purchased our boat in the Caribbean, we had very little money left over and had to find work almost immediately. Thereafter, for years, our "cruising kitty" would run out frequently in inopportune places or at inconvenient times, and we would be forced to hunt around for any way to scrape together some cash.

While this "cruise until you're broke" method is possible, it is rarely convenient and is often very stressful. Too often, the times that you run out of money are at the wrong time of year, or in the wrong part of the world. Having to face a winter in the northern latitudes or the hurricane season in an unprotected area of the tropics may be acceptable if you have planned and prepared, but for most of us it is a prospect that we would rather avoid. Also, having to stop and look for work without pre-planning may put you in the position of missing important passage deadlines. For instance, missing the autumn "weather window" to pass from Panama, north to Eastern Central America or the Caribbean, would force you to wait in that country possibly for nine months, or at least to face a heavy slog into the spring trade winds five months later.

Besides having to face inconvenient and possibly dangerous weather, running out of money at the wrong time can also strand you in countries where the work prospects are nil or virtually so. Many developing countries have huge unemployment problems and abominable wages, while their better-off northern neighbors often have tight immigration policies and strict work visa requirements. Also, as anyone who has

*Out of funds . . . out of luck.*

unexpectedly lost a job knows, the worst time to find a job is when you really need one. While you might see all kinds of prospects for work while you're still solvent, once you're broke and/or desperate you can be sure that whatever comes your way will be strictly the bottom of the barrel.

So, you might ask, why bother trying to work while cruising at all? Why not stick with my job until I can save X amount of money, which will last me for Y years, then take off and enjoy myself. After all, isn't cruising about getting away from the stress of the work world? Given the choice, why deliberately put myself back in a stressful situation?

All good questions, and that is what this book will address. For, as much as I believe that looking for work in desperate straits should be avoided, I also feel that work can be both a productive and enjoyable adjunct to a cruising lifestyle. This may seem a heresy to those reared on the traditional sailing literature that emphasizes escaping the "rat race" of modern life.

## MORE THAN AN ESCAPE

In the seventies and early eighties there was a generation of sailors who, with woefully inadequate planning, bought boats and went cruising in order to "drop out" of traditional society. They left filled with the admirable, if misguided, ideals of the hippy culture. Thinking that they could make a life off coconuts and fish, off love and goodwill, they inevitably found themselves stranded in some tropical backwater with little or no chance of earning money or of maintaining either their boat or their cruising life. In the mid-eighties we encountered these sailors throughout the Caribbean. Far from escaping the pressures of society, they often found themselves having to sell their boats for a pittance and return to the drudgery of their previous lives, or worse still, having to resort to stealing or smuggling to support their counterculture ideals.

By the early nineties, another generation of sailors arrived in the tropics. Refugees from the corporate belt-tightening of the late eighties, these were the people who inspired the term "yuppie." They were not concerned with trying to support themselves day-to-day like the "hippies." This generation had prepared themselves with well-found boats and generally good sailing skills. They too, though, had bought into the idea of "sailing away" as an end in itself. They thought, because it was what they read in all the books, that the cruising life should be, more or less, a perpetual vacation—the thrill and challenge of sailing interspersed with sight-seeing and socializing. These sailors found though, that after a year or two, the novelty of all this paled, and they were soon looking for a more rewarding life. In fact they often returned to their old jobs. Similarly disenchanted are many of the older retiree sailors. Many, many times Maggie and I have come to know older couples who, though they hate to admit it, are bored with their cruising dream but don't know what else to do.

The fault for all of these situations lies in the idea of trying to "escape work." One of the great aspects of the sailing life is that it gives you the freedom and perspective to look at things in a new light. You do, in fact, step outside of the traditional "system." This can be a powerful tool to allow you to redirect and focus your energies. The increased time and freedom can be used to examine your goals and feelings in ways that are simply too often impossible in our hectic society. Freed from the pressures and constraints of the nine to five world, the cruising sailor can develop new interests and explore old ones.

In this book we will examine these options under the broad title of "work"—intending much more than simply making money. In this context, work can be both a means to an end and an end in itself. Even for those without the need to earn money, having some productive occupation can stimulate the mind, improve self image, and often benefit others. In a broader sense, as more cruising sailors focus on "working" in some fashion, they will find themselves disbursing their skills to both the sailing community and the cultures in which they travel. People who choose this lifestyle tend to be talented, motivated people, so why not share the wealth? This is powerful stuff. It can engender a two-way interchange that will lift cruising sailors beyond the role of mere tourists.

As we lurch into the 21st century, the overall question of work, and its place in our lives, is becoming increasingly topical. Many industrialized countries are struggling with persistent unemployment and underemployment problems. Many people have found that despite what they were told in school, a long-term job or career just may not be available. In many ways, the cruising sailor has already sidestepped these concerns. In the cruising life one rarely looks for guarantees or long-term anything. Also, the two things that make for marketability in the sailing world—a diversity of skills and a flexibility in one's attitude towards work—are exactly what people may find they need in the shifting sands of the new century. Perhaps we as cruising sailors are leading the way to a new definition of work and its place in our lives.

Over the years, my wife and I have met many people who have shown us, through their examples, just what is possible. One of our great joys is to keep in touch with our cruising friends and follow them on their personal peregrinations through the years. It's always fascinating how cruisers carve out their unique niches in this amorphous society. Three special couples, who have inspired us by their examples, come to mind. For different reasons we "clicked" immediately with each of them and have kept in touch through all of our travels. I would like to introduce you to them and follow their stories throughout this book. They have, in three very different ways, all evolved their own solutions to the dilemmas of how to integrate working and cruising.

## THREE COUPLES

We first met John and Paula many years ago in the Bay Islands of the Western Caribbean, and we quickly became good friends. We swapped stories and, as always, were interested to hear how they came to be where they were.

As they related it, a few years earlier they had both been working in the urban sprawl of Los Angeles and had decided it was time to make a change. Both in their mid 40s, they were dynamic, motivated people but had the sense, as they neared the "big 50," that their lives were accelerating out of their control. The urban professional world and all its trappings of success just did not thrill them that much anymore, and increasingly they felt that they were working just to maintain their equilibrium, with little time for reflection or constructive change. They felt that what they needed was not more *things* but more *time*.

They both had successful careers, he as a public relations executive and she as an accountant. Recently, though, John's company had been downsized, and it did not look like he would be able to find another acceptable job without relocating. This had provided the impetus to go sailing. They had been hooked by the sailing lifestyle a few years earlier after a couple of bareboat charters, first in the Caribbean, then, more adventurously, in Polynesia. They figured why go through the stress of moving just to get another job, when instead, they could chuck it all and live the life of their dreams. They had read scores of books, subscribed to the right magazines, and even purchased their dream boat, or as close to it as they could afford. Paula, however, was still rather worried about the money.

Unfortunately, John's previous divorce and some untimely investments had taken the wind out of their financial sails. While they were comfortable at the moment, neither Paula, nor John if he was being honest with himself, saw how they could take off for an extended cruise on the small income they could generate. They could rent out their house. They had a few investments. But from everything they'd read, they figured they would need between 25- and 50-percent more income—if they were to avoid tapping into their capital. Even if they did want to work as they sailed, John realized there wasn't much call for PR men in the Caribbean or accountants in the South Pacific. What was their solution?

Steve and Irene, whom we met in the Virgin Islands, told a very different story. Twenty years younger than John and Paula, they were very much in love. We found their carefree, optimistic outlook refreshing. Although they owned nothing but the boat they sailed, they appeared to have few worries and eagerly awaited their first child. How had they arrived where they were?

The couple met on a beach in south Florida four years earlier. He worked as a windsurfing instructor. She was enjoying spring break from the university. After she graduated, they moved in together on a strong but rather scruffy steel sloop. Steve had picked it up for next to nothing from a stone-broke French sailor who wanted to go home. They found a free anchorage in which to moor and adopted a stray kitten marooned on an abandoned boat.

For the next three years, while they slowly outfitted their dream boat, they scrimped and scrounged in the boatyards of southern Florida. Despite an expensive Ivy League degree in modern history, Steve found that he was good with his hands. He developed a reputation as a hard worker and progressed from scraping boat bottoms to working as an assistant to a successful marine electrician who catered mainly to the well-heeled sportfishing fleet. Irene worked evenings as a waitress. She spent her days at the beach painting intricate, romantic scenes and dreaming of South Seas islands.

Finally, after years of pinching pennies and sweating bullets, their boat was ready to take them away. They were both aching to escape the banality of their Stateside existence, and yearned for the romantic freedom they had read about in all the classic sailing stories. Their only concern, and it was a big one, was money. Unlike the days of Bernard Moitessier or Tristan Jones, it seemed like now you needed a fistful of dollars to exist anywhere.

Working in the boatyards, Steve gossiped regularly with sailors returning home from the Bahamas or the Caribbean. They were usually sailing on boats whose electronics alone were worth more than his and Irene's entire boat. Worse still, these sailors told tales of how cheap groceries were in Florida and how expensive everything was "down island." These sailors' cruising budget, usually from a hefty retirement pension, was more than Steve and Irene could ever hope to earn Stateside, let alone in a foreign country. Also Steve had met many West Indian boatyard workers who had come to the U.S. precisely because they could not get work in their own countries. What chance did a young couple like Steve and Irene have to support themselves abroad? Perhaps it was best to stay where they were. Perhaps it was best to save their money until they had enough to live on, for a while. But that could take years! They were young, full of energy, and they wanted to go now! What to do?

Kent and Jan were at the opposite end of the cruising spectrum. They were sailing north, and Maggie and I on our way south, when we got to know them during the Carnival extravaganza in Trinidad. As we caroused with them through the mayhem of Port of Spain, they acted more like a couple in their 40s than their 60s. Through the course of several nights at the Trinidad Yacht Club bar, we came to hear their story. As we got to know them better, what set them apart from most other retiree sailors we'd met became apparent. It was their contagious enthusiasm. But as Kent told it, this had not always been so.

At age 61, an early and well-earned retirement freed Kent to pursue his dream. For years, as he worked his way up the ladder at a major U.S. auto company, Kent dreamed about the freedom of the sea. He kept a boat on Lake Michigan but was too busy to take it out more than once or twice a year. And, his previous wife had never cared much for sailing.

When he retired, and remarried, Kent decided not to put off his dream any longer. He sold his oversized house, the overpriced cars, the sailboat on the lake, and moved to Florida to live his dream with his new love, Jan. After a brief search, the couple found their dream boat. However, since Jan insisted on having most of their shoreside conveniences at sea, they spent another year subsidizing the marine trade community in Fort Lauderdale.

Then, like hundreds of other boaters every year, Kent and Jan set sail down the cruising path to the Caribbean. They saw dolphins and caught fresh tuna. They sipped rum punches at countless beachfront bars. They learned how to handle their boat and how to avoid bad weather. In the cockpits of other sailboats and at potluck dinners in the marinas, they passed innumerable nights swapping tales. Kent and Jan successfully made their way as far south as Trinidad and were getting ready to sail north again. But, though they were both loath to admit it, after some time, this life was just not as much fun as when they'd first set sail.

Kent had been a successful executive precisely because he had a lot of drive. Challenge stimulated him. In his years at the company, he

faced countless crises, and quite frankly reveled in his ability to sur-
mount them. His desire to go sailing and challenge himself was a logical extension of these traits. Jan had married Kent because of this, and
because she herself found the idea of change and growth exciting.
After too many years stuck in a unsatisfying marriage to a mediocre
salesman, she saw Kent as a ticket to a new and better life.

Kent and Jan's first few years of sailing fulfilled their dreams: new
challenges, unexpected beauty, intense and unaffected friendships. Now
though, the newness and challenge, which had stimulated them both
in the beginning, was waning. Increasingly, they found the topics of
their evening get-togethers as boringly predictable as the corporate
cocktail parties they'd left behind. Grocery prices, boat gear, breakdowns, and petty crime seemed to be the recurring themes that dominated their days. Also, after more than three years of sight-seeing, they
were both getting tired of feeling like perpetual outsiders, like voyeurs.
They felt that for all the time they'd spent in the islands, they still did
not understand the culture. They could not think of one local person
they would really consider a friend. They realized that they were moving in an isolated, floating community.

Ten years younger than Kent, Jan had spent most of her life working. First, she taught elementary school. Then, she taught piano. Finally, she worked as a volunteer in a local literacy program. Now, in
what should have been paradise, although she hated to admit it, Jan
was starting to feel a creeping sense that she was losing her motivation.
Day-after-tropical-day passed by. It seemed the days were all blending
together: cooking, sight-seeing, drinks in the evening, occasionally interspersed with a sail to a new island, then the same routine again and
again. It would sound crazy to her friends back in the States. Wasn't
this just the kind of monotonous routine that she had wanted to escape when she lived Stateside?

Kent was experiencing similar feelings, although he was doing his
best to force them out of his conscious mind. After all, wasn't he living
his dream? How many of his ex-colleagues would give their eyeteeth
(though maybe not their pensions) to be in his position: captain of his
own boat, moored in a beautiful, sun-drenched, tropical bay. And what
did he want to do? Go back to a retirement ghetto in Florida? Spend
his life on the golf course? Spend his days in restaurants, surrounded
by all the other pensioned off corporate soldiers? No, he didn't want to
give up the sailing life, with all the advantages and attractions he'd

*Another day in paradise?*

found. But he did thirst for new challenges. He thirsted for something that would hold his interest the way learning to navigate, scuba dive, or repair his diesel engine had in the beginning.

He thought of sailing across the Atlantic, as a new rung up the cruising ladder. But, though he would admit it to no one but himself, the sails were getting harder to hoist, and the night watches longer. Pushing 70, Kent was looking for something that would challenge his brain, not his brawn, such as it was. Plus, neither he nor Jan really wanted to leave the tropics. Life back in the cold weather just didn't appeal to them any more. But what to do?

All three couples had faced, as they described it to us, the question of how to integrate some form of work into their cruising lifestyles. John and Paula were looking for a way to supplement a small income with, as they saw it, few marketable skills. Steve and Irene had only minimal savings. They needed to support themselves but didn't know what the options were away from the U.S. And, they did not want to needlessly risk the little security they had. Kent and Jan didn't need to work to make money, but found, that despite its undeniable attractions, the cruising life just did not fully satisfy them. Perhaps there was something more?

## OTHER REASONS FOR WORKING

There are many reasons, other than the quandaries faced by these three couples, why someone would want to work while cruising. Some people may be looking for a new or second career. Others might want

*Finding his niche at last.*

to explore some skill or talent that they just don't seem to have time for lately. In our competitive, success-oriented society, there is often too much emphasis on visible "results" and not enough time to pursue "nonproductive" occupations. One can't simply leave a job as, let's say, a bank manager, take a few years off to play the sax, then expect to come back to any sort of career. Not to mention the financial drain incurred from trying to support a traditional lifestyle "ashore"—without the income of a "real" job.

However, if one has decided to live a cruising lifestyle, many concerns are lifted. With even a small, regular income, the money that you need to generate from your "new" career is minimal. The sailing life simply does not require the same kind of overhead as a traditional modern existence. Also, concerns of maintaining a career path, a respectable resumé, or keeping up with the Joneses all vanish. This can be a profound freedom for one accustomed to the rigor's of the modern workplace.

Our friend Bob had been trained as a dentist and worked in that career for ten, unsatisfying years. It was not until he went sailing and started exploring his talents, however, that he found that what he really enjoyed was repairing sails. While his family and friends back in New York were aghast that he would "throw away" his expensive education, the sailing community was happy to have a new artisan. He found that with a low-stress work load he was able to support himself comfortably in the adventurous, nomadic life that he loved.

There are also people who may have budgeted enough money for a cruise of a certain duration but find that the restraints of always sticking to a rigid budget limit their enjoyment. Having some source of extra income while you're sailing can often mean the difference between just existing and really living. Often it is that extra little bit that allows you to take advantage of cultural offerings, local restaurants, or entertainment that you would have otherwise gone without.

When we recently spent the winter in Lisbon, I was luckily able to keep a small income coming in by teaching English to local businessmen. It allowed Maggie and I to take advantage of concerts, restaurants, and classes that made the winter much more enjoyable. It would have been a different story had we spent months cooped up in the winter rain, unable to spend money on anything but the essentials! We have met many people on a "round the world" sail who have missed

*Living too frugally can mean missed opportunities.*

what were probably once-in-a-lifetime opportunities because of the necessity of sticking to a fixed budget.

Finally, there is no better way of learning or using a language than having to make a living using it. There are many would-be cruisers who study a language before leaving, often Spanish or French, only to find that, through laziness or just normal inhibition, they hardly ever use it. Getting out and working with a language quickly overcomes these barriers.

Our friend Russell was a diesel mechanic by trade, and hardly a language scholar, when he arrived in Guatemala. He saw, however, the opportunity to make serious money working on the sportfishing fleet of the local Spanish-speaking businessmen, so he quickly boned up on the language. Never one for learning out of books, he acquired most of his knowledge from his assistant, who spoke no English. Soon he was speaking like a local and enjoying his contacts with the new culture immensely. In fact, within a few years he had successfully wooed, courted, and married a beautiful Spanish-speaking woman from one of the local "families!"

While many people we've met have "fallen into" their new careers, there are many others onshore who are just not interested in stepping off the cliff without knowing what waits at the bottom. Certainly having some idea, in advance, of what might realistically be expected from the sailing job market would lift a lot of anxiety from people's minds. That, in essence, is what we aim to do with this book.

## KNOW YOURSELF

The first step, for those interested in pursuing the idea of working while sailing is to realistically assess your strengths, talents, and skills. Unlike the shoreside job market, where following one trade is the path to success, in the cruising world, diversity is strength. The more "arrows in your quiver," the better chance you have of profiting from opportunities when they arise. You need to think open-mindedly about where your skills and interests lie, so you can focus on and exploit them.

To help you focus on specific skill areas, we have provided a simple "Skills Questionnaire" on page 17. For each skill listed, think of relevant experiences you have had, and give yourself as objective a rating as possible. Don't sell yourself short or think about what is "marketable." Think about what you would do if you had all the time and money in the world. Think about what you're good at, and what you'd like to be good at. Be honest!

As a *general guideline* you can figure that if you score over 25, you will be very marketable in the cruising lifestyle. A score of 20 to 25 means that you will probably have several choices of work options, but will have to use some creativity in finding employment. The range of 15 to 20 means that your choices for work are fairly limited, but again, with creativity, you should be able to find something to suit you. A score of less than 15 would tend to indicate that your skills are concentrated in one area. Don't be discouraged though and assume that means you won't find any work.

Of more interest than the totals, really, are the areas in which you rated yourself a two or three. Make a note of these, and keep them in mind, as we look at the actual opportunities that exist while cruising. Your responses to this questionnaire will hopefully get you to think about strengths you've taken for granted or interests you've been meaning to pursue, but haven't yet had a chance. As you read through the following chapters, keep these in mind.

To sum things up, if you can see in yourself any of the following desires, you are probably interested in working while cruising in some fashion:

➤ The desire to use your boat now rather than wait until you have X amount in the bank

➤ The desire to supplement a regular income that is too small to live on, even while cruising

➤ The desire to have more freedom while you are sailing, so that you don't have to feel that you're pinching every penny

➤ The desire to start a new or second career that is just not feasible in your present circumstances

➤ The desire to explore an area of talent or interest that you have not had time for in your current situation

➤ The desire to interact more with the cultures in which you will be (or are) traveling

➤ The desire to stimulate your mind with new challenges

➤ The desire to enhance your self-esteem by being active and productive

➤ The desire to alleviate a sense of boredom or repetition in your cruising life

➤ The desire to learn a new language or really practice a language that you have learned

**Do you have skills (experience) or aptitude (talent) in these areas?**

| Working With Your Hands | | Professional Skills | | Artistic Areas | | Language Skills | |
|---|---|---|---|---|---|---|---|
| Sewing | | Medical | | Painting/Drawing | | | |
| Cooking | | Computer | | Decorating | | | |
| Carpentry | | Accounting/Financial | | Music | | | |
| Electrical | | Teaching | | Total | | | |
| Mechanical | | Sales | | | | | |
| Painting | | Writing | | | | | |
| Home Maintenance | | Restaurant Work | | | | | |
| Craft Work | | | | | | | |

**Scoring: 0=No Knowledge, 1=Some Knowledge, 2=Good Knowledge, 3=Expert.**

# CHAPTER TWO

# THE JOYS OF BOAT WORK

I remember Irene telling us about her first job varnishing for money. She and Steve had finally made the decision to leave the U.S. They had put a couple of thousand dollars in the bank, and Steve had convinced Irene that the Virgin Islands offered as good a chance for employment as Florida. After all, it was still a U.S. Territory, and they could both work there legally. They planned to work their way leisurely down through the Bahamas, keeping an eye out for employment possibilities, and hoped to arrive in the Virgin Islands before the start of hurricane season.

After waiting for the right weather, Steve and Irene finally crossed the Gulf Stream to the Bahamas. It was the first time there for both of them and they were stunned by the beauty and solitude of the islands. It was springtime and they were in no hurry. As they slowly picked their way through the myriad uninhabited cays of the Little Bahama Bank, they thought to themselves, this is why we went sailing.

Every day they were off, over the side of the boat, scouring the reefs in search of something for the table. Fish, conch, lobster, whatever they found would be landed and cooked, tasting fresh as only food caught with their own hands could. The days drifted by, turning into weeks. Two months after they left Florida, they hit Marsh Harbor, the first town of any significance. By then they both had allover tans and were as at home in the water as out of it. They were at peace with each other and in tune with the boat. The stock of groceries was getting a bit low though, and they thought they had better stop and provision.

Even after the stories they'd heard in the States, the prices in Marsh Harbor came as a shock. After parting with 200 of their carefully-hoarded dollars, Irene walked out of the store with three not especially large bags of groceries. In a flash, her money anxieties were back. That night, over drinks with Steve, she brought up the idea of trying to find a job. A bit skeptical about the chances of finding any-

thing in this backwater town, Steve told her that as far as he was concerned, she could go ahead and look around. He had several little
jobs to do on the boat, so there would be no reason to rush on.

Irene suggested they go into the waterfront bar and talk to some of
the other sailors about what work action there was around town. At
four dollars for a drink, Steve didn't see how that made sense. Weren't
they trying to save money, not spend it?

"You've gotta spend money to make it," Irene countered. "Think of
it as an investment."

"All right," said Steve, "but just for one drink."

It turned out that Irene's instincts were right. That night they met
another young couple who had been doing some varnish work, but
who were now getting ready to move down-island.

"But be careful," Dotty, who'd been doing the work cautioned Irene.
"This guy pays, but he's very picky. You done this work before?"

"Yeah, some." Irene thought of the interior varnish she'd touched
up on their boat. "A little bit here and there. It's not rocket science,
you know."

"Yeah you're right there. It's sure not rocket science," chuckled Dotty,
as she ordered another drink.

Eyeing her and Steve's empty glasses, Irene got up to go. "So, I ask
for a Mr. Myer on *My Toy II*, that big sportfishing boat at the yacht
club?" asked Irene.

"Yeah, I'll tell him you'll be coming. And Irene..."

"Yeah?"

"Good luck, huh?"

"Yeah, thanks Dotty. Hope we see you down the road."

"Me too. Bye now."

"Bye-bye," called Irene as she and Steve went out into the night.

"Isn't that great Steve? We're just here a couple days, and we've
already got a job. Doesn't seem so hard huh?"

"No, guess we just lucked into it. You gonna go over and see that
guy tomorrow?"

"Might as well. No point in procrastinating. Someone else might
get the job."

The next day Irene put on her "boatwork" clothes, old jeans and a
T-shirt, and set off in the dinghy at about 9:00 a.m. She knew the boat
Dotty had been referring to—a big 52-foot Bertram sportfisher that
was tied up at the small Marsh Harbor Yacht Club dock. When she

knocked on the hull, a voice called out, "C'mon aboard!" She stepped over the gleaming cap rail into a huge sportfishing cockpit, complete with fighting chair and a brace of designer fishing rods that was probably worth as much as her whole boat.

"You're Irene, the girl Dotty told me about." It was a statement not a question from the trim, grey haired man stepping out of the salon. "She stopped by 'bout half an hour ago. Told me she had a replacement. Myer, Tom Myer," he said, as he stuck out his hand.

"Irene," she replied, shaking his hand.

"Right. Glad to meet you. Done much varnishing before? Course you have. Not rocket science anyway. So, what I've got is this rail that needs recoating." Myer pointed to the slick cap rail that looked, to Irene at least, like it had just been varnished. "Few nicks and gouges. Etch those out. Give it a sand and a coat. No need to make a big deal out of it. Okay?"

Irene nodded.

"Varnish is inside on the table, sandpaper, rags, should be everything you need. It's all the stuff Dotty was using. Anything else you need, let me know. Fridge, microwave, if you want to heat up your food. Help yourself to a Coke, if you want, but don't touch my beer." He smiled, a joke. "I'll give you what I was giving Dotty, twelve dollars an hour. Keep track of your hours. I'll pay you at the end of the job. Is that okay?"

Irene nodded again.

"Right, any questions? Sorry to rush, but I've got a golf date at ten o'clock, I'll be back this afternoon. Anything else?"

Feeling a bit overwhelmed, Irene shook her head. "No, I can't think of anything."

"All right, see you later."

Myer ducked back into his boat, grabbed a canvas shoulder bag, and headed off onto the dock. Irene stood there, bemused, feeling that everything had happened too fast. As the sun climbed into the cloudless sky, the cockpit began to heat up, and in the glare of the white deck, she realized that she should have worn a hat.

Etching. She tried to remember what she had heard about etching. Myer had said that she should etch out the nicks in the rail. Now she remembered. Back in Florida one of her friends had mentioned the word. It involved some sort of scraping, with a razor blade she thought. Irene entered the cabin and looked around. There, on the spotless designer table, someone had spread a couple of towels and resting on them were several cans, sandpaper, brushes, and, yes, a package of single-edge razor blades. Okay, she'd start with that.

Slowly Irene worked her way around the rail. Although she hadn't noticed them at first, there were many small cracks and dings in the varnish. As carefully as she could, she scraped away at each one until she had reached bare wood. The sun was high now, and the white deck was brutally hot. The rail seemed to go on forever. The more she looked, it seemed, the more spots she found that needed etching. Keep at it, she told herself Remember, twelve U.S. dollars an hour, every hour.

Finally, she reached the end, that is, where she had begun, and she was ready to start sanding. This went faster, and as she worked, she remembered that she had forgotten to pack a lunch. No matter. She'd just carry on and grab a Coke later. She imagined that Tom Myer would be pleased with her progress when he returned. By the time she finished sanding and looked at her watch, it was already 2:00 p.m. The white deck was blinding. In fact when Irene first stepped inside the blissfully cool air conditioning of the salon, she could see nothing. Gradually her eyes adjusted, and she made out the refrigerator against the port wall. Reaching inside, she grabbed herself a cold Coke and sank down on the carpeted sole. God! She must really be out of shape. Only half a day of work and she was beat! Still, the preparation was the hardest part, she'd heard. The rest should be a cakewalk.

Irene looked at the varnish on the table. There was the better part of a quart can. Next to it a couple of brushes soaked in thinner. Might as well get right on it she figured. I've probably got enough time to get a coat on today. She polished off her drink.

Outside, the deck was scalding. Even the cap rail was almost too hot too touch. As Irene began to apply the varnish from the can, she noticed that she felt a bit light headed. At first things seemed okay, but as she worked, she noticed that the varnish seemed to be drying on the rail almost as fast as she applied it. She began to hurry. Then, looking down, she noticed a few drips on the pristine deck. Uh oh, she thought, and hurried inside to get a rag. Though she wiped at the spots, they only spread, and she realized that she had forgotten to put thinner on the rag. Hurrying back inside, she knocked the brush off the varnish can, creating another stain. She returned with the can of thinner and more rags and cleaned up the spots that had already started to dry. She went back to varnishing the rail, only to find that it too had dried, and her new varnish pulled and dragged where she had stopped. More varnish seemed to help, so she started applying a thicker coat.

The sun was now nothing short of murderous. Irene's frustration increased as drops of her own sweat ran off her nose and arms and landed on the newly applied varnish. Looking down, she saw more drips on the deck than ever, and as she stopped to wipe them up, she realized that a vicious cycle was developing. The growling in her stomach, the heat, the varnish fumes were all combining to make her feel sick and weak, but she told herself to stick to it. Grimly, she progressed down the rail.

"My God, woman! What're you doing to my boat?" It was Myer, back from the golf match. "I told you to varnish the rail, not the whole damn deck!" he shouted. "Holy cow, there're stains everywhere! And look at this varnish. It looks like crap!" He walked up to where Irene was applying the fresh varnish and ran his hand along the rail. "I don't believe this. You haven't even wiped off the dust! Now what am I going to do? This is a total friggin' disaster!"

Irene gave up. It was all too much. She sat down on the deck and began to cry. She couldn't help herself. She thought that she must look like a real fool. Of course that made her cry even more. Myer looked down at her sitting on the deck, still holding the varnish brush, blubbering that she was sorry, really sorry, and she'd leave, get off his boat. Just give her a few seconds. It would have taken a hard man not to be moved, and at heart he really wasn't too bad. Impatient, yes. Selfish, probably. But, like most men, he couldn't just stand there and watch a woman cry.

"Look, Irene, do you really have much experience with this work?" he asked, his voice softening.

"No. Yes. Well, you know, I've done a little interior varnish on our boat. Not a lot," she confessed, still crying.

"Well," said Myer, with the beginnings of an idea, "would you like to learn? Get some experience, some on the job training as it were."

"Sure." Irene looked up, tears drying, still holding the varnish brush. "You mean you'd keep me on?"

"See, what I thought was this," Myer explained, "I've got a guy, a local guy, who usually does the varnish for me. Lately he's been busy though, and he doesn't mind if I bring in someone else, as long as he's got work. That's why I put Dotty on. Just short time. Now what I thought is... If I could get him, his name's Joe by the way... If I could get Joe to come and finish this rail, and fix up this mess that you've made... Sorry... Well, you could help him out and get some good advice and experience. Mind you, I couldn't pay both of you. But if you want to do more of this kind of work, it's a good way to get started."

Irene was looking at Myer seriously now, thinking over what he'd said. "Yeah, if you'd like to do that, and if Joe will go along with the idea, that'd be fine with me. Look I know I messed up here, but I was doing my best. And, I'd just like to really know what I'm doing."

"Right then. Let's call it a day for now. I'll try to get hold of Joe this evening. Why don't you come by tomorrow. About eleven or twelve o'clock. We'll see what we can put together. Oh, and Irene?"

"Yeah?" she said, expecting some new criticism.

"Maybe you should put that brush in the thinner before it goes hard."

Irene looked down and saw that sure enough, she was still holding the brush that had precipitated all this aggravation. "Right, in it goes." She actually managed a weak grin. Tom Myer, in turn, gave her a smile. It told her that, while her twelve-dollar-an-hour windfall may have just self-destructed, things were, probably, going to end up okay.

"Hey hon, how'd it go? I guess we must be on a roll. I've got great news today too!" Steve was grinning at Irene as she climbed on board their boat from the dinghy.

Not feeling up to explaining her day quite yet, Irene took the easy option and asked Steve, "Great news, what's that?"

"Well, nothing, except that you're not the only one that's working here," Steve replied. "Just after you left, I had a visit from another cruiser, Jake on *Jolly Roger*. Somehow I guess he heard that I had electrical experience, and he wanted to know if I could come over and have a look at his alternator, he said that it wasn't working. You know these fancy boats... Without the damn alternator, they can't do anything. Anyway, I went over and sorted it out for him. Good God, what a mess his wiring is! He was real cool though. After I got the alternator working, we sat around and had a few beers. He said he'd like to have me straighten out some of the other stuff with his system. Looks like about two or three full days of work. Plus, he seems like a nice guy, fun, you know. We had a good time."

I can see you did, thought Irene, irrationally peeved with Steve's good luck. Well, at least *he'd* had a good day.

*Varnish Hell.*

"Be a doll and fix me a rum dear. I'm totally beat."

Irene slumped down in the cockpit and prepared to explain her disastrous day.

"You know," said Steve, chuckling as Irene finished her story, and he fixed them each another drink, "you know, it could have been a lot worse. Myer's no dummy. He'll be getting your work for free now. But he's right too. It is a good way to learn the basics. If this local guy's working for these rich sportfishing clowns, he probably knows what he's doing. And, at least I'll be bringing in some money. I should be able to get $20, maybe even $25 an hour from Jake."

"So you haven't fixed a price with him yet?" A little anxiety from Irene.

"No, not yet, but I've got a good feeling from this guy."

"That's great dear. Hey, since you had such a great day today, would you mind fixing dinner tonight?"

The next day on *My Toy II* was just as hot as before, but now Irene wore her floppy sun hat. She'd also brought a sandwich for lunch. She and Joe sanded down her work from the day before—it really did look pretty horrible. Then they started varnishing. Her job was to wipe down with a tack rag, ahead of Joe, and watch for and clean up drips. All went well. They were able to apply a full coat, and by the end of the day, Irene felt that she was getting the hang of things.

She got back to the boat before Steve and was mellowing out with a rum and lime when he appeared, smiling broadly, in the dinghy of a man she assumed was Jake. He certainly looked like someone who would have a boat named *Jolly Roger*, bearded with a pony tail, dirty T-shirt, and, inevitably, a gold earring. She wondered where the parrot was.

"Right then Steve, thanks for the help, man, I'll catch you tomorrow." Jake grinned as Steve climbed aboard, then he motored off, back to his boat.

"So, good day hon?"

Irene could see that it had been, from Steve's expression.

"Yeah, great. We got a lot done today. Straightened out some real half-assed repairs. Jake's real happy. Said I do more in a day than he could in a month."

"I'm not surprised, judging from the look of him," Irene commented dryly.

"You didn't happen to mention...you know...the money, did you?"

"Yeah, not to worry! He went for $25 an hour, no sweat. Said he was just happy to get the work done."

"Really? That's great. Here, let's toast to prosperity!" Irene passed Steve a dark rum and lime juice, just the way he liked it.

"To prosperity!"

The next morning passed quickly for Irene and Joe on *My Toy II*. By lunchtime, they had easily finished a second coat on the cap rail. Irene had to admit it looked pretty stunning. Joe had kept up a running monologue most of the time, telling her stories of the town and the islands—stories which she found fascinating. He also dropped pearls of wisdom about the finer points of varnishing and the correct way to handle people like Tom Myer. Joe's advice, which Irene pledged to remember: never commit to something you're not completely sure you can handle, especially when working for a wealthy boat owner.

That afternoon, their boss came around. It was obvious he was pleased. "Nice job you two." Myer was looking at the cap rail. "I'd say it's certainly up to your usual standard Joe. How was Irene, she didn't get in your way too much?"

"No sir, she was actually a big help. She did most of the sanding and a lot of the varnishing. I told her that she has a good touch."

"Good, good." Myer looked from one of them to the other. "Look, I don't really need anything else right now. That rail was the last of the touch-up work that Dotty didn't finish. Two coats'll hold it for a while I guess. Look Irene, since Joe says you saved him some time, it's only fair I pay you for your work. Any objection to half-wages for the 'apprenticeship,' six dollars an hour?" A touch of a grin played on his face.

"No, no, that sounds fair to me." Irene was pleasantly surprised that Myer was so scrupulous. He could easily have let her go without paying her a cent, which was in fact what she'd expected. This was a windfall.

"Okay then." Myer was obviously in a hurry, as usual. "Just add up your hours, each of you, and we'll settle up right now. Irene, are you sticking around or moving on?"

"Well, we thought we should push on. We'd really like to be in the Virgin Islands for hurricane season."

"Yeah, right. Well, if you're ever back in this harbor come by. I'll see what I can do. Okay let's get you paid. I've gotta run to a reception at six o'clock."

When she returned to their boat, Irene knew right away that something was wrong. First Steve was home already, second, his smile of the last few days was nowhere to be seen.

"What a lowlife, bilge-sucking, scumbag!!" He didn't even wait for her to get out of the dinghy. "My God, I can't believe the nerve of that guy. You know what happened today...with Mr. *Jolly Roger*, Mister $25-an-hour, Mister-you're-so-efficient?" Steve's voice was scathing.

"What?" asked Irene, although she thought she knew.

"That weasel's gone! He left the harbor! I waited for him to pick me up this morning. He said he'd be by around 10 a.m., or so. Well, when he wasn't here at eleven, I got on the radio and tried to call him. No answer. Somebody else came up though, Jim on *Sea Gypsy*, and he said *Jolly Roger* wasn't anchored next to him any more. Then another boat came up and said that they had seen him pulling up his anchor late last night. Well, I got Jim to give me a lift in to the club, and I started asking around. Not only is he definitely gone, people who know him told me that this isn't the first time he's stiffed somebody. I guess he's got kind of a reputation in the islands, and anyone who does business with him gets cash up front."

"So what can we do now? We can't chase him, not with almost twenty-four hours head start and no idea what direction he went. We can't go to the authorities. You've got no record of any agreement, and

*Stiffed.*

anyway, it was technically illegal for you to be working here. What can we do?" Irene looked at Steve as if he could somehow pull an answer out of a hat.

"Guess we can't really do anything... You know. Just chalk it up to experience. My God, we've sure had our share of experiences this last week. This working and cruising might not be such a piece of cake after all. Well, I know one thing we *should* do."

"What's that dear?"

"Have ourselves a good, stiff drink." Steve ducked below to grab the bottle of rum and a handful of limes as Irene bowed to the inevitable and collapsed against a cockpit cushion. When Steve reappeared she flashed him her irrepressible smile and said, in her best little girl voice, "There's one good thing, dear."

"What's that?" Steve was fixing the drinks.

"Well, that Tom Myer must have felt sorry for me. He ended up paying me anyway." Irene pulled three twenties from her pocket and laid them in front of Steve.

"Well, wha' da ya know," drawled Steve, affecting nonchalance. "I guess my girl's the breadwinner after all." He sat down next to her. As Irene snuggled beneath his arm, they smiled at each other in happy collusion, and began to plan the next leg of their journey.

## WORKING ON OTHER BOATS

One of the most obvious types of employment for cruisers is working on other boats. This is often the first type of work that cruisers fall into as they're traveling. After all, you've spent a lot of time and effort getting your own boat set up for cruising. Unless you are one of those rare souls who has had enough money to hire out all the work, (and usually these are exactly the people who never leave the marina), you will have picked up some marketable skills along the way. Almost anywhere cruising boats gather, you will find others who need some sort of practical work. Also, because you will be working on other yachts, you will, if discreet, rarely be troubled with shoreside regulations. However, as Steve and Irene discovered, working in a foreign port for people you don't know also involves risks and requires some foresight. Let's look at some of the lessons they learned that are applicable to anyone in this position.

### KNOW YOUR SKILLS—KNOW YOUR CUSTOMERS

There are several things that Irene could have done to avoid her debacle with Tom Myer. Obviously, if she'd been an experienced varnisher, she would never have gotten into trouble, but even with her rudimentary skills, she could still have found a good situation. If she had first admitted, to herself and to Dotty, just how sketchy her background was, she would probably never have started with Myer. As a beginner, it's not wise to start off with a top-dollar client. Nonetheless, there were probably other cruisers in the harbor who would have been happy to have her assist them with varnishing or painting, though for less money. On the other hand, if you are very competent, don't be shy about marketing yourself that way, especially to the high rollers.

## DON'T RUSH IT

Irene was so excited to get a job right away that she neglected one of the cardinal rules of working in new places: spend some time to get the lay of the land. By asking around, she would have found out more about Myer, his fussiness and impatience. It's never a bad idea either to talk to the locals who are working on boats. Joe could have provided her with loads of good information.

If you need to slink around hiding from the local workers you are probably competing with them too directly and are heading for trouble anyway. An excellent situation can be to work with a local person who has the lay of the land already.

Of course Steve should also have asked around before starting with Jake. If he had heard about the guy's reputation, he could still have worked for him, just been careful to get paid daily.

## DON'T COLD SHOULDER THE LOCALS

Irene was lucky that Myer had already gotten the okay from Joe to bring someone else on the job. All too often though, cruisers come into a port and either inadvertently or deliberately step on the toes of the local workers. Remember, it's their turf, and you can only get into trouble if you antagonize them. One option to avoid friction is to pitch yourself to a different market. Say, like Joe, the local guys don't want to work for sailors because they're too cheap, or they don't want to do small jobs because they're too busy. If you take up the slack, they're unlikely to complain. As long as there are no complaints from their own people, and as long as you keep a low profile, the immigration authorities will usually not bother with someone working casually on other boats.

Now let's take a look, category by category, at the different types of work that are available on other yachts.

## BOAT MAINTENANCE, DETAILING, AND VARNISHING

For better or worse it would be very unusual if in the course of outfitting your own boat you had not picked up the skills of painting, varnishing, and what's known as "boat detailing," that is polishing, waxing and cleaning. None of these are skills that require years to master, although neither are they something that you would want to make into a full-time career. Nevertheless, wherever you find yachts, you will find boats in need of these services.

With this low-level work, there is a distinct difference in how marketable your services will be in different countries. This depends primarily on the country's standard of living. In short, in countries with a low standard of living, and low wages, there is invariably a cadre of eager locals willing to paint, varnish and clean for a pittance. Unless you are very strapped for money, and hopefully you never will be, it is just not worth your while to compete with a local person in order to earn three, four, or even five dollars a day. On the other hand, in countries with a high wage scale, you may find it quite easy to live on what you can make working for "minimum wage." Also in many of these developed countries there are a greater number of yachts requiring maintenance services than there are workers. The locals have all the work they need and will not feel that you are taking bread from their mouths.

In general, when looking for these kind of jobs, you will do well to go where the fancier private yachts hang out. These boats are often carrying on a continual maintenance program and are looking to hire casual labor in almost every port. Again, in ports where wages are high, there is often an incentive to hire from other cruising yachts and avoid paying for somebody's ostensible "overhead."

An excellent practice, if you're serious about finding work, is to spend some money and take a slip in a fancy marina for a month. Though, as a simple cruising sailor, the idea of staying in such a place would never ordinarily cross your mind, this is one of the quickest ways to make contacts with the kind of boat owners and professional skippers who are the best clients. Being actually docked at the marina gives you full-time access to the "posh" yachts in a way that you could never achieve otherwise. This is an excellent tactic to use, in fact, when pursuing any type of work on other yachts. Believe me, the money invested in a month's dockage will be repaid several fold in better wages and more work.

## MARKETING YOURSELF

As we mentioned before, it is best to spend a week, at least, getting the lay of the land and a feel for how much tact is needed in pursuing work. Invariably, if prospects are good in a port, you will soon meet other cruisers working in a similar fashion. They will often provide you with an entree into the market. Failing that, try to find a local bar where the crews from the larger yachts hang out. Many times a professional skipper does the hiring. He may be busy with his responsibilities during the day thus more open to solicitation over a few beers at night. These guys are usually recognizable by their designer sunglasses, white Polo shirts, navy shorts, and deck shoes. If you are going to be working for the high-class crowd, it is not a bad idea to have at least one set of "blue and whites."

If after a few nights in the bar you haven't met anyone, try direct solicitation around the boats. Here it is essential to be neat and clean in your appearance, and to remember that on the big boats, one is judged very much by first impressions. If you present yourself as a well-groomed professional, and not just another cruiser looking for a job, it will go a long way towards landing a position. After all, varnishers are not that difficult to find, and a big bucks skipper is much more likely to hand the job to somebody who blends in with the rest of the spiffy crew. That being said, the pay on these fancy boats is often quite good, frequently one hundred dollars a day for basic varnishing, cleaning, and polishing. Remember, when your talking to the big-dollar crowd, you're never just "cleaning" a yacht, you're "detailing" it!

## THE MARINE TRADES

A step beyond general boat maintenance are the marine trades: sewing, carpentry, mechanical, electrical and refrigeration work. If you are lucky enough to already be accomplished in one of these trades, you will probably already know something of the market. If not, there are several ways that you can prepare yourself to work in these fields. The pay is almost always better than general maintenance jobs, and importantly, there is much more flexibility in where you can work. Look back at the Skills Questionnaire and see how you rated yourself in the Manual Skills department. Do you have a background in tinkering on cars, sewing, or fixing things around the house? If so there is a good chance that you already have the aptitude and some of the skills needed to begin working in the marine trades. Let's take a look now at each trade in turn.

## MARINE SEWING

If you have a background in domestic sewing, you are already well on your way to having your own marine business. Marine sewing consists of three fields: sail work, canvas work, and upholstery work. What's encouraging is that these types of sewing jobs require less intricate work and considerably less detail than what you will have become accustomed to if you've been sewing clothes onshore. All you need to do is learn the vocabulary and the tricks of working with the new materials, and you'll find yourself in the position of being able to command good money in a very salable trade.

The marketability of the three different sewing fields differs considerably, so it may be wise for you to specialize. Sail work, for example, really lends itself best to a fully equipped loft. While it is quite possible to effect small repairs on board, the physical bulk of sails, and the amount of specialized hardware and fabrics that are needed to market yourself as a real sailmaker, or even repairer, mean that usually you can not compete with a shoreside operation, even if their prices are higher. This does not rule out the odd repair in out-of-the-way areas where there is no loft onshore. But, if you do plan on making a career in sail work, you should really plan on being shore-based.

Quite the opposite is true of marine canvas work. Most marine canvas items (splash guards, biminis, dodgers, sail covers) are certainly of a size that is feasible to work with on board. A surprising number of boaters opt for the same colors, so carrying a stock of two or three of the most popular (navy blue, forest green, and maroon are good choices) is also fairly easy. The hardware for marine canvas work is not too various or expensive and can be easily stored. So equipped, and with a good machine (more on this later) you can tackle probably ninety percent of people's requests from an on board workshop. For some reason, it seems like canvas work is something that people are always wanting to either add to or improve on their boats, and in the tropics at least, nothing lasts more than a few years.

I remember when we were in the Virgin Islands in the mid 1980s we arranged to have a dodger made by Sandy. She and her husband had left Canada several years earlier, and she was making a steady

| | Advantages | Disadvantages |
| --- | --- | --- |
| Sailmaking and Repair | Good Pay<br>Possible to find work worldwide in established lofts<br>Good way to save money on your own sails | Requires an expensive machine to work commercially on your own boat<br>Materials are specialized and bulky |
| Canvas Work | Can be done onboard relatively easily<br>Supplies are not too diverse or bulky<br>Easy to find small jobs almost any time | Moderately expensive machine<br>Big projects like awnings may be too cumbersome to do on board |
| Marine Upholstery | Only requires a good domestic machine<br>Few specialty supplies needed<br>Most similar to domestic sewing | May be more competition from locals and/or lower wages |

income with her sewing. She was so popular in the Virgin Islands that we had to wait three weeks for her to start on our job. All her work was done from their 30-foot sloop. She told me that she rarely needed to make contacts when they came into a port, as word of her talents would already have spread through the cruising grapevine. She told us that she enjoyed her projects, and she especially enjoyed the freedom of being able to choose how much, or little, she wanted to work.

Marine upholstery is also very popular in countries that have distinctive local fabrics. Most of this kind of work consists of recovering cushions below decks. This is, basically, simply making a tightly fitting slip cover with a zipper or snap closure, and it's simpler than traditional furniture upholstery. An advantage with this work is that you only need to carry some good marine hardware (zippers, snaps, grommets, and such), then buy the fabric locally. Again, many times, we have seen that once the first job is done, other boaters come out of the woodwork with similar projects.

The table on page 33 summarizes the advantages and disadvantages of the different varieties of marine sewing.

## HOW TO GET STARTED

The best way to learn about the specifics of each of these types of marine sewing is to spend some time working in a canvas shop or sail loft before you set sail. These lofts usually have a fairly high turnover of workers, as they too leave to go sailing, and anyone with a background in domestic sewing should not have a hard time landing a job. In a few months working with professionals, you can gain invaluable experience.

Another way to gain experience is by working on projects for your own boat. The Sailrite Company publishes an excellent catalogue (see Appendix A) that sells virtually everything the do-it-yourselfer could want for sail, canvas, and upholstery work. They also have some excellent books that provide instruction in these fields.

Once you start working on your own, whether for others or just for yourself, you will need to make a decision on what machine to buy. For upholstery work, a good domestic machine will do fine. Some of the better models even do a serviceable job on canvas work. I have had an Elna brand (Swiss made) domestic machine for the last seven years and have done all the upholstery and canvas work on our boat with it. Nonetheless, for professional results with marine canvas, you need to move up to a machine with a *walking foot*. This means that the presser foot raises and lowers automatically and helps the machine advance the material—a critical feature when working with bulky canvas or slick sailcloth. Good brands are Reed's, Thompson's, and Singer. Some of these machines can be driven by a hand crank (useful in an emergency), and they often offer the option of a 12-volt motor. This is not really necessary anymore with the excellent, small, and cheap 12v to 110v inverters that are available. Expect to pay between $500 and $800 for one of these machines—new.

If you are serious about building and repairing sails on board, you'll have to get a full-blown commercial machine. These can be very cumbersome if they feature a separate motor and are never cheap. The Sail-Rite people offer two compact models, ranging from $1,400 to $2,300.

### MARKETING YOURSELF

If working from your own boat, word-of-mouth will be your best advertising. Once word gets out that there's a canvas worker/upholsterer in the harbor, it would be very unusual not to have someone approach you with a project. From there, inevitably, things tend to snowball. We've also seen boats with an advertisement sewn onto their splash guards, "CANVAS WORK," or "SEWING," or something similar. If you're not the shy type, this can also be very effective, especially if you're traveling and don't have time to stop and establish contacts.

Also, don't rule out landing a job in a sail loft or canvas shop while you're cruising. As we said, they are used to the transient life of cruisers, and if they need the help, they will often smooth the way with any authorities. I have even known of instances where someone has been able to arrange a swap situation where they work for six months, then go sailing, while another sailmaker comes in and takes over. Six months later, they swap again. Remember, flexibility is the key!

## MARINE CARPENTRY AND FIBERGLASS WORK

At the risk of being labeled sexist, I'll say that if the sewing trades are the province of handy women, then marine carpentry appeals to handy men. If you have been the type of guy (or gal!) who has always liked building things, puttering around the house, and dreaming up projects, you will probably find yourself doing much the same on your boat. Even more than a house, a boat provides the inveterate tinkerer with almost limitless opportunities to "improve" things. This is one of the best ways to get practice, before you try to work on someone else's boat. Of course if you have a background of land-based carpentry you have a big leg up, but don't forget, there are lots of differences between building a bookshelf in a house and building one on a boat!

## WHAT YOU WILL BE DOING

Marine carpentry work falls into two classifications: structural and cosmetic. Structural marine carpentry involves rebuilding hulls and decks, usually on older traditional boats. The work is relatively clean and esthetically pleasing, but often physically demanding. As there are fewer and fewer wooden boats, structural jobs are becoming harder to find.

Unless you find yourself working for a yard that builds new wooden boats, (of which there are few), you will probably be doing cosmetic work. This includes interior work, like adding shelves, cabinets, or other storage areas, and external work, like repairing rails or coamings, and building cockpit tables, etc. Most of this work is clean and pleasant and does not require either a lot of space or expensive, bulky tools. Increasingly, though, when working on modern boats, you'll find yourself working with fiberglass, whether it's bonding structures to the hull, encapsulating insulation, or reinforcing weak spots in existing structures. Also, it is hard to do any work for today's yachts without a working knowledge of the modern two-part painting and coating systems. While fiberglass and highly toxic paints are not the most romantic substances to work with, it's inevitable that you will find yourself becoming conversant with them in order to stay marketable.

## GETTING TRAINING AND EXPERIENCE

If you are interested in traditional wooden boat skills and construction techniques, several schools across the country offer excellent courses (see Appendix A). Bear in mind though, that as esthetically pleasing and rewarding as traditional wooden boat work is, there is not that much demand for it these days. For maximum marketability, you are well advised to add skills with modern materials (fiberglass, epoxy) to your repertoire.

Probably one of the best ways to get a broad range of experience, under supervision, is to find an independent craftsman and work with him. If you find someone carrying out a wide variety of repairs, you can learn a tremendous amount quickly. Whenever you come across a boatyard where work is being done (as opposed to just a storage yard), hang around and get an idea of who's doing the work. Is it the boat owners, yard workers, or the independent contractors?

The best time of day to approach anyone in a boatyard is in the afternoon, towards quitting time. Even somebody who would otherwise be happy to talk to you may give you the cold shoulder if you interrupt him in the middle of a time-sensitive gluing job or fiberglass layup. Even better, find out where the boatyard workers go for a drink after work (There is always somewhere!), and chat with them there. Buy them a few drinks and tell them how eager you are to learn. You'll be working and learning in no time!

Our English friend Martin arrived in St. Lucia from the Canary Islands with a new girlfriend, and no experience working on other yachts. Although he had fitted his own boat out from a bare hull, Martin had never actually worked as a marine carpenter before. After hanging around the local boatyard for a while, he met Mike, a fellow cruiser, who told him he was looking for someone to help him lay a big teak deck. After looking at the work Martin had done on his own boat, Mike gladly put him on. The owner was happy with the deck, and Mike decided to keep Martin for the next few jobs. After a year, Martin invested in more tools and went out on his own. When I met him in the Azores, he told me that in the two years he had worked on St. Lucia, he had saved more money than in his five years as an electrical engineer in the U.K. Plus, he now had a marine trade he could take anywhere.

Besides working for independents, you can also get a job directly with a boatyard. The advantage? You are guaranteed a regular salary and structured supervision. The disadvantages are that you will often be stuck doing one specialized type of work over and over. And, boatyards outside the U.S. usually, though not always, prefer to hire the local people for all but the most technical work. It never hurts to ask, though. A boatyard job may have other perks that make it appealing, such as free dockage or hauling.

In addition to practical hands-on experience, books can be both a good source of reference and of training. Recently, there have been several good how-to books written on marine carpentry, fiberglass repair work, and marine painting. If you don't already have these on board as reference books for your own boat, they may be well worth looking through. Check out Appendix A for titles and recommendations.

## MARINE MECHANICAL, ELECTRICAL, AND AIR CONDITIONING/ REFRIGERATION WORK

Now we're getting to the trades proper—jobs whose skills take years to master, and, unless you have a specialized background, for which you'll probably need professional training. Nevertheless, for someone who is mechanically or technically inclined, the investment needed to learn one of these marine trades can pay off several fold over the years. A big advantage of these trades is that when somebody needs you, they *need* you. Every year yachts of all sizes become more complex and more dependent on their electrical and mechanical systems. The cruising ketch whose freezer has just gone down, with six lobsters and twenty pounds of beef inside, or the charter boat whose electric anchor windlass won't work, are both in urgent need of specialized technical assistance. If you have the tools and skills to help them, money is usually the least important consideration.

So what, aside from the investment of time and money in training, are the downsides of working in these trades? Well, for one thing, to a greater or lesser extent, you are hamstrung by the availability of spare parts. There are only so many spares you can or want to carry, and in the case of marine engines or electronics there are simply too many different brands, each with different parts, to attempt to stock spares. Also, as systems become more and more advanced, many parts are quite simply impossible for the on board technician to repair. Integrated circuit boards or injector pumps are simply swapped out for new (or reconditioned) units. This requires that you have access to shoreside dealers/distributors, who often control the service end as well. Finally, even parts that can be serviced or rebuilt often require expensive and/or bulky equipment that is simply not worth investing in, unless you have a full-blown shop. The idea of carrying elaborate machinery like a lathe or an oscilloscope may appeal to the radical do-it-yourselfer—like Bob Pirsig who described making his own spares in his book *Zen and the Art of Motorcycle Maintenance*. But on a cruising boat where every pound must earn its keep, it just can't be justified.

All that being said, I know of many people who have made a good living in these trades while cruising. It's all a question of striking a balance. Peter was a New Zealander who had been trained as a mechanical/technical engineer by a large U.S. oil company. After he left them and decided to go cruising, he invested in a one-year night school course in air conditioning/refrigeration technology. They placed him with an established contractor with whom he worked until he completed his boat. When Peter left he decided what tools he absolutely needed for most of the repair jobs he would see, and what parts of the jobs he could farm out to shoreside services.

When I met him in Trinidad, Peter was booked up for weeks strictly on word-of-mouth from other sailors, plus he was keeping a couple of local machine shops and parts dealers happy with the work he was bringing them.

## What You Will Be Doing in Each Trade

### MARINE MECHANIC

If you intend to pursue work as a marine mechanic, in addition to studying marine diesels, you should definitely become conversant with the basics of outboard motor troubleshooting and repair. Outboard motors are gas engines, used in a punishing, salt water environment, usually with little maintenance. It's not surprising that they frequently break down. A lot of outboard repairs can be carried out by a skilled mechanic, on board, without expensive shop equipment. Jobs on outboards are not long, lucrative procedures as with some inboard work. Usually, however, the work is not physically demanding, and it seems that in any anchorage there is always someone having trouble with their outboard. Like the novel writer who supports himself with newspaper work, you'll find that outboards will often, at least, keep you in grocery money.

When working on inboards you will often be fixing problems with the fuel and exhausts system or ancillary components (starter, alternator, pumps). As with outboard work, these are often relatively quick, undemanding jobs, and they are very common on sailboats. However, on sailboats the "engine rooms" are often hellish places to get to, let

*On sailboats, engine rooms can be hellish places to get to.*

alone work in, and a good amount of both physical and mental flexibility is called for. Occasionally you will find yourself working on complete overhauls and large engines.

Large jobs and engines will be your bread and butter if you work for a land-based professional. If you're interested in the marine equivalent of working for a Mercedes-Benz dealer (as opposed to the local garage), it may be a reason to seek out a shoreside operation.

## MARINE ELECTRICIAN

As a marine electrician, you'll find yourself doing a lot of wiring systems troubleshooting. With the increasing complexity of modern electrics, there is a growing demand for electricians with efficient troubleshooting skills. Most marine electrical work involves crawling around in tiny spaces and installing things in out-of-the-way locations. If you are not very agile, or don't fancy spending a lot of time working with your head below your waist, consider working with an established firm that caters to large powerboats. A good knowledge of high-frequency radio installation and antenna design will add vastly to your marketability, as this is another marine problem area.

## MARINE AIR CONDITIONING/REFRIGERATION

Marine air conditioning/refrigeration work is concerned mostly with the repair of existing systems. More than any other piece of equipment on a boat (with the possible exception of the head!) marine refrigerators and freezers tend to break down frequently. In my opinion, this is the most marketable of all the marine trades, as well as being one that commands an excellent wage. Like electrical work, on sailboats you will often be working in tiny, cramped areas under difficult conditions. So, head for the large yachts if you want to stand up!

## GETTING TRAINING AND EXPERIENCE

Probably the best way to get training in one of these trades is through a private or public vocational school. These usually offer part-time, three to twelve-month courses, depending on the extent of the training provided. As a bonus, they often offer placement services after graduation. If you are in the planning stages, or have bought a boat but will be spending some time fitting it out, it may be well to think about making the investment of attending one of these schools.

When a good friend of mine, Russell, whom I mentioned earlier, decided he would switch from a sailboat to a trawler, he enrolled in a three-month diesel mechanic's training course in Miami. He felt that if an engine was going to be his only way to get home, he'd better learn how to fix it. He was mechanically inclined anyway, having spent a lifetime working on motorcycles. As post graduate training he completely rebuilt the GM 6-71 diesel in his new boat.

With the tools he had acquired to do that job, he set off for Central America where, in the absence of any local competition, he built a thriving business. He only works for wealthy power boaters and charges top dollar. As he told me, probably 80 percent of each job is done by shoreside shops, but his role is to provide the diagnosis, disassembly, and reassembly. He puts at least half the credit for his success down to successful marketing; selling people on the idea that *he's* the one they can trust.

## MARKETING YOURSELF

So, you've gotten your training and a bit of experience ahead of time. You've bought your tools. Now you're out cruising. What do you do? You've arrived in a port where you plan to stay for a while and as yet no one's come knocking on your hull desperate for your services. Do you look for work yourself as an independent, like Russell or Peter, or should you try to get a job with a shoreside operation? As with the other trades that we've discussed, there are advantages and disadvantages to either. To a good extent the route you choose depends on your personality as much as anything.

In general, finding work with a shore-based marine professional will see you earning money faster and more steadily than trying to go it on your own. Someone who already has an established business will be able to provide you with a regular paycheck, and, if necessary, smooth the way with any local immigration or work authorities.

In terms of abiding by the principle of not offending the locals, working for someone onshore gives you the advantage of being in a position where you are helping rather than competing with the local talent. Your boss will be making money from your services; that's why he's hiring you. In certain places, immigration people can get very touchy about someone trying to work on their own, however, once a local contractor decides your services are needed, there are, miraculously, no objections. Many times this is an informal agreement. A blind eye is turned, rather than implement some lengthy procedure with work permits, visas, etc.

Of course working for someone else entails the usual downside as well. Your hourly rate will be lower than if you were working independently, often by 100 to 150 percent, plus, you'll be locked into a fixed schedule, dictated by your boss.

Although it may take you longer to get started, working on your own, once you have started to make contacts, things will often pick up quickly. Word-of-mouth tends to work in an exponential fashion, i.e., one happy client tells two others, they tell four, who tell eight, etc. By hiring local workers to help you, and farming out work to local specialty shops, you can often smooth any friction with the folks who matter.

When I was working in the Virgin Islands years ago, I kept two local workers on the payroll. They did almost nothing. In fact, they rarely

*Thanks mon, keep up the good work!*

showed up. When they did, I encouraged them to spend their time on coffee breaks and naps, rather than risk the destruction that occurred when they tried to "fix" something! These guys were worth every penny though. They were related to the local parts distributors and transport companies, and by keeping them happy, I greased the wheels where it mattered and saved myself untold grief. Such is life in the islands!

## STEP BY STEP

In short then, my advice on how to proceed if you arrive in a new port and want to work in any of the above trades: sewing, carpentry/fiberglass, mechanical/electrical/refrigeration, would be to proceed as follows:

1. Spend a week or so getting the lay of the land. If there's a popular marina, consider splurging for a month's stay. Talk to the other boaters that have been there a while. Let them know what your area of expertise is, and try to get a feel for the local market. How are the wages? Are there big money boats needing work? Cruisers? What's the

local labor policy like? Answers that you get to these informal questions will serve to give you an idea of how to proceed.

2. If you can, wait around for a while longer. See if anybody comes to you needing work done. If the market is a rich one, you will often have someone contact you within the first couple of weeks. This extra time will also give you a chance to learn a little bit more about who the local players are.

3. If you can't wait around, or if nobody contacts you after three or four weeks, start checking out the shoreside businesses. Depending on your trade, talk to the local boatyards, sail/canvas lofts, and independent tradesmen. Be up front about your experience and how long you will be staying around, but don't sell yourself short. Avoid direct solicitation of boats, especially the big money boats, unless you are only looking for low-level detailing/varnishing work. Most professional skippers feel (quite rightly) that there is something fishy about a "professional" who has to come around like a traveling salesman. Don't leave business cards or advertisements until you know the area and local operators well. This kind of "publicity" can backfire by making it look like you're trying to cut in on the local businesses.

4. When you visit the local marine businesses have some sort of resumé prepared listing your training, if any, and "relevant" work experience. Keep it brief and informal. No one in the marine trades is interested in where you went to college or references from Kalamazoo. As much as anything, a short resumé will serve as some sort of record after you leave, just so they don't forget you once you walk out the door. A portfolio of photos is invaluable to show your work. It speaks more eloquently than any words. Reference letters are not worth the bother as people in the marine businesses don't pay attention to such niceties.

5. Start working!

## WHAT CAN I EARN?

The following table gives a guide to the approximate wages for the different marine trades. As a baseline I used the wages of southeast Florida in 1998. This is probably something like a worldwide average. California, Western Europe, Bermuda, Hawaii, and a few other islands may be a bit higher. Latin America, Australia, New Zealand, and Asia are somewhat lower. Nevertheless, as a rough comparative guide, it should give you an idea of what to expect and/or ask for.

| | Working for Yourself | Working for Someone Else |
|---|---|---|
| **Detailing** | $8-10/ hour | $5-8/ hour |
| **Varnishing** | $10-15/ hour | $8-12/ hour |
| **Sail Work** | $20-30/ hour | $8-12/ hour |
| **Canvas Work** | $15-25/ hour | $8-12/ hour |
| **Upholstery** | $15-25/ hour | $8-10/ hour |
| **Carpentry/ Fiberglass** | $25-30/ hour | $12-15/ hour |
| **Mechanical** | $25-40/ hour | $12-15/ hour |
| **Electrical** | $30-40/ hour | $12-15/ hour |
| **Air Con/ Refrigeration** | $30-40/ hour | $12-15/ hour |

# CHAPTER THREE

# Behind the Scenes in the Charter and Delivery Industry

Irene paused and looked at the rundown single-story house skeptically. Should she go through with it? The paint was peeling off the concrete walls, one screen was missing from the porch, and the screen door hung on one hinge. She thought for a minute. The midday heat was a physical force in the dead air of the lagoon, and, like every day since she and Steve had been in this mangrove-lined backwater in St. Thomas, she found herself subconsciously brushing off mosquitoes.

She decided to go ahead. We need the money, she thought to herself, and after all, John said at the bar last night that it was steady work for an established charter company. They're probably just investing their money in their boats instead of fancy offices. She knocked.

"Yeah, come in it's open. You the girl looking for a job?" A voice drawled from behind the door.

Irene let herself in. It was dim inside after the sun's glare and thankfully cool. Irene thought she detected a whiff of marijuana smoke as she closed the door. As her eyes adjusted, she made out a figure behind a desk who reminded her unpleasantly of Jake from the *Jolly Roger*. Baseball cap, T-shirt, and in a cage behind the desk an actual parrot. "My name's Peter, I'm the manager of this joint. Pull up a chair and let's talk," he said.

Ten days earlier Steve and Irene had arrived in the Virgin Islands. It was the beginning of June, and they were pushing the limits of safe travel before the onset of the summer hurricane season. Their target had been the V.I. because everyone they had met on their travels south had told them it was an excellent place to get work, both in terms of the availability of jobs and the wages. They had also been told there were secure "hurricane holes," anchorages where they could ride out a storm if the worst happened.

As it happened they were not just pushing the weather, they were also stretching their finances to the limit. The Bahamas had proven to be much more expensive than they had expected, and after their initial fiasco in the Abacos, they had both been gun-shy about working in a foreign country. They were pinning their hopes on the Virgin Islands, because at least it was part of the Unites States. They had the legal right to work, and would at least know the local culture. Or, so they hoped.

Shortly after arriving and anchoring in the crowded, noisy, and dirty harbor of Charlotte Amalie, they met another young American couple who had advised them to move around to "the lagoon." This was not only an excellent hurricane hole but was also the base of the fledgling bareboat charter industry and home to a busy boatyard.

Once securely anchored on the mirror-still waters of the inner basin of the lagoon, they quickly found the local watering hole. Using lessons they'd learned in the Bahamas, they decided to invest a few of their precious dollars in drinks at "Charley's Lagoon Saloon." This time, though, they both decided that they would not jump at the first job they heard about without getting more background information. At least that was what they promised each other.

When Irene heard about a "great" varnishing job on a boat at anchor, she first went around to look at the boat herself. What she saw was a half-rotten, 50-foot, wooden schooner. A grizzled, none-too-clean skipper sat drinking on the aft deck, and two growling dogs circled the cabin. Uh uh, she thought to herself, that looks like trouble before I even begin. And when Steve was offered a job rewiring a boat, he decided to meet the owner to discuss the project before offering his services. He found a half-finished ferro-cement hull and an owner who had to get "a little money together" before he could talk about payment. "But you can start work whenever you like," the owner had said. Steve knew that story all too well.

Steve and Irene were discovering one of the immutable truths about casual work, and especially casual boat work. It's invariably the jobs that nobody else wants that are offered to the newcomers. So, when John told the couple about an opportunity at Happy Daze Charters, they listened with enthusiasm. "Normally, you know, they only hire in the fall, at the beginning of the season. But a couple just left. I don't know why because no one goes sailing this time of year. Peter, the manager, was telling me today that he's really looking for somebody right away. I'm not sure they pay a whole lot, but it's steady work, a paycheck every week, and that's something. Especially now in the off-season."

The next morning Irene looked at the Happy Daze charter fleet—seven new, or nearly new, Beneteau sloops. Deciding it was worth a shot, she asked one of the men on the wharf where she could find the office. He directed her to a roof half-hidden in the nearby mangroves. Nothing ventured nothing gained, thought Irene, game, despite herself, for a new adventure.

Peter explained the job to her in the cool dimness of the office. "So that's what I need," he said, "sort of a general dogsbody. There's not enough work here in the summer to keep someone for both the office and boat maintenance. So if you could sort of take care of both ends, it would suit me fine. I'll tell you right now, we're not a big operation, so I can't pay you a lot. But you may find other "fringies" that'll compensate."

There was something in Peter's manner, Irene didn't know what, but despite the ramshackle "office" and his own seedy appearance, she just couldn't help liking the guy. By his own admission a fellow cruiser, Peter seemed as interested in having a good time as running the business. But there was something else, something that she had come to see in most long-term cruisers. She could only describe it as a basic honesty and a lack of BS and it made her believe what he said.

"All right. Let's talk about what exactly you can pay. But it looks like a good job. I think I'd like to give it a try." Irene had committed herself.


The lagoon at St. Thomas may have been an exceptionally protected anchorage, but it was certainly not an exceptionally comfortable one, especially in the summer. The surrounding hills blocked the weak summer trades, and the mangrove swamps and stagnant pools of water throughout the boatyard provided a perfect breeding ground for mosquitoes. The inevitable afternoon shower raised the humidity, but did nothing to cool things down. The thick air felt like the steam rising from the coals in a sauna. In her first few days at work, Irene thought more than once that a sauna was an apt metaphor for the atmosphere of the lagoon.

It was true that in the summer Happy Daze Charters did not have much business, at least not compared to the winter high season. Nonetheless as one of only two employees, Irene found that she more than had her hands full. The other worker was Graham, a British cruiser, who handled the mechanical and technical problems on the charter fleet. He took care of the inevitably blocked heads, flat batteries, drowned outboards, and any other repairs that needed doing. In the winter he usually worked with another mechanic, but now he was alone and like Irene found himself constantly on the go.

Irene's day was broken into two segments. During the mornings she took care of maintenance on the fleet. When a boat returned from charter, she would change all the linens and check for any missing items. Then she would give the whole interior of the boat a good wash down. Next she would clean the heads and galley, paying particular attention to the former. It never failed to amaze Irene in her first weeks on the job that people who would never dream of fouling a friend's bathroom, let alone their own, would treat the heads on a chartered boat like a public facility in Times Square, or perhaps in the men's case a kind of urinary pin-the-tail-on-the-donkey. Anyway, once she got through that she would go through the inventory list of below-decks items: galleyware, navigation equipment, safety equipment, and all the odds and ends that had gone out with the boat. She would make a note of whatever was missing for Peter.

Then, finished with below decks, she would clean topsides. Once done with the cleaning, she would perform an inventory of all the items topsides. Finally, she would run up the sails and check to make sure there were no tears or other damage.

When she started the job, Irene was hard pressed to get through this drill before lunch. As she gained experience, however, she found that if she pushed it, she could knock out two boats in one morning. Occasionally four boats would all return at once with two or three scheduled to go out the next day. When this happened, she cranked them out, but in the summer heat it was brutal work that left her dripping and exhausted at the end of the day.

After the hard, hot work of the morning, the office's air conditioned cool was bliss. Here Irene took care of all the administrative details of the business. She had never had any experience with office work before and was surprised to find that rather than disliking it, as she had expected, she actually enjoyed many of her tasks. She also realized she was getting good training, especially when she found out that Peter's bosses had recently installed a new computer system, and she and he were both in the same boat when it came to learning the software.

Irene and Steve began to find that there were many benefits to her having a job with a shoreside business. To start with, Peter encouraged them to make use of the showers at his office. This was a real blessing in the heat of the summer as a solar shower in the cockpit could just never match the real thing. Also, Peter had a car and was happy to let them borrow it as needed. This allowed Irene to shop at the large supermarkets downtown and Steve to find cheap boat gear in the warren of marine stores in Charlotte Amalie. Moreover, Peter had told Steve that if he needed to, he was welcome to use the workshop onshore. Several times Steve took advantage of this and was able to use tools, like a big vise, drill press, and a small arc welder, all items that he could never have had on his boat.

All in all, she and Steve reckoned that the fringe benefits of the job more than compensated for the low pay. And, though Irene was making only a little more than minimum wage, by living at anchor and keeping their expenses down, they were able to put some money away each week. Bit by bit their "cruising kitty" grew.

Now all they needed was for Steve to find a job. There was not much going on that summer in the boatyard, other than some long-term, low-budget projects by locals. The boatyard shops did not need anybody right now, though they told Steve to try later, maybe in the fall. Although he was keeping himself busy with projects on board their boat, the summer heat and his lack of success on the job market were beginning to get Steve down.

Then one Friday, in the Lagoon Saloon, they were having drinks and a burger—their weekly treat. Steve got to talking with Neville, a Kiwi temporarily marooned in the Virgin Islands. After having sailed his engineless home-built steel ketch for more than 15,000 miles from New Zealand, Neville had been dismasted in a freak squall off Virgin Gorda. He limped in under jury rig and currently had his boat at anchor in the lagoon. Like Steve, Neville had heard that it was a safe spot to spend hurricane season.

Unfortunately his budget was also stretched pretty thin, and he had no money for a new rig. He'd been looking around for work, but being a foreigner and not having any technical skills he had not been having much luck. A couple days earlier he had heard about a boat that needed to be delivered to the States and had gone to talk to the owner. The owner was impressed with Neville's credentials and agreed to have him move the boat, provided he could get it to South Carolina by the end of the month. As it was already the end of the first week in July, and because the boat was a 38-foot ketch of mediocre sailing qualities, they would have to hurry. The owner told Neville that he would pay him on arrival, which Neville didn't like but was desperate enough to accept.

"Look," Neville told Steve over his Budweiser, "I'm taking this delivery for cheap, real cheap. But I need the money. I also need someone else to crew. You seem like a good guy. You got your boat down here by yourself, so you obviously know what you're doing. How about coming along?"

Steve was tempted. It would be a way to get out of the heat and boredom of the lagoon.

"How much will I get paid?" he asked Neville.

"I'll be honest with you Steve, at what I'm getting for this delivery, I can't afford to do more than cover your food. But I'm sure the owner will spring for a plane ticket for you to get back here. He's doing that for me. And I'll tell you, if you're thinking about getting into the charter business or working as a skipper, this'll give you good experience, a good reference for other deliveries, and sea time towards your captain's license."

That was tempting to Steve, he did need experience on other boats. He was in fact thinking of trying to work as a skipper either on a bareboat, or for a private charter boat. If serious about getting his U.S. Captain's license, he needed all the sea time he could get. Plus, he didn't have much going on here at the moment.

"Sure, sign me on. Why don't you tell me where the boat is and I'll meet you there tomorrow. Then I can meet the owner, and we can set up a timetable."

"You got a deal Steve. Can I get you and Irene another rum and Coke?"

Two days out of St. Thomas, Steve and Neville lost their engine. They had been motoring in light and variable winds for the previous 24 hours when suddenly the engine, an old Volvo, coughed and died. Neville had never liked the thing in the first place, and since he claimed to know as little about diesel engines as he could get away with, it fell on Steve to dive into the suffocating heat of the engine room.

*"Well, it is a sailboat, isn't it?"*

What he saw a few minutes later convinced him they were in for a long and potentially difficult delivery. The Racor fuel filter was filled with a whitish grunge, like an oily milk shake. More worrying still, when Steve pulled the fuel lines off the injectors, the same slime oozed. Obviously water had gotten into the fuel tank a while ago. Mixed with the diesel fuel, it had formed a perfect medium for the growth of algae. Now, after 24 hours of motoring, they had sucked enough of the viscous mess into the Racor filter to overwhelm it, and the injectors were undoubtedly shot.

When he broke this news topside, Neville's response was characteristic. "See, I told you. Never trust the damn things. Now I guess we'll have to be sailors. Anyone ever taught you how to whistle for a breeze?"

Steve didn't reply. He was thinking about their conversation three days earlier as they'd been getting ready to leave.

"The whole thing is Steve," Neville had been explaining, "we're leaving damn late in the season. Too late. But that's the way it is, so we've got to make the best of it. Now, the only thing we can do is make a straight shot and get it over with as quickly as possible. We'll put on lots of extra fuel. We can lash jerry cans on deck, and if we have to, we'll motor all the way. You can't trust the trades this time of year, especially once you get north of the Bahamas. You a religious guy?"

Steve shook his head.

"Superstitious?"

Steve said maybe a little.

"Well whatever kind of good luck charms you use, bring them with you. I've got a hunch we might need them before we get to Charleston."

Now here they were, 150 miles north of the Dominican Republic, rolling on a lazy swell without a hint of a breeze. They talked aimlessly throughout the day, as much to take their minds off the punishing heat as anything else. Neville said that when a breeze did come up, he still wanted to make for Charleston rather than head south to Samana in the Dominican Republic.

Weeks later, when he finally got back to St. Thomas, Steve got a lot of mileage, and free drinks, out of the story of the rest of their trip. To cut a long story sideways, as they say, for the next two days they rolled around becalmed. Finally a breeze came up and began to build. Unfortunately it was from the northwest, just where they wanted to go. They lay off, heading due north, as close to the wind as they could manage. For the next 24 hours the wind continued to build until the were sailing at six knots under staysail and mizzen. Finally even this was too much, and they lay head to the wind under just mizzen. By now the wind had clocked around until it was west, then southwest, so they were being blown out into the Atlantic. Neville reckoned that an early season depression must have been tracking north of them.

After another day hove-to drifting northeast, the wind went down, leaving them rolling murderously in the leftover seas. Grimly, they hung on and were rewarded twelve hours later when finally the beginnings of an easterly trade wind began to blow. Then followed six days of near perfect conditions in which they logged some 800 miles towards their goal. By then they were entering the Gulf Stream and figured they were only one day out of Charleston, as long as the wind held. It didn't.

Incredibly there was not a breath of air, not a puff, not a hint, for the next 60 hours. During that time, they sat helplessly in the grip of the Gulf Stream and watched as they drifted some 120 miles north. When they finally got wind, it was a fluky southwesterly, which was their course now to Charleston. Rather than fight both the wind and the Gulf Stream,

Neville decided to put into Morehead City, North Carolina, the nearest accessible port.

When they finally called the boat's owner from Morehead City, they were over 17 days out of St. Thomas, more than five days overdue on their ETA. Neville said he could hear the owner's relief over the phone. Although the owner was not happy that the boat was not in Charleston, he agreed that under the circumstances there was nothing else Neville could have done. Covering airfares out of Morehead City for Neville and Steve was not a problem, and the owner said he'd have the money for the delivery waiting for Neville upon his arrival in St. Thomas.

Back on board his own boat once again several days later, Steve told Irene his feelings about the trip. "Well, I guess in the back of my mind I wanted adventure, and I sure got it. I don't know. I mean in one sense it was a terrible trip, and I probably came close to getting myself killed for nothing. But on the other hand, I'd always wanted to do a delivery, and I'd always wondered how I'd hold up in really bad weather. Well, in one shot I got both. Anyway, it's certainly not something I'd like to make a habit of. And definitely not at those wages. Good thing you've got a steady job!"

"Don't worry hon," Irene responded. "You'll come up with something sooner or later. Why don't you look into this skippering idea of yours. If you get the right job, it might be steady work, and maybe even good money too."

"Yeah, I guess I will. I'll see if Neville has any contacts."

For the next few weeks Steve and Neville canvassed the St. Thomas charter scene. Thanks to Peter's car they were able to go into Charlotte Amalie in the evenings and hang out at the Yacht Haven bar, a watering hole for most of the big-dollar skippers. Steve put notices with Peter's telephone number on several bulletin boards. He even went to see a professional placement agency in town. Unfortunately, when they found out he had no experience and no formal qualifications, they were polite but firm in their answer. Sorry, but no way.

By now it was nearing the end of the summer and Steve was starting to feel he was wasting his time. Then suddenly good news came from an unexpected quarter. One afternoon when she was working in the office, Irene was surprised to hear Peter say to her, "You guys might be in luck. I just got off the phone with one of our charterers. He's been coming here for years. Nice guy to do business with. Well, the reason he's calling me this time is he's just retired. He decided to buy himself a boat of his own and cruise the Caribbean. His only problem is, he doesn't have much experience, and even though he's retired, he still doesn't have a lot of time. So he's asking me if I know a couple that could take care of his new boat and help him sail it when he comes down. He wants somebody who's honest and hardworking, but not necessarily "pros." He said he was more interested in enthusiasm than a lot of professional experience. So I told him I might just have the right couple, and that I'd talk it over with you folks and get back to him. So what do you think Irene? Does it sound like something you and Steve might be interested in?"

"Geez Peter." Irene was overwhelmed. "I mean, yeah, sure. It definitely sounds like something we'd be interested in. I mean, I'd have to talk it over with Steve, but I'll let you know first thing tomorrow morning. Gosh, it almost sounds too good to be true!"


One week later Steve and Irene met with Stewart Fielding of Naples, Florida. He had flown in two days earlier. After meeting them for dinner at one of the fancy resorts on the island where he had booked them a room for two nights, Stewart said, "Look, we're going to be on very close terms if you're running my boat. I need to get to know you well now. So let's just pretend we're all on a little vacation here together."

Irene and Steve enjoyed the lush life of the resort, but were also conscious that they were being subjected to a subtle yet rigorous interview. After two days with Stewart, as he insisted on being called, they had the feeling they'd passed the test.

Before leaving the resort, Steve and Irene had breakfast at the pool with Stewart. They were meeting with him to discuss what would happen next.

"So," Stewart began after his food had arrived, "The boat's going to be delivered down here sometime around the end of November, as soon as the delivery skipper feels good about the weather. If you're going to take this position, I'll need you to have everything sorted out by then. I assume you'll want to put your boat up, out of the water, and Irene, you'll have to wrap up your job with Happy Daze. Steve, I'll need you to fly up to Florida before the boat leaves and advise me on what I need to get in terms of tools and spares for maintenance. I don't want to have to go hunting around for things down here. But I'm serious. If you two want the job, I'd be happy to have you. You seem to have all the skills I'm looking for."

Stewart continued, "Irene, you have experience cooking underway, provisioning, and keeping a boat clean with a minimum of fuss, and Peter tells me you're cool under pressure, all of which are good. Steve, you can handle most mechanical and electrical jobs, and what you can't, you can supervise. You know how to navigate around reefs and shoal waters, and how to get along with the locals. Good again. Plus, most importantly, we all get along together. As I told you, after my wife died, I didn't really want to marry again, but I don't want to miss out on what I enjoy either. Sailing's one thing I enjoy. A lot. But, you know, I really can't see myself as a singlehander, nor do I want to be, so I want somebody to sail with me. Plus I need somebody who can maintain the boat while I'm gone. I think you two could do that. So that's the pitch. Are you willing to sign a one-year contract with me? It'll mean putting your cruising life on hold for a while. What do you think?"

The night before, in the luxury of their hotel room, Steve and Irene had discussed just this possibility. They figured that they would have to make at least a one-year commitment to Stewart. They knew it would mean putting their home up in a boatyard and not seeing her for months, maybe the whole year. They knew that it would mean giving up their independence for a while. But on the plus side, the salary Stewart would be paying them was generous, if not extravagant. It would all go in the bank. They figured that after one year, they would have enough saved to extensively upgrade their boat and probably still cruise for two years without having to think about money. They did have to admit that while they had enjoyed their adventures so far, they didn't think they wanted to keep repeating them. After all, they thought, at some point they should be doing more than just barely getting by. They felt they had years of sailing ahead of them, and having some money in the bank would give them the freedom to explore other interests more fully.

"So?" Stewart looked at them expectantly.

"Sure," said Irene.

"Why not?" added Steve.

They all smiled and shook hands as Stewart called for a round of Mimosas.

## WORKING IN THE BOATING BUSINESS

During their summer in the Virgin Islands Steve and Irene learned some valuable lessons. These are lessons that Maggie and I have seen new sailors learn time and again over the years. First, they found proof, yet again, of what they had discovered the hard way in the Abacos: that if you are looking for work, unless you are very lucky, the first jobs you are offered will be the bottom of the barrel, that is, jobs that nobody else wants. Now this doesn't mean that you should never take them, sometimes this is the only way to break into a competitive market. But be aware, like Steve and Irene were this time—sometimes it's just not worth the aggravation.

Second, Irene learned two things from her experience with Happy Daze. One was that she actually enjoyed working in the office, something she would not have expected. By not being afraid to try new things, she found herself heading in new and unexpected directions. Also, she found that working for a shore-based marine business has all kinds of fringe benefits which may make accepting a low wage worthwhile.

Also, that summer in the Virgin Islands, Steve experienced the Delivery-From-Hell. This seems to be almost a rite of passage among male sailors. For some reason, almost everyone we've met (myself included) has experienced a low-budget delivery gone awry. Like Steve said, if you're looking for adventure, this is a good place to find it. On the other hand, if you're looking to earn some money or to build up your experience and sea time, it's much safer, not to mention less stressful, to stick with professional delivery skippers and established outfits. The delivery business today is a serious and competitive business. Companies, or skippers, don't last long if they take chances, and a bad reputation carries far in the boating world.

Finally, Steve and Irene learned that sometimes opportunity knocks on unexpected doors. By being linked with an established business, Irene gained both credibility and contacts. Without experience or formal credentials, an entry-level position with a bareboat company is a great way to get a start in the charter business.

## WORKING FOR A BAREBOAT CHARTER COMPANY

So what's the best way to go about looking for a position with a bareboat charter company?

Since these jobs are very transient at the entry level, your best bet is to do what Irene did—just "bang on doors." If you're the very organized type and have a good idea of what your cruising itinerary will be, you may want to write or fax ahead with a resumé. Don't expect a lot of commitment from the company. Staffing requirements are very seasonal. Most companies have no interest in making you a job offer, then having you arrive two, three, or even four months later than expected.

An interesting point to note is that over the last decade a dramatic consolidation of companies has, in a way, simplified working in the charter world. When Irene was working for Happy Daze, the bareboat charter industry was in its infancy. In places like the Caribbean there were dozens of small operators, often each with only a handful of boats. Over the years, though, as bareboat chartering became big business and spread throughout the world, the little guys were squeezed out or bought out. Today, with a few exceptions, the bareboat charter industry is dominated by a few huge conglomerates with branches throughout the world. Take a look in the back of any sailing magazine, and you will get an idea of the scope of their operations.

What does this means for the cruiser? If you find you like this kind of work, you may be able to move laterally through the corporate network as you cruise throughout the world. Our friend John, for instance, worked as a skipper for a large charter company in the Caribbean for two seasons before moving up to become manager of one of their bases. When he finally decided to leave the Caribbean to cruise the Mediterranean, his boss made some phone calls. He ended up receiving a tentative commitment from the regional manager of the company's Mediterranean operations who said that he would try to find a spot for John the following summer. The last we heard, John was managing a charter base in Greece, spending the winters on his boat in Turkey.

## WHAT YOU WILL BE DOING

If you decide to work for a bareboat charter company, there are basically four areas in which you might find yourself, though they are not necessarily mutually exclusive.

### SKIPPERING

The first is skippering. Although called "bareboat" charters, often the boats really aren't "bare." If the charterers wish, they may elect to have a captain on board for a nominal fee. Most charter companies are happy to provide this service as it minimizes their risks. Also, in the Mediterranean, a popular form of chartering is the "flotilla." This is a group of several bareboats led by one boat with an experienced skipper on board. Although the unskippered boats have control over how they sail and how they spend their time in harbor, it is the single Captain who makes decisions as to route planning, navigation, and safety (whether to go out in a blow for example). Also many charter companies offer one-way or "dead head" charters. They rely on their skippers to bring the boats back to the home base from their final destination.

Most companies like to see some kind of formal certification from their skippers, like a U.S. Coast Guard Captain's License or an RYA Certificate. Often, though, they are willing to accept cruising experience (i.e. you got your boat there) as enough qualification. Bear in mind, though, that these skippering positions are usually on a demand basis. In other words, the company will only be paying you if it has work. If they don't need a skipper for a week or two, you don't work, and you don't get paid!

## MECHANIC/MAINTENANCE PERSON

Another position with a charter company is that of a mechanic/maintenance person. Every charter operation is continually fighting a war against breakages. Depending on how busy they are, they may have one person, even a whole staff, to handle all the minor breakdowns that come along. If you have a general background in marine maintenance, as most cruisers by necessity do, you can probably market yourself for one of these positions.

## HOUSEKEEPING

Then we have the housekeeping positions—jobs like Irene had. They involve a lot of "domestic" work, keeping the fleet clean, stocking the boats with food and sundries, and keeping track of the inventory. I'd be lying if I said that these jobs were not a lot of hard, generally thankless work. However, as a short time seasonal job with, as we saw, possibly good perks, housekeeping is something to consider.

## OFFICE

Finally, every charter firm needs one or more people in the office. If you have basic secretarial skills, this could be for you. Often the folks in the office have a lot of contact with the charterers, so it is good to be a "people person" as well. Again, like the housekeeping positions, a lot of the work here is menial, but the fringe benefits can be good.

Working for a charter company has another advantage. In foreign countries, if the company wants you, they will generally smooth the way with immigration. Our friend Ann was from New Zealand. When she decided to spend the winter on her boat in Turkey, she asked at the local charter company about jobs. She found that they desperately needed an English speaking person in the office. Thanks to the charter company's connections, she was able to get legal papers to work in Turkey, something that would have been difficult and expensive to do on her own.

## WHERE TO LOOK FOR WORK

Where are the best areas to look for work with a charter company? By far the highest concentration of bareboat charter companies can be found in the Lesser Antilles in the Caribbean, and Greece and Turkey in the Mediterranean. However, as we mentioned earlier, the large companies have bases all over the world. You can find companies like The Moorings in locations as far flung as Tonga, Thailand, Australia, and Turkey. For a complete listing of bases, consult the companies' Web sites. A general listing of charter companies can be found in Appendix B. And, ads in the back of the larger sailing magazines, *Sailing*, *Cruising World*, and *Sail*, for example, offer excellent resources.

## PLUSES AND MINUSES

In summary, here are the pluses and minuses of working for a charter company:

### PLUSES

➤ Very often there are good "fringe benefits" associated with charter work

➤ It is a good way to get experience in the charter industry in preparation for other, more lucrative positions

➤ Working for a large company may give you job security as you move around the world

➤ In foreign countries the charter company will often take care of the legal visa-related requirements

### MINUSES

➤ Usually relatively low paying

➤ Seasonal work may leave you unemployed part of the year

➤ May be fairly high stress at the height of the season

## BEST WAY TO GET A JOB

The best way to get a job with a bareboat company? Show up in person and speak with the manager of the base. Highlight your skills, especially mechanical/technical skills and any clerical/secretarial experience. Emphasize that you work well with people.

## WORKING FOR A PRIVATE CHARTER BOAT OR PRIVATE YACHT

The job that Steve and Irene finally landed taking care of Stewart's yacht was a plum. For many professionals in the captaining and crewing business, working on a large private yacht for a mostly absentee owner is the gold ring—the prize to which they aspire. Others, for whatever reason, prefer the more high-pressure world of a private charter yacht. Taken together, these two types of jobs constitute the world of professional crewing.

Private yachts, both charter and pleasure, are big business. Large amounts of money change hands in their purchase, upkeep, rental, and the salaries paid to their crews. If you want to put some real money in the bank and still work on boats, this is the way to go.

So what exactly is the difference between a private pleasure yacht and a private charter yacht? Obviously a charter yacht is rented out to whomever can pay for it, a pleasure yacht isn't. Beyond this, from the crew's standpoint, the two are markedly similar. A private charter yacht may only be chartered for a few weeks out of the year, and the owner may live on it the rest of the time. Or it may be on charter 52 weeks a year, and the owner may never see it. Or it may be available for charter but never, or hardly ever, go out.

Similarly, a private pleasure yacht may be lived on and used by the owner full-time, or he may simply allow guests to stay on it and only pop in for an occasional visit. Or he may keep the boat in port with captain and crew and not see it or use it for years. On one extreme the owner may want a personal, casual relationship with his crew, like Stewart had with Steve and Irene. On the other, the boat may be owned by a corporation and the crew held to the strictest professional standards.

One point to note, however, is that sometimes a job on a private yacht will enable you to do more "cruising" than a job on a charter boat that basically works one area. It is not uncommon, for instance, for a wealthy owner to keep his yacht in New England for the summer and the Caribbean for the winter. One couple we know landed a job with a recently-retired doctor who wanted to circumnavigate, but needed crew for his 67-foot ketch. This couple spent two years crewing his boat around the world, with the doctor flying out to meet them in various ports. After two years they left the boat, returned to the Caribbean, and resumed their own circumnavigation. Now, however, they had experience with the route they planned to take, plus a hefty bank balance.

The differences are more from boat to boat rather than between charter and pleasure yachts. Let's look at professional crewing as a whole. What will you be doing if you choose to become a professional captain or crew?

As mentioned previously, available jobs run the full gamut from rather casual to highly professional (and highly-stressed). To some extent the levels of stress, and standards expected, are proportional to the size of the boat (and the salary). But not always.

Our friends Cathy and Steve landed what most crew professionals dream of—a high-paying, low-stress position. They were captain and crew on a 65-foot sportfishing boat based in the Bahamas. The owner, an older wealthy businessman, would literally go years without using the boat. The only responsibility Cathy and Steve had was to keep the boat clean and ready to go, should the owner happen one day to call and decide to use it. They were drawing a very generous salary and had almost nothing to do. What could be the downside of such a job?

The very real downside, as with any professional crewing job, was that their lives were not their own. With a regular nine to five job, when you leave work, you leave the job. You can do what you want. Not so when you are professional crew. Although you may not actually be working, you are on call, and you are often physically on board the boat 24 hours a day. What you do, how you dress, how you act, must at all times be in keeping with the standards of the yacht you're on.

Say you're working as a mate on a 75-foot private yacht, and you pull into port in Nassau. You may have the day off, but that does not mean you can throw on a pair of old jeans and go hang out at one of the comfortable, but sleazy, fishermen's bars, though this might be exactly what you'd do if you were on your own boat. No, you have to wear your spotless blue and whites, and, if you want a drink onshore, it had better be in a high-class yachtie or tourist bar. Of course having more than one drink is frowned upon by the captain, so maybe you'll just stay on board and read a book.

The bottom line is, if you can't live with being "on the job" 24 hours a day, don't get involved in this kind of work.

Suppose you can live with that, what kinds of positions are available?

## CAPTAIN

To start with of course, there are captains' jobs. These are the ones with all the responsibility and stress, but also the biggest paychecks. Many people don't know it, but the captains of larger yachts often command six figure salaries. Your responsibilities vary with the size of the boat of course, but in all cases, you will be responsible for the navigation and handling of the yacht. Usually, you will have to deal with the paperwork and handle negotiation with foreign officials, marinas, yacht clubs, and the like. On larger yachts you will also have to manage the rest of the crew. Like any manager, you will be caught between the people below you and the people above. Captains on larger yachts earn every penny they are paid.

## COOK/MATE

Another position that really earns its money is the cook/mate. On smaller yachts, say under 90 feet, this is usually one position. On the larger yachts, however, there is usually a dedicated cook, and there may be one or more mates. On the smaller yachts (45 to 90 feet) the captain and the cook/mate are often a couple. Owners like the solidarity of a couple working together. If you are thinking of getting into crewing, marketing yourself with your significant other as this kind of couple makes sense.

A cook/mates' position involves doing everything the captain does not do. You will of course be cooking meals for all on board, (and doing the dishes) as well as acting as hostess, housekeeper, yacht detailer, and sometimes even baby-sitter/tutor to the kids. If the captain has the most responsibility, the cook/mate probably works the hardest of anyone on board.

## ENGINEER

In addition to the above two positions, the larger yachts usually have a full-time engineer on board. His responsibility is not just to repair breakdowns (in fact often these are handled by a specialist shop onshore) but also to prevent trouble through regular maintenance. On the larger yachts the mechanical/electrical systems are large, very complex, and critical to the operation of the yacht. Today's full-time yacht engineer is a highly-trained specialist.

Large mega-yachts in the 100-foot plus category also usually have several deckhands and stewards. These entry-level positions take care of all the myriad of little details involved in running one of these floating hotels. They polish the chrome and serve the guests, help with the housekeeping, provisioning and varnishing. I would not recommend cruisers pursue these low-level positions. If you are going to make the sacrifices required to be professional crew, you should at least be well compensated. It is worth the effort to get the qualifications needed for the more professional positions.

So, you may ask, if this professional crewing is such a serious business, how does it fit in with the casual nomadic cruising lifestyle? The answer is, usually it doesn't! Most of the time if you decide to pursue a job as a professional crew, like Steve and Irene, you need to put your cruising life on hold for a while. This will usually be for a minimum of a year, although you may luck out and be able to swing a more creative schedule.

Our friends Cathy and Steve, for example, were able to convince their boss, after they had spent two years on the job, that there was no reason for him to keep his boat in the water in the Bahamas during the dangerous hurricane season. They offered to lay it up for him in a Florida boatyard in June, then recommission it at the end of October. This gave them a chance to cruise with their boat and explore other interests for four months a year.

More often, however, you must make a trade-off with these jobs. In exchange for the chance to make good money, and put most of it in the bank, you must temporarily forego your cruising lifestyle.

Also, most of these jobs require either several years experience in the charter business, professional credentials, or both. It is certainly possible to work your way up from bareboat charter companies to larger and larger private yachts. At some point, though, anyone in a captain's position will probably find it necessary to get a license. If you are thinking of going cruising, and this line of work appeals to you, there are several excellent schools that can prepare you for the Coast Guard Master's exam (see Appendix B).

If you are seriously thinking of working on larger yachts in any of the positions mentioned above, there are also many schools which offer specialized training, certification, and job placement assistance. If you already have experience, or think you qualify for this kind of work, you can list yourself with some placement agencies that specialize in linking up boats and crew. Listing with these agencies is probably the best way to find work, if you are not currently working in the charter industry and don't have current contacts. Information on all of this can be found in Appendix B.

## PLUSES AND MINUSES

We can sum up the pluses and minuses of working as professional crew as follows:

### PLUSES

➤ Pay is good to excellent depending on the size of the boat and your position

➤ Chance to travel and see new places and get paid for it

➤ Working conditions can be excellent

### MINUSES

➤ Requires a commitment of time when you will have to give up cruising

➤ Requires a 24-hour-a-day commitment for days or weeks on end, and you must conform to the standards of the yacht

➤ If you develop a bad relationship with the owner or captain, you may not be able to easily get out of it

## CHARTERING YOUR OWN BOAT

And now we come to a topic that everyone wants to know about when it comes to making money in the charter business: namely, what about chartering your own boat? For many people contemplating the idea of a cruising life, the concept of chartering their own boat seems like a perfect way to combine business with pleasure—almost the perfect adjunct to a cruising life. Would that it were so!

I remember reading a book years ago on this topic. It was the story of a middle-aged executive who bought a sailboat and moved to the Caribbean, intent on making a living chartering. After a couple years of trying to make a go of it, the author came to the conclusion that you could charter for fun *or* profit, but not both. I'll always remember that line.

Remember, the charter business is just that—a business. Unless you've worked in the field, you may not realize just how much hard work (particularly if the captain is also the owner), goes into keeping a charter boat running smoothly. It's even worse if the boat is also your home.

These days professional, full-time operators have saturated virtually every lucrative market. Gone are the days when you could pull up to the dock, hang up a sign, and attract guests to come on your "romantic" little boat. Nowadays, most charter guests, even those on a budget, expect, and get, excellent professional service on well-maintained, well-appointed yachts.

Plus, local governments now have their fingers in the pie as well. In some countries you can not even retain ownership of your boat. It must be sold to a citizen of the country who will then give you a share of his company! At the very least, you must often retain a local partner, who in many cases is required to hold a majority stake in the business.

This is not to say that the law always makes chartering your own boat impossible. Given enough time and determination, it is usually possible to charter legally almost anywhere. No, the point I'm trying to make is that, like working as professional crew, it may be hard to integrate a charter business with a cruising life.

If, after this, you are still interested in chartering your own boat, I recommend you read one or more of the books in Appendix B. These are real-life stories of cruisers who did it. They outline both the pluses and the minuses of this demanding business and delve into many of the details that you need to be aware of before committing yourself and your boat.

Now, after having said all this, and probably having discouraged you from the idea of chartering your own boat, I should make one point. There is one type of chartering that can be done successfully by the casual cruiser. This is what I call informal or occasional chartering. Basically this is having acquaintances, or acquaintances of acquaintances, come "visit" you in some exotic locale.

This scenario works best if only done on a part-time basis and in areas where there is little, if any, direct competition from established operators. You will be working in a bit of a grey area as far as the law is concerned, and you definitely need to do your research ahead of time regarding the policies of the country you are in. I am not in any way advocating that you flaunt the law, and again this can in no way become an established business. Nevertheless, we have known many people over the years who have made a bit of extra money by having people stay on their boats.

Establishing a relationship with a travel agent in your home country is one method of arranging this type of charter. The agent recommends your boat to adventurous vacationers. It is made clear that this is an "adventure" and not strictly a charter. If necessary, the guests are signed on the boat's crew list when they arrive as crew rather than passengers. Approached in the right way, this type of "informal" chartering can actually be a way to strike that elusive balance between fun and profit.

So here are the pluses and minuses of chartering your own boat:

**PLUSES**

➤ You have the freedom of being your own boss

➤ If you develop an established business, the money can be quite good

➤ If you are a very social person, being a charter operator allows you to be an "entertainer"

➤ Doing occasional "informal" charters can actually be fun and it puts a little money in your pocket

**MINUSES**

➤ With a busy charter business the workload of an owner/operator can be crushing

➤ The legalities of the host country may be daunting or even prohibitive

➤ Using your home as a charter boat can be very stressful and will contribute inordinately to wear and tear on your boat's equipment

➤ The time needed to run a successful charter business may preclude any actual cruising

➤ It may take years to build a reputation

## SEASONAL NATURE OF ALL CHARTER WORK

One thing to bear in mind when considering any aspect of chartering—working for a company, crewing on a private yacht, or chartering your own boat—is the seasonal nature of the work. Different parts of the world have different charter seasons. In the Caribbean it is the winter (December-May), in the Mediterranean it's the summer (May-October), and in the Pacific it varies with the region, but is whenever it is not typhoon season.

If you are working at an entry-level position with a bareboat company, there is a good chance you will be let go in the off-season. Similarly, Irene's lucky break notwithstanding, it is generally difficult to find a job in the off-season. If you are working as a deckhand or steward on a mid-sized charter boat, you will also probably be out of work for part of the year. However if you are a captain-cook/mate pair, or an engineer on a larger yacht, you will probably be kept on year round. In the off-season it will be your job to have the boat hauled and the yearly maintenance performed. You will also need to take care of all the million and one odd jobs that don't get done during the charter season.

If you will be chartering your own boat, think of what you will do during the off-season. One couple we knew chartered out of the Antilles in the winter, and spent every summer cruising the coast of Venezuela. Another New Zealander chartered his schooner during the summer in the Mediterranean then went back to live on and sail his 30-foot sloop during the Southern Hemisphere's summer (November-April).

## DELIVERING YACHTS

As I said earlier, it seems that at one time or another nearly every male cruising sailor has a fling with delivering yachts. On the face of it, this should be a perfect complement to the cruising lifestyle. After all, what could be better than getting paid for what you already do for fun? And so, with this reasoning, time and again, otherwise sensible people find themselves at sea in the wrong season, on unsafe boats, under a captain with insufficient experience, bad judgement, a tyrannical attitude, or possibly all three. And, like Steve, they are often lucky if they break even on the trip.

There are of course many professional delivery skippers and agencies who rarely experience any problems beyond the ordinary, and also make a decent living. But like chartering, it is hard work and a 24-hour job while you are on a delivery.

If you are thinking of crewing on deliveries as a way to make money, I would strongly suggest that you sail only with reputable, recognized delivery skippers or established agencies. If someone approaches you to crew on a delivery, find out what kind of experience they have and how many similar deliveries they have made. It is not enough just to be a good sailor. A delivery skipper must also be able to assess the seaworthiness of a boat *before* it leaves port, troubleshoot most minor problems underway, and be familiar with the peculiarities of the local weather. Don't be shy about asking to see a skipper's qualifications or asking to check his references. Remember, however tempting things might look in port, it will be *your* life on the line if something goes wrong. Finally, make sure you get all the details of payment, airfare, and your obligations on board ironed out before you get on the boat.

If you are already an experienced sailor, you may be interested in working as a delivery skipper. Once you establish a reputation (and this may take years), this can in fact be a useful money-making adjunct to the cruising lifestyle. While the pay for delivery skippers is not extravagant, especially given the demanding nature of the work, it is adequate, and the nature of the work allows you to put a decent chunk of cash straight into the bank.

So how do you get started? Call the established agencies to see what kind of qualifications they require. You will almost certainly need a U.S. Coast Guard 100-ton Master's License or an RYA Yachtmaster Ocean Certificate to work as a professional delivery skipper. Agencies may also require lifesaving, navigation, or other formal credentials. The sea schools in Appendix B can provide you with information on how to acquire all of these credentials.

If you can convince the agency that you have the qualifications, you may luck out and have them take you on as a skipper. Otherwise, you may be able to get your foot in the door by crewing on deliveries with the agency. One way to find these agencies is through the advertisements in the back of yachting magazines. Another is through online listings, some of which can be found in Appendix B.

If you are very qualified, put an ad in the yachting magazines yourself. This is not cheap, and there is no guarantee it will bring any business, but if you want to start you own delivery business, this is as good a way as any to get your name out there. A less costly alternative is to advertise in local, free yachting newspapers and place ads on all the bulletin boards of the local marinas, yacht clubs, and chandleries. You may also want to design a Web site and get linked to the various nautical portals. More than one skipper is doing that already. A good book for anyone contemplating the delivery business is the *Passagemaker's Handbook*, listed in Appendix B.

Whatever you decide about the delivery business, you should be aware of the following pluses and minuses:

## PLUSES

> ➤ The pay, especially as a skipper, is not bad

> ➤ The work can be integrated into a cruising life

> ➤ Deliveries can be interesting in terms of sailing different boats and visiting different places

## MINUSES

> ➤ The work can be very difficult and sometimes dangerous

> ➤ It may take a while to develop a reputation

> ➤ You need a safe place to keep your boat while away on deliveries

# CHAPTER FOUR

# Alternatives to the Rat Race: Casual Work on Shore

The smell of chicken grilling and the laughter of sailors mixed with the music of Jimmy Buffet, singing about mother ocean. The marina regulars had gathered on D dock to congratulate John and Paula on their departure.

"Well I'm glad someone's really doing it," said Sam, John's former golf partner and sailing buddy.

"You know how much we all envy you, you bastard. I wish I could chuck it all for a life of adventure. I hope you know that we all expect to get postcards from every exotic palm-covered island you visit."

"Don't envy us too much Sam," John joked. "We might be back in six months asking for a job, or a loan."

Everyone laughed at John's sense of humor except Paula, his wife. Surveying their friends gathered on the dock, she thought ironically, look at them, there's not one in the bunch that would sacrifice their careers for the sake of "adventure." Unless of course they had a bullet-proof bank account. They wouldn't believe that we're actually going to leave without knowing how we're going to make ends meet. They think John made a killing in the market. If they really knew he'd lost his shirt, they'd be sending us to a shrink, not throwing us a party. Well, we're committed now, for better or worse.

Last week Paula had collected her last paycheck and said good-bye to her colleagues at the CPA firm where she had worked for 12 years. After the obligatory promises to stay in touch and send everyone postcards from Polynesia, she walked out the door for the last time and, surprising even herself, felt nothing. No sadness, no sense of loss, not even a sense of relief or freedom. Just nothing. In a certain way, she realized, she was already living in the future. For the last few weeks her body had been in the office, but her mind had been on the boat.

She had been mentally reviewing her checklists. Lists of provisions she had stowed, lists of charts and guidebooks they had bought, lists of equipment purchased, lists, lists, lists. And then, always coming back to the money. As an accountant, and as a well-raised conservative, hardworking American, Paula just could not get the issue of money out of her head. As much as she tried to adopt the freewheeling, devil-may-care attitude that she supposed was what "cruising sailors" had, she just couldn't live with the idea that if she and John cruised for five years, they would deplete their bank account by nearly 50 percent.

This was the hard cold truth, and however much John talked about "picking up jobs as we go along" and "we'll figure something out" she just couldn't see it. But then she came back to their initial reasoning. They were both in their forties, and they weren't getting any younger. They were both healthy and loved sailing. At this point in their lives there was really nothing they wanted more than to change their lives, take a chance, and explore new horizons. And as John had said, if every-thing bombed out and they had to reenter the job market, they were a hell of a lot better off doing it at age 49 than at 55 or 60. There was no reason to wait, he said.

She looked again at her friends from the marina. She wondered how she'd feel next week when she and John were away. Would she miss them? Or would she again feel nothing? How much did she really know them anyway? Really, how much quality time had she and John been able to spend with anyone these last five years? She felt as if for several years she had been living her life second hand, not really engaged. If she felt that way now how would she feel in another five or ten years? Money be damned, she thought, we've only got one life. Let's do it!

Three weeks later *Drifter*, John and Paula's secondhand Crealock 38, was lying at anchor in the beautiful pine-ringed harbor of Morro Bay. Despite urgings from their friends to sail direct for the South Pacific, John and Paula had opted for the less romantic, but in their minds more sensible, option of spending the summer cruising the coast of northern California. They even thought they might get as far as Seattle.

*Adios to the "good life."*

If we spend the summer on the U.S. coast, John had reasoned, we can get our feet wet without making an irrevocable commitment. If we still like the life at the end of the summer, then we can head south. But if we don't, or if something goes wrong, we're still in the States and can bail out.

Now that they had finally left the urban sprawl of southern California, John and Paula were starting to feel their attitudes towards many things changing. The last three weeks had been one daysail after another. John had insisted that they go out in all weathers in order to intimately learn their boat as quickly as possible. They were even planning on giving San Francisco a miss.

"Just another big city," John had said. "We're sailors. What are we going to do in a big city?"

Paula could have thought of a few things, like maybe take in a play or eat out for a change. She was getting a little tired of cooking *every* meal. But then the question of money raised its head again, and she agreed it was best they keep moving.

The last two days though, they had been forced to stop. It had been blowing 20 to 30 knots on the ocean, and although the anchorage they were in was wonderfully protected, conditions like these would make the bar at the river's entrance extremely treacherous. As a result, *Drifter* stayed where she was, and John and Paula had a couple of days to explore their surroundings.

An old fishing town, Morro Bay was now metamorphosing into a small time tourist destination. There were a couple of funky inns and three or four fish and seafood restaurants. The population appeared to be a nice mix of urban drop outs and locals, and John and Paula found themselves relaxing in the town's ambiance. They had even treated themselves to dinner, the last couple nights, at a comfortable waterfront dive called The Captain's Cabin, rationalizing that it was half the price of Los Angeles and, after all, didn't they owe themselves a treat after all the sailing they had been doing?

That night as they were finishing their meal, Paula remarked to their waitress that she and John were hoping for a break in the weather as they wanted to get sailing again.

"Oh, so you're sailors too?" Sheila, their waitress remarked.

"What a coincidence! George and I live on *Goblin*, that little Pearson sloop in the anchorage. Are you on *Drifter* the boat that just came in?"

Paula said they were.

"Hey, why don't you folks stay around for a bit? This is a great anchorage and this town really grows on you. George and I came here a year ago, and we've been here ever since!"

Paula said they really would like to keep moving up the coast but given the weather would probably be around another couple of days.

"Great. Why don't you folks come over for dinner tomorrow night? It's my day off, and I'm sure George would like to meet you. Can you come by about seven?"

"Sure," said Paula, a little taken aback at hospitality so freely given. "What can I bring?"

"Oh, just yourselves, that'll be fine. Well, gotta run, they're calling me in the kitchen. See you tomorrow."

So the next night John and Paula were treated to Sheila's home-made seafood chowder and salmon steaks. During the course of the meal Paula happened to mention their concerns about not having enough money. She told Sheila about John's idea of "finding jobs along the way" but said that she didn't think this was very likely, given their lack of skills.

"So what exactly did you two do back in the "unreal world?" asked Sheila.

"Oh, I was a CPA and John was a public relations man. Nothing too marketable now I'm afraid," Paula replied.

"Well I've got an offer that might tempt you two to stick around a while longer. It's in my own selfish interest. We don't have a lot of liveaboard boats here, and I like the company. About three days ago one of our waitresses quit. It's just the beginning of the season, and Larry, our manager, wants to find a replacement. The quicker the better. If I put in a good word for you, I'm pretty sure I can get you the job Paula. You don't happen to have any waitressing experience do you ?"

"No, not really. Hold on, I did wait tables for a summer once back in college."

"Great, that'll be fine. Anyway I didn't have any experience either before I started. I'll teach you everything you need to know."

And so, three days later Paula started waitressing at the Captain's Cabin. John at first wasn't too crazy about the idea as he had really wanted to spend the summer sailing. He had been looking forward to getting to know both the boat and themselves. After the first few days though, he noticed a real change in Paula as her immediate money anxieties began to fade. She became markedly more relaxed, and little things that had bothered her before, like his habit of leaving his shoes on the salon floor, now went unnoticed. Plus, he had to admit, that it was nice to see money going into the bank account instead of out of it.

However, every night for the first week that she was working, Paula came home exhausted. She was working the dinner shift, and since the restaurant didn't close until 11:00 p.m., she couldn't get back to the boat before 1:00 a.m.

"Good God!" she said the first night as she crawled into their bunk, "I'd forgotten waitressing was such hard work. Tomorrow I'm going to buy some good walking shoes. And from now on I'm leaving everybody a bigger tip when I eat out!"

After the first week Paula counted up her tips and announced to John, "Well if this week is average, and Sheila says it'll get busier as the season goes on, I figure we should be able to bank almost half of what I make."

John said that was fantastic. But there was something in his voice that caught Paula's ear.

"C'mon, what is it?" she asked, "Why is it you don't sound exactly overjoyed that we're in the black instead of the red?"

"I don't know," replied John, "I guess I had just expected to be doing more than this. I mean, it's great that you're working and all, but I'm sort of feeling useless sitting around on the boat. If we were sailing or going someplace it'd be different. But just sitting here, and then waiting for you at night. I guess it's just not what I'd expected."

"Well what would you think about getting a job too?"

"Sure, but what would I do? I don't see a lot of PR firms around here. And I'll be honest Paula, I really would rather not work in a restaurant. It's just not my thing."

"I was thinking of something different. I was talking with Gary, the bartender at work, the other night. His brother's a contractor here. He was saying that they're framing up a big custom home this summer and they don't have enough guys to stay on schedule. I told him about you. I said that you had done some good basic carpentry projects around the house and that you were handy in general and picked things up quickly. He was a little worried about your age and asked if I thought you could keep up physically. You would have been proud of me, hon, I said that you had the physique of a man half your age. What do you think about that?"

"You'll get me into trouble yet, before you're done." But John was grinning. "So what'd he say? Does he think there's a chance they'll hire an old geezer like me?"

"Gary seemed to think so. He said he'd talk to his brother and let me know. He's working tonight, so I should get some information. Do you think that would be something you'd like to try?"

"Yeah, I think so. I mean that's why we're doing this isn't it, to try new things? And, sure, I've always been interested in woodworking. I just haven't had much time for it in the last ten years. I don't know what it'll be like working with a bunch of hammer-wielding twenty-year-olds. But you know what they say, "If it doesn't kill me, it'll just make me stronger!"

So John went to work as a framer for Henry Grundig, Gary's brother. The first day he worked alongside Gene, a pre-law student from Stanford who was trying to save a little money over the summer and also get out of the city for a while. They got along well, and John quickly picked up the basics of framing. He was amazed at how much carpentry had changed since he had worked on a building site as a college student. Now they had chop saws and nail guns, and the work wasn't nearly as demanding as he had feared.

Nonetheless, when he got back to the boat that evening, he found his arms and shoulders hurting in places he hadn't felt in years. As Paula rubbed Tiger Balm into his aching muscles he commented, "Boy that brought me back, today. I'd forgotten how much fun it can be working on a building site. Did I ever tell you that I spent three summers in college banging nails?"

"Uh, uh."

"Yeah. It was okay, like today. Just the guys hanging out with the guys. You can get away with saying a lot of stuff that you can't say anywhere else. Nowadays it seems like everywhere you look there's someone monitoring your political correctness."

"Saying what kind of things?" Paula stopped massaging his shoulders.

"Oh you wouldn't be interested. Just guy talk, nothing special. Listen, I'm beat. Let's get to sleep."

"Mmmm," Paula thought, wondering, as she turned out the light.


And so John and Paula passed the summer in Morro Bay. As the weeks went by, they became quite friendly with Sheila and George. George, it turned out, was a retired physician. Seven years ago, at the age of fifty, he decided he'd had enough of the U.S. medical system. He was fed up with the greed and lack of ethics he saw in many of his colleagues and, like John and Paula, decided to let his love of sailing lead him in new directions.

George had managed to save enough money over the years so that now he and Sheila would not have to worry. Nevertheless, in keeping with their new philosophy of simplifying their lives, they elected to buy a smaller rather than larger boat. A vintage 32-foot Pearson fit the bill perfectly. As he told John, he and Sheila had never intended to "sail the world." They were quite content to stay on the West Coast and get to know a few places well. Until the last winter, they had spent the summers in northern California and winters in Mexico.

Last year, however, Sheila had decided she was missing the social interactions of shoreside life. She decided to try her hand at waitressing after hearing from another boater that the Captain's Cabin was hiring. She found she enjoyed socializing with her co-workers, as well as with the customers. She also enjoyed the sense of having something definite to do each day. After six years the routines of the cruising life were getting to be just that, routine. The waitressing job was actually a pleasant change.

This suited George just fine. A few years earlier he had taken up something he had always meant to try, painting. Sheila's job allowed him the privacy he needed to indulge what had become his new passion. One night, when John and Paula had come over for dinner, he brought out some of his latest landscapes. Paula especially was impressed.

"Wow, George, in this one you really caught the feeling of this place."

George's paintings were tiny, barely four inches square. Nevertheless, with an almost Japanese sense of minimalism, he had managed to capture the sense of both tranquility and power that Paula felt in the northern California forest.

"Well, I don't know if they're any good or not, but I'm having a lot of fun playing around. Anyway, Sheila and I have decided that a year here is long enough. We're going to sail down to Mexico for the winter. I'm looking forward to trying out some of my new ideas with the Mexican landscapes. Hey, that reminds me, I wanted to ask you, would you folks like to sail down with us? I know you were talking about going south. If we sailed down together, we could show you all the spots we know. We've cruised that coast four or five times now."

"That sounds like a great idea," said John. "Paula and I were just talking about that the other night. I still don't think we're ready to make the jump to the South Pacific. But going down the Mexican coast, that sounds like a good plan."

It was now the middle of August, and as the two couples discussed their plans, they decided that if the weather was okay, they'd leave around the middle of September. George said he wanted to be in Los Angeles at least before the beginning of October, which was when, he said, all hell usually broke loose in the northern waters. As he and John discussed route plans and anchorages, Paula and Sheila talked about leaving the Captain's Cabin.

"You know, Paula, I'm going to miss that screwy place. After a year here it almost feels like a family."

"I know what you mean. I've only been here a couple months, but we've all had some good times together."

In fact, Paula was surprised at how close she had become with the restaurant staff. She thought of Gary the bartender. An ex-film producer from San Francisco, he had left the city after watching one too many friends die of AIDS. Now he rented a large falling-down house with his boyfriend Alex, and almost weekly the crew from the restaurant would end up there for a post-work get-together. And there was Felicia, another waitress. She was supposedly writing a novel, though she would never let anyone read it, nor would she say what it was about. And, Fred the cook, a Morro Bay local once became so angry with a customer, who complained about the chowder, that Fred sent him a charred fish head as an entrée.

As Paula thought about her co-workers, who had now become her friends, she realized that they were the kind of people that she would never have talked to in what she now thought of as her "old" life. Her friends then had been other up-and-coming professionals like herself. They would meet for a hurried lunch at a downtown bistro, or perhaps cocktails at the latest hotspot. But Paula could never remember sharing the kind of casual craziness that she had with the Cabin's staff. The nights when Gary had them all in stitches with his wickedly funny pastiches of certain obnoxious customers. Or the "women's club" when she, Felicia, and Sheila would meet for a morning coffee and wile away hours with local gossip.

Later, on board *Drifter*, she mentioned this to John.

"I know what you mean," he said. "I feel the same way about a couple of the guys on the crew. You know, I think part of it is that none of us has anything to prove. We're not trying to advance our careers. We're not trying to show off any status symbols. We're all here trying to make a buck, plain and simple."

As John and Paula continued to talk late into the night they both realized that the summer in Morro Bay had changed them in ways that they never would have imagined. Having discovered a whole new side of life in just three months, they were more determined than ever to continue their cruising. They were eagerly looking forward to the trip down the coast with George and Sheila.

*You know, maybe this is the good life.*

A couple of weeks later the two boats pulled into John and Paula's old marina in L.A. It was still warm in southern California, and as the two couples sat drinking beer in *Goblin's* cockpit, John decided to call his friend Sam on the cell phone.

"John, buddy, how are you?" Sam's voice came over the phone, blustery and upbeat as ever. "Welcome back! How long you guys in town for? Just a couple days? Yeah, I'd love to get together but this week's really crazy. A client's in from Japan, and I gotta show them around, shmooze 'em. You know the show. What? No, I'd love to come down to the boat, but I'm pretty tied up this week. Can we pencil something in next week? Oh, you are? Well have a great trip! You don't take passengers on that boat do you? No, I didn't think so. Wish I could go with you! All my best to Paula. Bye now."

After Sam hung up, John sat back, looking bemused.

"I think I'll call Carol at the office," said Paula picking up the phone. "Maybe we can do lunch tomorrow." Paula dialed the number of her old firm. "Hi Jody. It's me Paula. Remember me? Yeah. Anyway, is Carol in by any chance? Oh, she's in New York for the week? I see. What about Ted? He did? He took a job in Washington? Well, good for him. I'm sure it was a step up. No, there's no one else I need to talk to, thanks Jody. Have a good day." Paula put the phone down. "Well, there's no one else I have a burning desire to see. How about you John?"

"Nope, can't think of anyone." John turned to George and Sheila.

"What do you folks want to do tomorrow? You want to go around and see the city, check out Hollywood, the tourist stuff?"

"To tell you the truth John, L.A. has never done much for me. You know where I'd really like to go? To Mexico!"

"Me too," said Paula. "To Mexico!"

"To Mexico!" from Sheila.

"To Mexico!" said John.

Then all four, raising their beers together, said, "To Mexico!"

## CASUAL WORK ON SHORE

Waiting on tables, bartending, working as a cashier or on a construction site; these are jobs that people do not usually associate with a cruising life. Also, many people may feel that they went to college precisely so they would *not* have to work at these kinds of "menial" jobs. And yet, in many ways, casual work onshore meshes very well with a cruising lifestyle, as John and Paula found out. They saw that not only are casual jobs relatively easy to find, they also pay enough, at least in the United States, to allow cruisers to actually put a good portion of their income in the bank.

John and Paula also found out something that they did not expect. For someone used to the fast-paced, high-pressure professional life of the States, working at a low-skilled job can be pleasantly refreshing. And for longtime cruisers, as Sheila found, working at a shoreside job can provide a break from the routines of the boat life and the chance to get away for a while from incessant "boat talk." So, since these casual jobs can play an important role in the cruising life, let's look at them in more detail.

## RESTAURANT WORK

A perennial favorite among land-based as well as nautical transients, restaurant jobs are classic "easy-come, easy-go" jobs. In addition to not requiring any special skills and very little training, working in a restaurant as either a bartender, waiter, or waitress can, in the United States, pay anywhere from two- to four-times the minimum wage, depending on the restaurant. The American custom of tipping between 15 and 20 percent can, in a busy restaurant, add up to a hefty amount of money for waiters and waitresses. In other developed countries the tipping scale is not quite so generous, but restaurant work still pays well, relative to the skill level required.

One question I'm often asked is which is better, waiting tables or tending bar? As someone who worked in the restaurant business for years, both as a waiter and bartender and later as a manager, let me say that my personal preference is always to work behind the bar. As a bartender you have control of your domain (the bar) as well as a chance (sometimes) to actually carry on conversations with your customers. As a waiter or waitress you are constantly on the move, shunting between the bar, kitchen, and the tables. You seldom have a chance to say more than a few passing words to the customers. And, you're at the mercy of both the kitchen and the bar. If you do not stay in the good graces of the cook and bartender, both can cause you serious grief. Believe me, I've seen it happen!

Bartending does require some specialized training. If you have not worked in the field, probably the easiest way to get a job is to attend a bartending school. There are scores of these all across the country (see Appendix C). The courses usually run two weeks part-time or one week full-time and are relatively inexpensive. You practice making drinks behind a real bar and are also given advice on such relevant topics as how to "shut-off" a customer who's had too much, how to break up a fight (what that long Galliano bottle is *really* for), and the new legal liabilities of bartenders.

What about working in the kitchen? One of the drawbacks to working as either a bartender, waiter, or waitress, is that your income (tips) depends on your being in a good mood. If you are not a "people person" or have off days when you just don't want to deal with anyone, you may want to consider working as a cook. In the kitchen, no one sees you and you can act as you want. You can yell, curse, abuse the waiters and waitresses, whatever you want (and many cooks do).

One drawback to working as a cook is that until you get to high priced restaurants, which demand highly-trained kitchen staff, cooks usually make much less than waitresses and waiters, often only one and a half to two times the minimum wage. This is because the restaurant must actually pay their salary; they're not subsidized by the customers. Also, cooking jobs are less transient than those of bartenders, waiters, and waitressess, making them more difficult to find.

However, if you enjoy cooking but haven't tried it as a regular job because of money or career concerns, this might be the time to give it a whirl. Cooking can certainly provide more challenges than the rather repetitive work of bartenders, waiters, and waitresses. Cooking schools and resources are listed in Appendix C.

## WHERE TO FIND RESTAURANT JOBS

The only place to seriously consider restaurant work is in developed countries. This is because in developing Third-World countries, wages are so low that even for the most destitute cruising sailor, it just isn't worthwhile to bother. For example, while we were in the Bay Islands of Honduras, my wife Maggie and I were so desperate that she took a job as a bartender at the local "yacht club." When I found out that her salary was twenty U.S. dollars a week I figured that at least she might make out all right with the tips. Then I found out that in Honduras nobody tips bartenders!

In all honesty I have to say that, as an American, the odds of being able to get work in a restaurant abroad are not too good. Probably your best bets are other English speaking countries like Australia or New Zealand. Landing a restaurant job in a foreign country, however, should be treated as a windfall and not something you can count on.

In terms of the legalities of working abroad, restaurant owners are sometimes willing to turn a blind eye to the immigration formalities for their floor staff. Usually they will know the legal situation (in terms of what risk they are running) better than you, so if there is any question, just ask.

One thing to remember is that Americans can also work legally in U.S. possessions and trust territories. These include the Virgin Islands, Puerto Rico, Guam, American Samoa, and the Northern Mariana Islands. Employers on these islands like to hire continental Americans because they are perceived as hard working and honest. For cruisers in either the South Pacific or the Caribbean, these U.S. possessions and affiliates can be useful bases for shoreside work.

## HOW TO GET A JOB IN A RESTAURANT

The only way to find restaurant work is to apply in person. Often restaurants have hiring policies based on age, race or gender, which of course they can't tell you. The only way they can tell if you'll suit their criteria is to see you in person. And a word to the wise after all my years in the business; if you're looking for a job as a bartender, waiter, or waitress, *never* say that you have no experience. Always say that you have worked in at least one other establishment, preferably two. Restaurants in the mid- to low-price range seldom call to check references. If they do, and can't reach your references, you can just say they must have moved or gone out of business. Once on the job, you will pick up what you need to know very quickly.

If you arrive in a location with many restaurants, start at the ones that are busiest. Remember, that the amount you earn is directly proportional to a restaurant's sales, the busier the better. Also remember that on the floor, appearance is everything. If you've been out sailing for a while, invest in a good haircut, and dress appropriately for the caliber of restaurant you are applying to. In other words don't go into a fancy restaurant in shorts and a T-shirt and don't apply to a casual beach joint in a blazer and tie.

Assuming there is an opening, ask some key questions. Find out the hours of the restaurant. If it's open until one or two in the morning, it may influence your decision. Also ask whether you will have to work split shifts (both lunch and dinner). This can be a killer. Ask how much side work you will have to do; that is, work not directly associated with serving, such as setting tables, putting away flatware, filling salt and pepper shakers, etc. In some restaurants, this is done by the bus people, in others, by waitresses and waiters. A lot of this side work can really add to your hours. By asking these questions, you'll also show the manager that you know something about restaurant work.

Finally, after speaking to the manager, or perhaps later in the day, try to talk to some of the other employees to get a feel for the atmosphere of the place. If you hear a lot of grousing, there's probably a reason for it, overwork, underpay, abusive management, something. On the other hand a good work environment is usually also evident in the staff's attitudes. By taking the time to do these preliminaries, you may avoid getting yourself caught in an unpleasant situation. Of course, you may not have the liberty of being so choosy. But it doesn't hurt to try!

## PLUSES AND MINUSES

To sum up, let's review the pluses and minuses of restaurant work as it applies to the cruising sailor:

### PLUSES

➤ Generally easy to find work

➤ Pay can be very good (especially on the floor)

➤ The right environment can make the job a lot of fun

### MINUSES

➤ The work can be physically demanding

➤ The hours can be very long

➤ Abusive customers or management can make the job hell

## OTHER CASUAL WORK ON SHORE

Other than restaurant work, a whole host of other jobs fall under the category of "casual work." Virtually any entry-level or low-skilled job can be taken by a cruising sailor as a short-term way to beef up the cruising kitty. Jobs such as cashiers, salespersons, clerks and even the much maligned "burger flippers" all have similar attributes and detractions, so let's look at them together.

On the plus side, these low-skilled, entry-level jobs are usually easy to get in most parts of the U.S. As long as the unemployment rate remains low, this country will have a shortage of people who want to work in these positions. The reason is simple. Most of these jobs pay minimum or close to minimum wage. These days it is hard enough for most people to support themselves, let alone anyone else, on that kind of money. In fact, there is not too much difference between the benefits one receives on welfare and what one makes as a cashier at a convenience store.

But this works in the cruising sailor's favor by making these jobs readily available. And if you're living on your boat at anchor and don't have a car or other high overhead items, even the minimum wage from low-level jobs can be enough to live on and still put money in the bank.

Our friend Rick was an example of how a minimum wage job can, at times, suit a cruising sailor. Self-taught but highly intelligent, Rick built up a thriving bar/nightclub business in Detroit during the 1970s and '80s. Upon turning forty, he decided to sell the business and retire. He certainly had enough money to live on, but his personality and drive made it necessary for him to be doing something.

During the winter Rick lived on his boat at anchor in Miami. When I first met him, I was surprised to learn that this articulate, well-read man was working as a dishwasher in a nearby hotel. One day he explained to me what were, for him, the advantages of the job, and I began to see his point.

He had a short commute, about 50 feet from the dinghy dock. He was on good terms with the manager of the hotel and was treated to all kinds of fringe benefits. He had the use of the hotel's pool and laundry and was given a hefty discount on any meals he ate there. Whenever he wanted to, he could take a few days off to go sailing. He had a very low-stress job and actually found the mindless work relaxing. Furthermore, he told us that since all the money he made was gravy, he was able to treat himself to all kinds of little luxuries. Rick's attitude and life style got

*Liberated by the mindless work, Rick's fantasies took flight . . .*

me thinking about the ways in which minimum wage jobs can benefit cruisers.

During that winter I talked with many of the "snowbirds" who had come down the Intercoastal Waterway (ICW) on their boats. Most of these sailors were planning on either heading back north or over to the Bahamas in the spring. For now though, they were spending the winter on the hook in Miami. Many of them picked up jobs as cashiers or clerks as a way to both stay busy and have enough cash to enjoy the restaurants and nightlife in the city.

Of course on the downside, these jobs don't provide you with much training for anything else. Also, even though for some, like Rick, the very mindlessness of the work is relaxing, for others, that kind of repetitive, menial work can be excruciating. It's a matter of temperament. The moral to the story is that if you're cruising in the United States, don't disregard minimum wage jobs. In some cases they may be just the ticket.

## TRADE AND SKILLED WORK ON SHORE

Many other shore jobs are also suitable for cruising sailors, of course. As we saw earlier, John did well in construction work. Construction work can mean everything from entry-level manual labor jobs to highly-skilled trade work. If you enjoy working with your hands and making things, even if you have no previous experience in the building trades, at least consider construction work.

One good thing about construction work is that the more experience you get, the more marketable you become. Also, the skills you acquire in shoreside construction work can be used to your advantage working on boats. Many sailors who develop good carpentry skills find that they can move easily between marine and land-based carpentry depending on the job market. If, as you work in construction, you make an investment in acquiring your own tools, you will be well on your way to having your own business.

Our friend Tom was a high school history teacher for twenty years. After meeting the love of his life when he was forty, he decided to get out of the system and go sailing. When he and his wife sailed into the Virgin Islands a year later, he had intended only to stay a few weeks. Their boat needed repairs badly, however, and rather than dip into his savings, Tom took a job on a local construction site. He had always enjoyed woodworking projects and had renovated the interior of his ferro-cement ketch himself.

Working on the finishing touches of a custom home, Tom not only honed his carpentry skills and put money in the bank, he also bought himself a good inventory of professional power tools. Later, after returning from a six-month cruise "down island," he went to work on his own, making twice what he had earned as an employee.

The last time we cruised through the Virgins, Tom had a thriving construction business of his own, though he still managed to get away several months a year to go sailing. When I asked him if this had all been part of a plan, he chuckled. Tom told me that if, when he was teaching history in Cincinnati, somebody had told him that one day he would have a construction business in the Caribbean, he would have laughed in their face. No, he said, one thing just led to another, and he didn't regret any of it!

One positive aspect of construction jobs in a warm climate is being able to work outdoors. Also, as John found, it is certainly a way to stay fit. Moreover, the easygoing nature of a construction site is something that many people appreciate. You can dress how you like and act how you like. As long as the work gets done, you can get away with a lot of "horsing around" that would be frowned upon in other jobs. For people accustomed to the conservative office life, this can be very refreshing.

On the negative side, the physical demands of a job on a construction site may be too much for some people. If you have difficulty with heavy lifting and carrying, this kind of work is probably not for you. Also, depending on the construction methods used, you may find yourself doing a lot of very repetitive, menial work. In buildings with a lot of concrete in the structure, for example, many of the crew are kept busy mixing cement, carrying blocks, etc. Often the only "carpentry" involved is the nailing together and tearing apart of plywood forms for the pouring of concrete. This kind of work is dirty, tiring, and not very rewarding.

## WHERE TO FIND CONSTRUCTION WORK

Where, other than in the United States, can you find decent paying construction work? Like restaurant work, reasonably high wage scales for construction work can only be found in developed countries. This rules out almost the entire Caribbean, and most of Latin America and Asia. While you may luck out and be able to find construction work in Europe, Australia, or New Zealand, generally, the legalities will keep anyone from hiring foreigners. As with restaurant work, it is almost never worth the time and expense to try to get official work papers for these kinds of jobs.

Outside of the United States, any construction work you find should be considered a lucky break rather than something you can count on. Also, as with restaurant work, remember that you can work legally in all U.S. possessions and trust territories. In fact, contractors on these islands are often desperate for hardworking, skilled people and are sometimes willing to pay more than you could make on the mainland.

## HOW TO GET A JOB IN CONSTRUCTION

Like restaurant work, and most casual work onshore, the best way to get a construction job is to apply in person. Simply find building sites and ask to speak to the person in charge. A verbal description of your skills and experience is all that is needed. Generally if there is an opening, you will be hired on the spot. One thing to bear in mind when discussing wages is that sometimes construction workers in the United States are paid on an "informal" (i.e. cash) basis. This means that you are responsible for your own taxes. Clearly your take-home pay will be quite different depending on whether taxes are withheld or not, so this is a point worth asking about.

Another thing, make sure you understand exactly what you'll be doing on the job. As I said earlier, some types of construction work can be grueling, unrewarding, and only loosely related to traditional carpentry.

Let's summarize the pluses and minuses of construction work:

**PLUSES**

> Provides training that can be applicable to boat work as well
> As you become more skilled, or work for yourself, the money can be quite good
> Working conditions can be pleasant

**MINUSES**

> Work may be too physically demanding for some
> You must (literally) get your hands dirty
> Some aspects of the work may be very boring and/or repetitious

## MANAGING RESORTS ON SHORE

Clearly, if you are thinking about spending a lot of time sailing in Third World countries, casual work of the type discussed so far will not provide good income opportunities. Are there any shoreside jobs open to cruisers without specialized skills traveling in undeveloped countries? In fact, there is one category of work that lends itself particularly well to the cruising lifestyle—that of resort management.

All resorts need educated, honest people to work as managers. In the tropics it is very difficult to find and keep good people in these positions. Although experience is always desirable, in out-of-the-way locations, resort management positions are frequently open to anyone who can pick things up quickly and who is willing to apply themselves. Experience in restaurants or hotels in the United States is good preparation for resort positions abroad. Mechanical and technical expertise is also a plus.

When Pete and Annie sailed their Bristol Channel cutter into the beautiful bay in Honduras' Cayos Cochinos, they had only come for the snorkeling. When they went into the bar at the island's dive resort for a drink that night, however, they were almost immediately buttonholed by the bartender.

"Look," he told them, "I'm one of the owners of this place. Our last managers disappeared two weeks ago, and we're desperate for someone to take their place. Would you two be interested in running things here for at least six months?"

He did look desperate, and though Pete and Annie had never even thought about running a dive resort until that moment, they started discussing the idea with John, the owner. As it turned out, they ended up managing the resort for six months. Afterwards they used the experience they gained to get management jobs in the Virgin Islands and the Marshall Islands.

Although it sounds farfetched, this story is absolutely true. In fact, it is surprising how many times during our travels in the tropics we have run across almost the same scenario. An honest couple (couples are preferred for managing small resorts) willing to work hard, can find job opportunities managing resorts more often than one would think.

In many way, these jobs are similar to working for a bareboat charter company. The skills required are much the same. Office skills (basic secretarial and accounting) are desirable. The ability to troubleshoot systems, make minor repairs to keep the machinery going, is also a necessary trait. Being a sociable "people person" helps. A key part of a resort manager's job is being able to supervise the staff. These are usually local people, and, from what we have seen, a resort manager ends up being a combination motivator, moderator, expeditor and policeman.

Like working for a charter company, managing a resort may not pay the greatest wages, but very often good fringe benefits come with the job. Many times you will have the opportunity, if you wish, to live onshore at least part-time. You can eat free at the resort and have the use of their facilities such as laundry, repair shop, etc. Sometimes free dockage for your boat is included.

Also, like a charter company, a resort that wants to hire you will often smooth the way with immigration formalities. Pete and Annie did not even bother getting involved in securing a Honduran work permit, a monumental task. The resort's owner had the connections to facilitate everything.

A good sense of humor and the ability to laugh at the absurd (and yourself) is a necessity in the resort business. The quintessential account of life in this business is Herman Wouk's *Don't Stop the Carnival*. Anyone contemplating a job running a resort should read this hilarious and all-too-true account of a New Yorker's travails running a resort in the Caribbean.

Other than working as a resort manager, you may also find work as a resort dive instructor. In the Caribbean and South Pacific, resorts are always in need of certified dive staff. If you enjoy diving, consider getting your divemaster certificate before you leave (see Appendix C).

## WHERE TO FIND RESORT JOBS

Something to remember for anyone who is looking for a resort manager's job but who doesn't have much, or any, experience, is that the more isolated, inaccessible, or backward an area is, the greater the likelihood that you will land a job. It is in isolated and out-of-the-way areas that resort owners are hardest pressed to find and keep managers. The resort where Pete and Annie got their start, for instance, was the only business of any sort on an island with a population of less than two hundred. Other friends of ours had a similar break on a tiny island in Micronesia. So, while there are, of course, resorts everywhere in the tropics, concentrate on the oddball locations, and you'll have the best luck with entry-level qualifications.

## HOW TO GET A RESORT MANAGEMENT JOB

Resorts in out of the way locations are usually in need of someone quickly and on short notice. To a large extent, you have to rely on being in the right place at the right time. When you arrive at a new port, ask around for possible openings as soon as you arrive. Go to all the resorts around and ask whoever's in charge if they need anyone.

If you have some experience in the resort industry or specific qualifications, you may want to send your resumé to resorts where you think you will be sailing. There are several good databases on the Web that list resorts worldwide and their web sites (see Appendix C). Again, however, don't expect too much of a commitment until you actually arrive. You may also want to consider listing with a hospitality industry job placement service (see Appendix C). The disadvantage with this, of course, is that the jobs they come up with may not coincide with your sailing plans.

To conclude, we can summarize the pluses and minuses of managing a resort as follows:

**PLUSES**

> These jobs are often found where other semiskilled jobs pay too little to consider

> It can be an excellent way to get to know the local culture and/ or practice a language

> Good fringe benefits

**MINUSES**

> Small resorts in out-of-the-way places don't usually pay much

> The job can be very stressful and can be, though isn't always, a "24-hour-a-day" job

# CHAPTER FIVE

# GETTING A LITTLE SERIOUS

The setting sun lit the restaurant at the Trinidad Yacht Club, casting long shadows on Kent and Jan's table as they sat with their evening gin and tonics. Not that they needed any more to drink, thought Kent. The last week they had gone crazy in the lunacy of Trinidad's Carnival. Now, their heads still foggy from too many late nights, Kent and Jan began to discuss the future.

"I think it's time we made a break," Kent said. "We've been studying Spanish for what, three months now?"

"Yeah, about that." But as Jan thought back, she couldn't exactly remember when they had started their private lessons with Juanita. It must have been about three months ago, though she couldn't be sure. These days, more and more, she experienced a sort of a fuzziness of memory, a blurring together of the days.

"Anyway, it's been long enough," Kent said. "We're not going to accomplish anything staying here any longer. Everyone's told us how great Venezuela is. Let's just go and have a look."

As he spoke, Kent began to feel a sense of direction that he hadn't felt for months. In fact, for the last year he'd had a feeling that he and Jan were just drifting. Seven months ago, they had completed their second circuit through the Lesser Antilles and parked themselves here in Trinidad. It had been all too easy to stay; the dockage at the yacht club was very reasonable for their 47-foot ketch, and the social scene kept them occupied.

But looking back on it now, even through the post-Carnival haze, Kent saw a side of himself he had never been aware of before, and he didn't particularly like it. He and Jan had begun to slide down a slippery slope, and the end result he saw every night at the Yacht Club bar. The five o'clock cocktail hour was a ritual for most of the boaters living at the club, and it was obvious that for many of them, this was far from the

*Yet another night at the yacht club bar.*

beginning of the day's drinking. In fact, Kent thought, several of his friends at the club seemed to be in a constant state of inebriation. The combination of booze, hot weather, and their advancing years had combined to sap all initiative from these sailors. Kent knew for a fact that many of them hardly ever even went into the nearby city of Port of Spain anymore, let alone explored the island or sailed their boats.

When he and Jan arrived at the yacht club, they had vowed that this would never happen to them. In fact, they had originally intended to stay for only a couple of months, until the end of hurricane season, and then head back up-island. One thing had led to another, however, and after several months they found more and more excuses to stay. They wanted now to go to Venezuela but had decided that they first needed a rudimentary background in Spanish. Hence the private lessons. But as the weeks turned into months, Kent gradually realized that they were being dragged into the same tropical ennui that they had sworn to avoid. He realized now that they needed to make a move and to make it fast.

"We're pretty well stocked up aren't we?" Kent Asked.

Jan nodded.

"What would you think of leaving Saturday, three days from now? We're only paid up until then, so it'll be as good an excuse as any to get out of Dodge."

"That's fine with me dear. You know I've been trying to get us out of here for weeks."

Kent wasn't so sure this was true, but said nothing. He watched the shadows play on the table, but in his mind he was already beginning to plan the trip. It would all be new territory for them, a new language, and a different culture. He began to feel the stirring of the old enthusiasm, the sense of adventure that had brought them this far.


It was now three months later. *Osprey*, Kent and Jan's Hans Christian 47, was anchored in the harbor of the small fishing town of Morrocoy on the north coast of Venezuela. From the open hatch came the sound of the first movement of Beethoven's Moonlight Sonata. Suddenly it stopped.

"Damn it! I hate this piece." Then, "I don't care, I'm going to get it if it kills me." And the sonata started again from the beginning.

Despite her frustration that day with Beethoven, Jan was pleasantly surprised at how quickly her piano skills were coming back. It had been six years ago, before she met Kent, that she had last practiced seriously. A month earlier as a very special gift on their anniversary, Kent had surprised her with the piano, a top-of-the-line electric "baby grand." He had picked it up in Caracas, he said, and thought that she might like to start playing again on the boat. She was enthusiastic but thought it would take ages to get her form back. Now, however, though she was not as far along as she had been several years ago, she could feel herself making progress daily.

And today she would be giving her first piano lesson in almost ten years. Patti, an American sailor whom Jan and Kent had met last month in the Venezuelan islands of Los Roques, had asked if Jan could help her brush up on her own skills. A week ago, when she came to visit, Patti had been amazed at how tiny Jan's new piano was and the quality of the sound it produced. She began a campaign to convince her husband Sam that it was just what she needed as well. He had tactfully suggested that maybe she should play for a while with Jan, before they made the investment and sacrificed the precious space on the boat.

So that afternoon Jan helped Patti start to relearn her rusty arpeggios and half-forgotten etudes. The time passed quickly, and before she knew it, they had been at the piano for almost three hours. Suddenly Jan realized that even more than playing herself, she was enjoying being back in the role of a teacher.

Jan had never really considered herself a professional teacher. Nevertheless, for most of her life she had taught in some form or another. First were the years teaching piano to youngsters. Then she became active in the local Girl Scouts organization, which involved teaching in all kinds of capacities. Finally, working in an adult literacy program, she taught adults for the first time.

Patti left that afternoon with promises to return tomorrow, and Jan got to thinking. She realized, that since they had been sailing, she had gradually come to miss the interactions with her students. Helping Patti through a difficult chord progression, Jan had experienced once again that peculiar thrill that comes with a successful teacher-student exchange. She wondered, were there any other boaters around who wanted piano lessons?

While Patti and Jan worked through the intricacies of grace notes and modulations, Kent was off in the Venezuelan countryside. The week before he had been invited out to the ranch of a wealthy Venezuelan family he and Jan had met in Morrocoy. The Hernandez family kept both a house in Caracas, where they had their business, and the ranch down on the north coast, near Morrocoy, where they went for holidays and long weekends.

Last week Andre Hernandez, a retired businessman slightly younger than Kent, had asked Kent if he would like to come out to his ranch over the weekend for a little shooting. Maybe they'd get a few birds, nothing too serious, but it would be a chance to get out in the back country for a while. Kent had asked Jan if she would mind his being gone for a night. The boat was securely anchored, and the May weather was incredibly stable. Besides, Patti and Sam were there if she needed any help.

"Sure," she said, "Go out and have a good time. It'll do you good to get away from the boat for a while."

Jan got her privacy for a couple of days, and Kent got a chance to see the "weekend place" of a wealthy Venezuelan. "Just a small spread," Andre had said of their 700-acre ranch. "We're not serious about doing anything with it to make money, so we only have enough land to give us some privacy, just a place to play around."

When Kent returned the following evening Jan told him about the lessons she had given Patti. "You know, the great thing is that not only am I enjoying myself, Patti thinks it's fantastic too. She told me that although she's been thinking about getting back into her piano playing for the last couple of years, she's just never had the motivation. Now, with me here, she said she feels it's more fun."

"It's funny," said Kent, "I was mentioning to Andre yesterday that you were giving some piano lessons. He asked me if we were going to be staying around long. I said I didn't know. It seems that his daughter is looking for someone to help her with her own playing. She used to study in the city, but now she's living down here full-time and can't find anyone to help her out. I told him that your Spanish is pretty minimal, but he said his daughter speaks pretty good English. Interesting, huh?"

"Yeah, I'll say. What do you think about staying around here for a while? I mean this seems like a good anchorage. Morrocoy's a comfortable town. And we're south of the hurricane belt. If we stay down here for the summer we won't have to worry about hurricanes, this year at least."

"I've been thinking the same thing. Anyway, it's not like you have to make any kind of big commitment to Andre's daughter or anything. Andre seemed to think that she would appreciate any help you could give her."

Andre's daughter, Fiona, turned out to be an outspoken woman of thirty-five. She did, in fact, speak excellent English and wasted no time in giving Jan her views on Venezuelan society.

"Boy, I envy you Americans," she said. "We're still back in the nineteenth century here in Venezuela. All the men think about is guns and money. All the women care about is having kids and raising a family. Well, that was never my thing, I can tell you. I went to a university in the States, got a degree in education, and spent ten years in L.A. teaching Spanish. I liked it there. But in the end my family comes first. My father hasn't been very well the last couple of years, and I decided it was better for me to be here in Venezuela in case anything happens. But I'm not going to be one of those typical Latin women, staying at home and gossiping. That's why I'm living down on the coast now, I'm going to be starting a school in Puerto Cabello."

"What kind of school?" asked Jan.

"English. Teaching English to adults. English is the language of business, the language of the future, though a lot of people in South America don't want to hear that. Anybody who gets in on the ground floor in the next several years is going to have the chance to build a good business. There are already a dozen schools in Caracas, but here on the coast nobody's opened one yet. I'm going to be the first."

As they worked through the piano lesson, Jan was thinking about what Fiona had said. Later, over cocktails on the boat, Jan mentioned Fiona's ideas to Kent.

"Well, she's certainly right about English being the world language of business. If there's a conference anywhere in the world between several different nationalities, English is going to be the language they speak. And another thing. Now with the communications and information technology revolutions, more people are going to need English than ever before. It's not just traveling executives who will need it. It'll be anyone who has to fax back and forth with foreign suppliers, or who has an e-mail relationship with customers abroad. I think we're just seeing the beginnings of the need for people to learn English. Fiona's right. It's a great business to be getting into."

Jan said it was a shame she didn't have any formal background in teaching, or for that matter even know that much about English grammar, or she might be interested in trying something like teaching English. Oh well, she'd stick with what she knew and did well, teaching the piano.

Meanwhile Kent was having his own bout with language learning. He had made a serious commitment to learn Spanish and was spending several hours a day studying. He hired a local teacher, whom Fiona had recommended, and worked two hours a day onshore with her. For another couple hours he worked on his own on the boat. He invested in the latest tapes, videos, and books. Nevertheless, despite all his efforts he was still finding it heavy going. At the age of 68, learning a new language is a daunting task for anyone, regardless of his intelligence or aptitude. Nonetheless Kent was determined to stick it out. If there were two things he had plenty of, they were time and persistence.

He had found that there was much about the Venezuelan culture he really liked. The friendliness and openness of the people, the freewheeling nature of the society, the love of wild salsa music and small children. Most of all, he had the sense that here was a country with a lot of potential. It was a place where there was still a lot to be done.

But Kent realized that he could never really get to know the culture until he learned the language. He would always be an outsider, condemned to seeing only the surface of the Venezuelan society. Kent realized now that in Trinidad he and Jan had been little more than dilettantes, playing at learning Spanish. Their minds had been dulled by too much booze and their initiative sapped by their boring routines. Besides, there wasn't any chance to practice the language outside the classroom.

Kent now realized how important it was to really use a language, not just learn the rules. Already he saw that in his day-to-day dealings with the Venezuelans he was using more and more Spanish. And the more he used it, the more he understood what was said back to him. Despite the difficulties, he was very excited about his study of Spanish and optimistic about his progress. Here again was a challenge, something he could sink his teeth into. It felt good.

Jan's lessons with Fiona were also proving rewarding. Fiona had her own piano, a real baby grand brought down from Caracas, and the lessons were given twice a week in the cool of her sprawling ranch house. She was hardly a highly-skilled musician, but what she lacked in technique she made up for with enthusiasm. Frequently the lesson would be interrupted as the two women dissolved into giggles over one of Fiona's particularly off-color remarks.

One day Jan mentioned to Fiona that she was interested in being involved in Fiona's school, only she didn't have any experience or qualifications.

"Rubbish," Fiona proclaimed, "Of course you have qualifications. You're a teacher aren't you? Didn't you tell me that you've been teaching in one form or another most your life?"

"Yeah, but I don't have any qualifications for teaching English. Plus I don't know a participle from a preposition. How could I ever teach foreign students about our crazy language if I don't even understand it myself? Plus my Spanish isn't up to it. I mean I can do all right buying groceries and stuff like that, but I'm sure not conversant enough to get up and teach in Spanish."

"Jan, if that's all that's bothering you, don't even worry about it." Fiona was adamant. "Look, nowadays the new methodology in language teaching is not to use the students' native language at all. Everything is done in the language you're teaching, in this case English. In terms of having formal qualifications and learning grammar, there's a simple solution: go up to the United States and take a certificate course. That'll teach you the basics of language teaching and give you a good start on learning English grammar. There are three schools back in the States that'll give you what's called a Cambridge Certificate. This is recognized everywhere in the world. I'll tell you, it's a damn good course too. Not easy, but damn good. A couple of my friends in L.A. took it. If you're interested I'll give you the names and numbers of the schools."

"Wow Fiona, that'd be great! If I could feel that I knew what I was doing I'd really like to give this English teaching a whirl. Yeah, get me the names of those schools. I'll call them up and see what the chances are of getting into one of those courses."

Two months later Jan was wondering what she had gotten herself into. She was halfway through her Cambridge Certificate course in San Francisco, and she felt like her head was going to explode. Past perfect continuous, modal auxiliaries, L1, L2, pair work versus teacher talking time; she felt like she was learning a whole new language, maybe even two.

She had been told up front that the one-month course would be intensive, but she had never bargained for this. For four hours a day she was in teacher training classes. Here she learned the basics of the new "communicative approach" to language teaching. She also got a good grounding in English grammar. Then in the afternoons, for three hours, she was either teaching or monitoring other students' teaching. Afterwards the students all sat down with an instructor and analyzed each other's strengths and weaknesses in the classroom. By the end of the day, at five o'clock, she was wiped out. She found out though, that in order to stay on top of the course work, most nights she had to spend about another three hours on homework.

In short, it was a 12- or 13-hour day, and all of it intense. On weekends she usually had about four or five hours of work a day. Now, halfway through, she was pretty confident that she'd be able to finish the course. During the first week and a half, however, she had serious doubts and wondered if the whole idea had been a big mistake. The thought of going back to Kent and admitting that she had failed spurred her on.

Now, although she was exhausted and figured she'd probably be a quivering wreck by the time she finished, Jan was very glad she had made the decision to take the course. She could see that by the time she had finished, she would have learned a tremendous amount about the realities of teaching English, far more in fact than she had ever expected. Not for the first time, she silently thanked Fiona for pressing her to take the plunge and explore her dream.

Months later, Jan and Kent were sitting together watching the moon rise over the Los Rocques archipelago. They relaxed in the comfortable silence of a couple who doesn't need to be talking in order to communicate. Jan was thinking that there were few things in life better than freshly-caught grouper grilled on a beachfront fire, and washed down with plenty of icy cold beer. It was the beginning of February and almost a year since they had left Trinidad. Drifting with the beer and the warm tropical night, Jan thought about their life now and how changed it was from a year ago.

A few days ago Jan had finished teaching her first term at Fiona's school. She and Kent had decided to snatch a quick cruise out to the islands before the next term began. In spite of her training in San Francisco, Jan found that she had worked harder over the past three months than she had in years. It was worth it though. As she started to become more comfortable with her role in the classroom, she relaxed and began to enjoy herself. Her students were mostly young professionals who had learned some English in school but wanted to improve their fluency. There were a few students with whom she had established real friendships, and at least two of them would be with her next term.

She was still playing the piano and still tutoring Fiona. As her friendship with Fiona deepened, she realized that there was something else that had been missing in her life since they had been sailing. While she and Kent had met plenty of cruisers with whom they shared laughs and good times, the very nature of their transient life meant that Jan had never had the time to develop a close friendship with another woman. Now, after six months of working and playing together, Jan and Fiona had formed a bond that really meant something.

Jan thought too about how different Kent's life was from a year ago. His perseverance in studying Spanish finally paid off. While he tended to play it down, the truth was that Kent could now do just about anything he wanted with Spanish. Jan had even seen him bantering in a bar with some of the local fisherman whose staccato dialect was impossible for her to understand.

He was also spending more and more time with Andre. Jan wasn't too clear about what they were doing out on the ranch and Kent was strangely reticent about what he was up to. She knew it must be something Kent was serious about because he bought both a cellular phone and a personal computer and was talking about getting Andre "hooked up" with something called the "Internet." Kent said the Internet was going to revolutionize business. She was glad he was happy, anyway, and was sure she'd find out what was going on when he felt confident that his project would be a success. It was good to see him back to his old dynamic self.

The moon was high now, and *Osprey* was silhouetted in its light, fifty yards off the beach. Looking out on their home as she lay peacefully at anchor, Jan was suddenly seized by the conviction that after three years, and 3,000 miles of sailing, their adventures were just beginning.

## PROFESSIONAL WORK ON SHORE

Over the years we have met many professional people, teachers and medical people especially, who have wondered, sometimes before they went cruising, sometimes after, if they could integrate their professional life with a sailing life. The kind of commitment, amounting to almost a vocation, that motivates people to pursue careers in teaching or medicine is such that often they do not want to give up their profession completely. Somewhere down the line, these professionals very often have the desire to work in their field again. Let's see how it can be done.

### ACADEMIC TEACHING IN THE SAILING LIFE

Anyone who has been a teacher will understand that sometimes it doesn't matter *what* you teach, what's important is simply *that* you teach. On the other hand, sometimes teaching professionals want to continue in their chosen field. Not only do they feel comfortable teaching subjects they are familiar with, they also find that this is the best way to make a living.

If you have been a professional academic teacher in the United States, you are undoubtedly familiar with what is required to work there. If you will be continuing to cruise in the continental United States and want to continue teaching, you may want to take advantage of some of the Web-based job placement services for teachers in the United States (see Appendix D).

What many people don't realize is that teaching jobs in countries that are affiliated with, or are possessions of, the United States can often be significantly better than corresponding positions on the continent, both in terms of conditions and responsibilities. The reason for this is the same reason you can find jobs managing resorts so readily on these islands. Basically, it is because of the difficulty they have finding and retaining good people.

Our friend Anne, for example, was a special education teacher in the United States for twelve years. After she and her husband had cruised the Bahamas and the Caribbean for several years, she started to feel an urge to work again. When they returned to Florida, Anne got a job at a small town elementary school. She hated it. The conditions were terrible: large classes, no support from the administration, harassing parents. Plus the pay was terrible.

Anne lasted a year before she and her husband left to go cruising again. After they were gone, she wondered, had she changed that much since they'd been sailing or had conditions in U.S. public schools deteriorated?

Three years later she took a teaching job on St. John in the Virgin Islands. It was, she told me, heaven. She only had two students in her class, to whom she could give all the attention they needed. There had not been a special education teacher on the island for several years and the children's families were so happy to have their kids under the care of a professional that they couldn't do enough for Anne. And, since the school system had a perennial staff shortage and such vacancies created a budget surplus, the pay was generous. Anne was making substantially more than she had in Florida.

This is by no means a unique or even unusual story. Other friends of ours have had similar experiences in Guam and the Marshall Islands (affiliated with the United States through a Free Association agreement). We have heard of the university in the Marshall Islands paying the airfare and a generous housing per diem to attract teachers from the mainland. This means that for cruisers who are also teachers, substantial opportunities exist for working within the American education system even outside the United States.

What are the drawbacks? Isolation and a lack of contact with the mainland culture are things that many transplanted continentals complain about. For cruisers, accustomed to a life where they are frequently isolated and out of touch anyway, this is not usually a problem. On all of these islands the cost of housing and food is very high. Again though, cruising sailors do not need to worry about housing costs, and if you are working, the cost of groceries, even if high, should not be too onerous.

Finally, many mainland Americans simply don't like, or can't relate to, the local culture on these islands, which is something you'll have to work out for yourself. This is why it is a good idea not to arrange a job in the islands ahead of time, however tempting it might be. Get to your destination first and spend some time there to see if you can fit in. If, after a few weeks or a month you are already sick of the culture, you can be pretty sure that you don't want to sign a one year contract. Don't be tempted to jump into a situation where you'll be unhappy just because the money is good. After all, that's why we're cruising, so we can have control of our lives, not the other way around.

## PLUSES AND MINUSES OF ACADEMIC TEACHING: TEACHING IN THE UNITED STATES

### PLUSES

> Allows a teacher to continue his/her career

> Opportunities exist in U.S. possessions and affiliated countries that may dovetail with cruising plans

> Pay scale for an experienced teacher may be good

### MINUSES

> May be difficult to find jobs as a transient

> Working conditions in U.S. possessions or affiliated countries may not suit some Non-Academic Teaching

## ACADEMIC TEACHING ABROAD

If you want to teach outside the U.S. system, what are your options? In nearly every country you can find what are called *international* or *American* schools. These are primary and secondary schools that offer an international baccalaureate degree. This allows the graduates admission to most American and British universities. Most classes, if not all, are taught in English, mostly by native-speaking teachers. The students are a combination of well-to-do locals and children of United States and British expatriates.

The standard of the education at these schools varies, but tends to be high. They usually expect their teachers to be highly qualified, with a minimum of several years teaching experience. The pay at these schools also varies but is usually about the same in proportion to the cost of living as that received by a teacher at a private high school in the United States. For anyone interested in continuing a professional career in teaching abroad, the listings of international schools on the Web, and the international teaching placement services (see Appendix D) will be invaluable.

There are some points to consider, however, for anyone who wants to integrate this kind of a career with a cruising lifestyle. The first is the location of the schools. In many countries these high-caliber schools are located only in the capital and other large cities. As a sailor, you will either need to find schools in cities located on the water, with facilities for your boat, or make the decision to move ashore for a while. And that could be quite a while. All these schools require that you sign at least a one-year contract, and most require you to commit for two years. To leave your boat and move ashore for this long is a big decision, and one that you should be aware of before you start applying.

A second factor is that, while occasionally an international school may hire "walk-in" applicants, it is far more usual for them to place candidates well in advance. This means that the best way to find a job is to send resumés directly to schools, or list yourself with a placement service. However, it's likely that this will place possibly severe constraints on your sailing plans, depending on where you get a job and when you have to be there.

None of these obstacles is insurmountable and it is certainly possible that you may end up finding a school on the water, with a harbor nearby, in a country that you're planning on sailing to, with a job that will be starting when you expect to be there. It is possible, just not very likely. So, despite the undeniable attractions of teaching at a high quality school in a foreign country, and earning a good wage, a professional teacher who is also a cruising sailor may want to consider other options for working abroad.

## PLUSES AND MINUSES OF TEACHING AT PRIVATE INTERNATIONAL SCHOOLS ABROAD

### PLUSES

➤ High standards may appeal to experienced professionals

➤ Wages can be quite good

➤ A contract provides job security

### MINUSES

➤ May be difficult to find jobs that match cruising plans

➤ Two-year, or longer, contract may be too long a commitment

➤ Location of school may force a move ashore

## CASUAL TEACHING

Whether you are a highly-qualified teaching professional or someone like Jan, don't discard the idea of nonacademic, nontraditional teaching opportunities.

What can you teach? Virtually anything that you have a specialized knowledge of and that others want to learn. We have known people who, like Jan, taught music, people who taught computer skills, handicrafts and scuba diving. The list is endless, and it's really a question of your imagination and market demand.

Who do you teach? One obvious answer is other boaters. One difficulty with trying to teach boaters, however, is that they're always leaving for somewhere! One way to get around this is to plan to teach during a season when few people are sailing. In the Caribbean and the Pacific these are the hurricane and typhoon seasons, respectively. In the Mediterranean, it's winter. During these periods sailors often hole up in one spot, and a small community develops among the boaters. In such a situation it is easy to canvass the other cruisers and see if there is an interest in a particular topic.

One friend of ours had been a dance instructor in the States. While spending the winter with a group of boaters in Lisbon, she asked around and found that many women were interested in a yoga dance class. She rented a space from the neighboring private school for a nominal fee and held class there twice weekly. The concept was a success with the boaters as it gave everybody a way to get some exercise during the dark, rainy winter months. It was also a great way for everybody to get to know each other. Amy, the instructor, made a little money out of the program, but more important, found herself once again doing what she really enjoyed, teaching.

If you are in a non-English speaking country and are fluent in the native language, boaters will always welcome the opportunity to practice one-on-one. During one rainy summer we passed on Guatemala's Rio Dulce. Maria, a native Mexican sailing on a Canadian yacht, had the idea of giving private Spanish lessons. Again, the boating community welcomed the concept. Before long she was teaching three lessons a day, making a bit of money, and having fun.

Of course, you don't have to confine your teaching to other sailors. If you speak the language of the country you're in, or if enough people speak English, you can also offer classes to the locals. Consider asking at the local schools, or perhaps the yacht club to see if there is interest in one of your areas of expertise. Many times in developing countries, foreigners (especially Americans) are seen as possessing cutting-edge information.

Roger, an American sailor who spent the winter with us in Lisbon, offered a series of workshops on the Internet at the private school where I was teaching English. At first he was just instructing the teachers, but there was so much interest from the students that he began offering classes to small groups of them as well. The topic of the Internet was at the time very "cool" and the students were keen to find out the latest about the "information superhighway" from someone in the know.

Although he had originally intended to only hold a few classes, Roger ended up giving over fifteen workshops during the course of the winter. He told me that it was a great way to get to know the local people of Lisbon. He spoke no Portuguese when he had arrived in October, and said that before he started giving the workshops, he had felt shut out of the local culture. By the end of the winter, however, he had a whole circle of *Lisboeta* friends with whom he socialized regularly. He even learned a bit of Portuguese. When it came time to go, he said that of his four winters in the Mediterranean, this one had been the most fun, and that next winter he would definitely try to do some teaching again.

The bottom line with any of these ideas, however, is that they require initiative to make them happen. This means you can't be shy about your talents. If you have a skill that you think others might benefit from and you're in a situation where you can market yourself, get out there and do it! While you'll never get rich, you can make a few bucks and more importantly, you'll be sharing something you enjoy. Also, as Jan found out, it's a great way to meet people and can lead to all kinds of other opportunities.

## PLUSES AND MINUSES OF CASUAL, NON-ACADEMIC TEACHING

### PLUSES

➢ Can be a good way to meet other cruisers or locals

➢ Generally low-stress

➢ May lead to other opportunities

### MINUSES

➢ Generally, the money is not very good

➢ Logistics may be difficult

➢ Requires setting things up yourself

## TEACHING ENGLISH AS A FOREIGN LANGUAGE (EFL)

If you are looking for a formal teaching position but want more flexibility than is offered working for an international school, consider what Jan decided to do, teach English as a Foreign Language (EFL). As Jan found out, teaching EFL is a booming business today, with opportunities in virtually every country in the world. The nature of the schools, and variety of programs, means that you have a selection and flexibility unmatched by traditional teaching positions.

What is the typical EFL position like? Well, if there *was* a typical EFL position that would be an easy question to answer. Unfortunately there's no such thing! I will say, however, that the majority of EFL positions that would be suitable for cruisers are with relatively small, private schools. Usually you will be teaching adults (over 18 years old) who need to learn English, or improve their English, for their careers or professional lives. Sometimes you will be involved with a school that specializes in readying students to study in the U.S. or British universities, preparing

*Exotic locales add spice to an EFL career.*

them for the entrance exams required by those universities. Sometimes you may be teaching younger students, though usually not younger than high school age. Because of the tremendous number of EFL schools that have sprung up in the last ten years, you will often have the opportunity to choose the type of situation you want.

In addition, after you have worked for a while and gained some experience you will probably want to consider giving private lessons. This can be either a way to supplement your income from the school or your sole source of income. Although it takes a while to build up a "portfolio" of students, once you have acquired a number of steady clients this can be substantially more lucrative than working for a school.

And speaking of being lucrative, how much do EFL teaching jobs pay? On the average, EFL positions pay about the same, relative to the cost of living, as positions in U.S. public high schools. In other words, not a lot, but certainly enough, if you are living on board and keeping your overhead down. Of course, as you gain experience and work for better schools, or if you teach privately, the wages can be substantially more.

Like most teaching jobs you'll never get rich teaching English. It can, however, be very rewarding. It is particularly satisfying to be able to empower people to change their lives for the better. In many countries this is exactly what you're doing by teaching English. For people in poor countries, learning English is often the key that opens the door to a whole range of opportunities.

Teaching English is also an excellent way to get to know a culture better. You have direct contact with the local people, and the classroom can provide you with the opportunity to ask all kinds of questions about the students' country, its politics, and its culture. I have found that taking the students' minds off "learning English" by getting them to talk about politics and current events dramatically helps their fluency. Plus it is a great way for the teacher to learn as well!

## GETTING CERTIFIED

Although not all schools require certification to teach EFL (for instance, the larger "diploma mills" in Japan will hire almost anyone), you will find that to land any desirable jobs, you will have to become certified. And as Jan found out, the certificate course is much more than a "pay your money, get your ticket" course. You will actually practice by teaching real students in a real classroom. You'll also learn a substantial amount of current pedagogical theory and English grammar.

Although many certificates are offered by many different schools, there is only one that's worth getting. This is what's often called the Cambridge Certificate or, more properly the Royal Society of the Arts Certificate of English Language Teaching for Adults or RSA/CELTA.

What sets this certificate apart from others is this: although it's offered by schools all over the world, both the curriculum and teaching methods are designed and closely monitored by Cambridge University in England. Because of this standardization the certificate is recognized worldwide by virtually every reputable EFL school as being the guarantee of a certain level of teaching ability.

To their credit, by introducing this CELTA certificate, and rigorously upholding its standards, Cambridge has gone a long way toward standardizing and professionalizing EFL teaching worldwide. There are three schools in the United States that offer the RSA/CELTA course:

one in San Francisco; one in Fort Lauderdale, Florida; and one in New York City (see Appendix D for more information).

Admission to these certificate courses is not open to anyone. To be admitted to the course, you will have to convince the admissions officer that you:

> ➤ Have a good command of spoken and written English

> ➤ Have the ability to learn (not that you know already) details of English grammar

> ➤ Have a legitimate desire to teach and the ability to relate to your students

> ➤ Can function well in a team environment

While the schools prefer applicants to hold a university degree (bachelor's or master's), they will waive this requirement if other strengths are present. Prior teaching experience, time spent living abroad, and the ability to speak another language are all looked upon as desirable.

As Jan found out, the one-month course is very intensive. For someone pressed for time, this is a good option. However, everyone I have ever met who has taken the course (including myself), has felt like Jan did at the end of it, wiped out. The school in Fort Lauderdale offers as an alternative a three-month, part-time course. I would recommend this to anyone who has the time because it allows you to assimilate the large amount of information over a more realistic time span.

## WHERE TO FIND EFL JOBS

As we said earlier, these days you can find EFL jobs almost anyplace in the world (even in the United States). Around the world, however, both the quality and quantity of available jobs vary considerably. In the United States for example, the demand for Certified EFL teachers (as opposed to those holding bachelor's or master's degrees) is primarily confined to smaller, lower paying schools geared towards immigrants and low income students. In Argentina and Southern Brazil, on the other hand, there is a large, growing, and well-paid market for skilled teachers of business English. And so on. Anyone interested in pursuing a career in teaching English would be well advised to read one or more of the very good books available on the subject (see Appendix D).

## HOW TO GET A JOB TEACHING ENGLISH

There are several ways to get a job teaching English. To begin with, get the names of schools where you plan to be traveling, and send out resumés. As with other jobs, however, don't expect a lot of commitment until you actually arrive. When I last crossed the Atlantic, I planned to spend the winter in Lisbon. Knowing that the EFL market there was booming, I sent off about twenty resumés in June. I did not get a single response.

I was not too optimistic, then, about finding a job when I hit the streets of Lisbon in September. Imagine my surprise when I received two job offers within the first two days, both from schools that had received but not responded to my resumés! I ended up working for a school whose director of studies actually remembered my application. She said that she had liked my resumé but had not been able to make a commitment so far in advance. The moral to the story is that though sending resumés in advance might not actually get you a job, it can't hurt, and the schools might even remember you when you walk in the door.

Another way to look for an EFL job is to utilize online placement services either before you leave or after you arrive in a country (see Appendix D for a list of these services). The advantage in doing this is that you are dealing with close to real-time information and you can actually find schools that have a current need for teachers. The disadvantage is that a school must list with the service in order for you to find them. There may be many schools abroad who are not yet savvy enough, or don't care, to list with online placement agencies. As their databases grow, however, these services will probably become more and more valuable.

Finally, of course, you can just arrive at your destination and "bang on doors." This is what I did in Lisbon, and have done in other places, and it works fine. As in many other relatively transient jobs, if a school needs you, they will frequently hire you on the spot.

One thing to consider when looking for an EFL job are the hours you will be working. You will usually be teaching professional adults, so you will often find yourself called on to work odd hours that coincide with the students' free time. It is not uncommon for a school to offer one or two classes during the lunch hours as well as several in the evening. Some schools also offer classes in the early morning before work.

This means that you may find yourself teaching one class in the early morning, one at lunch, and three in the evening. In such a scenario you would start work at seven in the morning and not finish until ten at night, though you would only get paid for five hours (most schools only pay you for the actual time you teach). Before you take a job, make sure you find out what your schedule will be. If it seems too arduous, try to negotiate with the school for something more acceptable.

Another point to be aware of is that frequently schools contract with businesses to provide teaching on-site, at the company itself. If this will be the case, find out if you will be compensated for travel time and expenses. Also find out how much traveling you will be doing. Will you be teaching all day at one company, or will you have to shift from one place to another several times a day?

And finally, a word about legalities. In most of the world, if you land a job with an established school, they will handle the paperwork. However, it is becoming increasingly difficult for Americans to get work legally in countries in the European Union. There are still opportunities in Spain, Portugal, and Greece; however, it's hard to say how much longer this will last. For a cruising sailor who will probably not be staying more than a year or two, it is generally not worth the bother to go through the whole rigmarole of getting EU working papers for an EFL job. If you're thinking of working in Western Europe, research the current situation before you go. Of course Turkey, not being an EU member, continues to offer good possibilities, though with lower wages than Europe.

## PLUSES AND MINUSES OF TEACHING ENGLISH AS A FOREIGN LANGUAGE

### PLUSES

➤ Many job opportunities world wide

➤ Excellent way to meet local people and learn about their culture

➤ More flexibility than traditional teaching positions

### MINUSES

➤ Wages not very high (especially at entry-level positions)

➤ Usually requires a commitment for at least one academic year

➤ Hours may be long or inconvenient

# WORKING AS A MEDICAL PROFESSIONAL

Many opportunities exist throughout the world for health care professionals to continue their professional lives after embarking on a cruising lifestyle. Over the years we have met retired doctors who volunteer in clinics, nurses who return to the United States every year or two to work, dentists who set up practices on their boats, and a host of others in the health care fields who continued to work in one form or another as they sailed.

There seems to be something about the health care professions that makes it difficult for people to give up their work permanently. Fortunately, several options allow one to integrate work in the health care field with a cruising lifestyle. Let's take a look at them.

## WORKING AS A MEDICAL DOCTOR

If you are a licensed medical doctor in the United States and want to continue to work while you cruise, you will have several options. If you wish to get paid while you practice, there are a few agencies that specialize in placing doctors worldwide. Most of them place American doctors in areas of other English speaking countries, mostly Australia, New Zealand, and Canada, that are under-served and in need of personnel (see Appendix D for more information).

While these countries do not usually offer reciprocal licensing status to American doctors, they are willing to make exceptions in areas where doctors are needed. These positions usually require a six month- to two-year commitment. If you think you will be cruising to one of these countries and wish to work in your profession, it is worthwhile to make contact with these agencies and see what they can offer. Unfortunately these are fixed-term appointments, and you will not be able to work indefinitely in the country without going through a lengthy and expensive certification process.

Fortunately, most American M.D.'s who decide to go cruising, will not need to work to support themselves under way. What is far more common is that doctors, even after they "retire," can't get doctoring out of their blood. We have known many retired doctors, and dentists too, who find that the challenges and rewards of volunteer work fill the gap. This volunteer work is usually in developing countries desperately in need of health care professionals, making the rewards both immediate and lasting.

Several years ago my wife, a semi-retired R.N., found a position assisting a retired doctor who was running a clinic on the island of Utila, off the coast of Honduras. The clinic itself was tiny, only a couple of rooms, and the doctor and my wife did everything. I can remember eagerly waiting for her return in the evenings because hardly a day went by when there was not some exciting, hair-raising or unique experience at the clinic.

The doctor and my wife were doing everything from setting bones to treating advanced cases of malaria. They were delivering babies, stitching up drunks after knife fights, and treating venereal disease. My wife had worked thirteen years in Manhattan intensive care units but had never seen anything like what she encountered in that tiny clinic. For many people accustomed to the specialization of the American medical system, the very diversity that they encounter in volunteer work in developing countries is a big attraction.

If you are an American trained doctor or dentist interested in volunteer work abroad, you're in luck. There are many agencies that specialize in placing medical volunteers worldwide. Several of them are listed in Appendix D. If you intend to be spending much time in the Third World you should certainly be able to line up something that will fit in with your cruising plans.

## WORKING AS A NURSE

Like doctors, many nurses do not want to leave their career in medicine behind just because they have left to go sailing. As a nurse, what are your options in a cruising lifestyle?

If you are cruising in the United States the answer is straightforward. Virtually every state offers licensing reciprocity so, although you must apply for a new license in each state, you can work anywhere. While the nursing shortage of the 1980s may be over in most of the United States, it is safe to say that a nurse interested in working in a hospital should be able to find work anywhere. In fact, in the U.S. possessions and affiliated countries the job market for nurses is similar to that for teachers. Hospitals and clinics are often desperate for skilled people.

The caveats for nursing in the islands are similar also. Many Stateside nurses find working conditions in these locations to be unpleasant and unprofessional. Others enjoy the casualness and lack of red tape. So, although you may want to research these job markets before you get to one of these islands, I suggest you avoid committing to anything until you have had a chance to check out conditions in person.

For nurses interested in working overseas, there are several placement services (listed in Appendix D) that can advise you on the job markets. The markets for nursing worldwide are continually changing, however, so any specific recommendations I could make here would probably not be valid by the time this book is in print. As with doctors, if a country needs your services, they will honor your U.S. credentials. The catch is they must need nurses. If there is not a shortage, it will probably be difficult or impossible to get licensed.

Nurses also have the same opportunities as doctors for volunteering. We have met several nurses in developing countries who were running clinics on their own. For someone accustomed to working under M.D.'s in the United States system, the idea of having autonomy and the freedom to set things up as you want can be a powerful inducement.

During our stay in the Bay Islands we met another nurse, Pauline, in the Cayos Cochinos. During the winter she operated a free clinic out of a tiny house onshore. Then, every spring she and her husband would sail back to Florida and spend the summer with family and friends. While in the States, Pauline would contact hospitals and clinics in her area and solicit donations of outdated, but still useful drugs, dressings, and other medical supplies.

Single-handedly this exceptional couple was staffing and equipping the clinic at virtually no cost to anyone. They were making a tremendous difference in the lives, not only of the inhabitants of Cayos Cochinos (who otherwise had no health care), but also to poor Hondurans up and down the coast. Pauline told us that it was nothing for coastal Indians to paddle forty miles in a dugout canoe to bring a family member in to be treated! She said she was just happy her husband had a small pension so that they were able to carry on with their work. She said that the last four years running the clinic had been the best in her whole thirty-year nursing career.

Cruising nurses can also avail themselves of volunteer placement services (see Appendix D). As with positions for doctors, there are opportunities worldwide and anyone who is seriously interested should be able to find something that will fit in with a cruising lifestyle.

You should be aware of two things when considering volunteer work as a health care professional. One is that working in poor developing countries may entail putting up with less than sanitary conditions and exposing yourself to tropical diseases. For some people, used to working under the hygienic conditions of the States, this may come as a shock.

A second point to keep in mind is that a volunteer job may turn into a much bigger commitment than you initially bargained for. More than once, we have seen health care professionals who became so embroiled with not only the medical problems but also the personal lives of their patients that the job ended up dominating their lives. But is this necessarily such a bad thing?

So, what then, are the pluses and minuses of working in the health care professions? Let's look at working for wages and working as a volunteer separately.

## WORKING FOR WAGES IN THE HEALTH CARE PROFESSIONS

**PLUSES**

> If the host country needs your skills, licensing requirements will be waived

> Working in a small community abroad may be a pleasant change from the work environment in the United States

> If the situation dovetails with your cruising plans, it can be a good way to put some money in the bank

**MINUSES**

> Available positions may place unwanted restrictions on your sailing plans

> Especially for doctors, wages may be much less than you're used to

> The working environment may be a "step down" from the United States

## WORKING AS A HEALTH CARE VOLUNTEER

**PLUSES**

> Can be very rewarding

➤   Much more diversity and freedom than found in the United States

➤   Many positions open worldwide

**MINUSES**

➤   You may be working in unhealthy or unsanitary conditions

➤   The job may turn into more of a commitment than you had expected

To conclude this section, in my opinion, both teaching English and working abroad in a the health care field epitomize work for cruisers at its best. Both fields allow sailors enough flexibility to integrate the work into their sailing plans. Both professions provide material benefits to the people of the host country. Both professions can reward cruisers in material as well as less quantifiable ways. Finally, they can both provide the opportunity for sailors to really get to know the culture of the country they are in. In short, I feel that anyone with an interest in these areas should seriously consider exploring them further.

## WORKING AS A COMPUTER PROFESSIONAL

If you are fortunate enough to be have an Information Technology (IT) background you are certainly aware of the myriad opportunities for short-term contract work in this field. Internationally, the demand for skilled IT professionals far outstrips the supply and is likely to continue to do so for the foreseeable future. Also, the trend for companies to hire IT professionals as temporary workers for fixed-length contracts is growing. Over three-quarters of some 1,500 IT companies surveyed recently said they regularly hire IT professionals as temporary workers.

What this means for a cruising sailor who also happens to be a qualified IT professional is that there is a good chance of finding short-term contract work almost anywhere in the world. The most opportunities exist, of course, in developed countries. The United States, Western Europe, and Australia all have booming IT sectors and are constantly recruiting temporary workers.

Probably the best approach for a sailing IT professional is to contact several of the worldwide placement services (see Appendix D). These services list tens of thousands of jobs available worldwide and provide an interface between companies in need of short-term help and skilled workers. This is one of those areas that is changing so rapidly that predicting what the market will look like in the future is virtually impossible.

Two years ago we saw a graphic example of how the qualified IT professional is in demand worldwide. Our German friend Gunter had worked for a large American software development firm for three years while living on his boat in Miami. His specialty was designing and implementing software packages for financial institutions. His firm kept him very busy, signing him up for one six-month contract after another. One day, though, Gunter realized he was spending all his time working and none sailing. When the next contract came up he declined, telling his company that he was going back to Europe. They told him to stay in touch because they might have work for him there, provided he was interested.

That spring Gunter single-handed his steel sloop across the Atlantic via the usual route of Bermuda and the Azores. In September he arrived in Lisbon where we met up with him for the first time in several years. After a couple months of hanging out in Lisbon, and with the prospect of a long and wet winter ahead, Gunter rang his old employer.

"Lisbon!" they said. "Perfect, we've got a contract starting there next month. You interested?"

Gunter thought for a minute and said, "Sure. Why not." With almost no effort on his part, Gunter had transferred his skills across the Atlantic.

You need not be a computer programmer or systems analyst to work in the IT field these days. Anyone with a good grasp of the basics of PC's, Windows, MS Office and the Net, can, with some studying, become a Microsoft Certified Systems Engineer (MCSE). This certificate, awarded after successfully passing a comprehensive exam, qualifies one to work as a troubleshooter in corporate intranets. As more and more companies implement their own private networks, they are finding that they need qualified personnel to keep the nets up and running and to instruct their staff in the most efficient way to make use of the network. These companies look for people with the MCSE Certificate, and anyone holding one is virtually assured of a well-paying job.

Another area in which non-programmers can shine is in Web page design and content management. Worldwide, more and more businesses are jumping on the Web as a venue for marketing. Companies that specialize in designing Web pages are proliferating, and they are constantly in need of qualified personnel. If you are an expert with software, such as MS FrontPage (and especially if you can work with the HTML programming language) you will be in demand in virtually every corner of the globe.

These of course are just a sampling of the IT jobs available. The IT market is growing every month. It is safe to say that for the foreseeable future, jobs in this field will be plentiful. They will also be diverse enough to provide anyone who qualifies and desires to integrate an IT career with a sailing lifestyle many chances to do so.

## OTHER PROFESSIONAL WORK OVERSEAS

In addition to the specific professions addressed so far, there are of course others that a cruising sailor may pursue abroad. We have, over the years, met cruisers who worked in a wide range of professions: engineers, accountants, management consultants, and scientists to name a few. Obviously, to cover the opportunities that exist for all these jobs in all the different countries of the world, is outside the scope of this book. If you are currently working in a professional capacity in the United States and are wondering about your work options abroad, I would strongly suggest checking out some of the resources on the subject that are listed in Appendix D.

Those considering professional work abroad are probably interested as much in the immigration policies and restrictions of various countries as in the job markets themselves. Also in Appendix D is a listing of resources for finding out more about the current immigration policy of any country you are interested in.

## WORKING OCCASIONALLY BACK IN YOUR HOME COUNTRY

At this point I'd like to comment on an approach that many cruisers we have known have used to practice their profession; that is, occasionally returning to work in their home country without their boat. One way to do this is to keep a residence, a house or condominium, that can be rented while cruising and lived in when you return to your home country. Many people have found that this combination of part-time work in one's home country and part-time cruising allows them to combine the best of both worlds.

Many people, like Kent, find themselves, after several years of full-time cruising, looking for something more. They don't want to return to their old life full-time, but neither do they want to pursue a job in a foreign country. By mixing a few months of work in their home country with a few months of cruising, they can take advantage of opportunities offered in each way of life.

Our friends Mike and Liz have been doing this successfully for over six years now. They maintain a house in the suburbs of Toronto and a sailboat in the Mediterranean. Whenever they feel the urge, often during the cold, wet Mediterranean winter, they put their boat in one of the secure, long-term storage yards that are becoming increasingly common and fly back to Canada. While they rent out the main section of their house year-round, there is a small addition in the back that they live in whenever they return.

Mike is a management consultant and Liz is a registered nurse. Mike works on a contract basis for a large firm in Toronto and Liz can usually find a job in home healthcare through a local agency. One day I questioned Mike and Liz on their arrangement. It seemed almost too good to be true. Surely they couldn't both be assured of landing jobs every time they went back? Mike agreed that there were certainly no guarantees. In fact, occasionally one or the other of them could not find work. Nevertheless, they both had established reputations in their fields, and over the six years of "commuting" between the Mediterranean and Canada, each had been able to work about 80 percent of the time.

The rental income from their house covered maintenance and taxes. In effect, this allowed them to live rent free whenever they went back. Storage fees for the boat, while they were away, were minimal, and their only real cost for the trip was airfare. So, Mike said, even if in one year neither of them could land a job, it would not be catastrophic. In short, he was very happy with their situation. It allowed them to not only put some money in the bank every year, but also to stay active in their careers, see their friends in Toronto, and keep variety in their lives.

There are two things to note in Liz and Mike's story. First, as more and more boats join the cruising fleet, more and more cruisers are following the path taken by Mike and Liz. This has made it economically feasible for an increasing number of boatyards all over the world to cater to people who wish to store their boats out of the water for months or even years at a time.

These yards offer minimal or no services, except security, and are surprisingly inexpensive. Usually the charges are only 25 to 35 percent of what you would pay for a marina berth in the same area.

The second factor that has made this part-time cruising option increasingly viable is the growing acceptance of short-term contract work in the workplace. The concept of a lifetime career with one company is as outmoded as communism. Increasingly, employers are discovering the benefits of hiring independent contractors, often on a short-term basis. We will discuss this trend in more detail in the next chapter. One point to note here, however, is that when you take a job as an independent contractor, be very cautious about telling an employer up front that you plan to return to your boat in a short time. Even though you may only sign a contract for a few months, many employers like to think that they will be able to keep you on indefinitely if they like your work. They want to have their cake and eat it too. Of course after you develop a relationship with an employer, as Mike and Liz had, you will probably be able to lay your cards on the table.

As a result of these developments, the concept of regularly flying back to one's home country for work, which ten years ago would have been much more difficult, is now practical from virtually any of the world's popular cruising grounds. Nowadays we know of cruisers who regularly:

➤ Leave their boat in Trinidad to return to work in Europe

➤ Leave their boat in Australia to work in the United States

➤ Leave their boat in the Mediterranean to work in New Zealand

➤ Leave their boat in Florida to work in Canada

The options for structuring such an arrangement are endless and are as varied as the cruisers who pursue them. The point to remember is that if you are a professional who wants to go cruising, but are reluctant to forgo your professional working life completely, this approach may be the best way to integrate your work with your sailing.

# CHAPTER SIX

# THE ENTREPRENEUR ONBOARD

The boat was a mess. There was sawdust and debris everywhere, but Steve and Irene didn't care. It was just good to be back home again. Steve was in the middle of three projects at once: installing a new watermaker, a refrigerator, and a new diesel engine. Inevitably chaos reigned. At the same time, he and Irene were planning what they would do next.

It was a month and a half now since they had finished their contract with Stewart, and as Steve reflected back, he thought that it had been a good two years. While running Stewart's boat he and Irene had cruised most of the Eastern Caribbean. From the Dominican Republic to Venezuela, they spent time at almost every island, dove a good percentage of the reefs, and even ventured inland for a couple of weeks in South America. They had also managed to save a sizable amount of money, some of which was funding the new improvements to their boat.

Stewart had proven to be a good man to work for. He was fair and honest, and Steve had to admit that he and Irene would have been hard-pressed to find a better situation. Of course, occasionally the work was stressful and the days long, especially when Stewart arrived with three or four friends. Overall though, it had been a good job, and both Steve and Irene were glad to have had it.

However, after two years, they both felt they needed their freedom. Irene met a young couple in St. Martin who seemed like they would be good replacements. With Stewart's permission, she and Steve had taken them aboard for a month to show them the ropes. Stewart was sorry to see Steve and Irene leave, but understood their need for freedom, and when they left, he showed his appreciation with a handsome bonus.

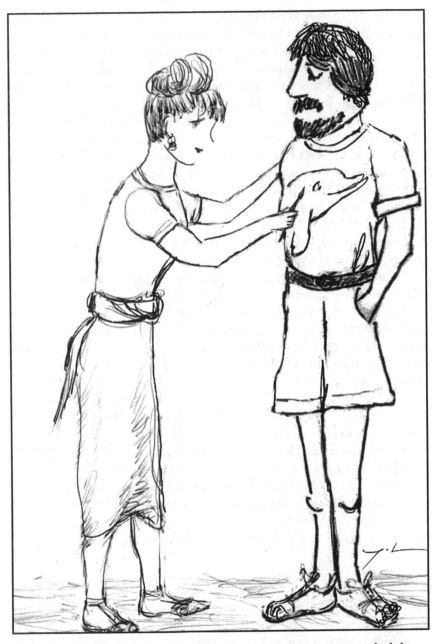

*Onboard crafts can be lucrative ways to earn money on your own schedule.*

While Steve worked on the boat, Irene was spending time with Judy, a friend of hers on St. Thomas. Judy ran a small tourist boutique. A few weeks ago, when she saw some of Irene's sketches of tropical scenes, she became very enthusiastic. She told Irene that hand-painted T-shirts were all the rage among tourists this year, and encouraged Irene to try her hand at it. Irene had never even thought of such a thing, but with Judy's urging she decided to see how it went. Working at Judy's boutique would at least be a way to escape the chaos on board her boat.

Once she got over her initial shyness and her hesitancy about publicly displaying her work, Irene found that she was really enjoying herself. Many of the motifs that she had been sketching privately for the last few years—parrots, dolphins, beachfront scenes—worked very well on T-shirts.

Even more surprising to Irene, her work sold. A few weeks after she began, Judy was pressing her for more shirts.

"I can't keep the darn things in the store," Judy told Irene one day. "I'll take as many as you can give me."

The shirts were selling for twenty dollars each, which Irene thought was outrageous. She was making ten dollars a shirt, and although she and Steve were no longer strapped for cash, it was gratifying to Irene to receive monetary confirmation of her work's worth. She thought that this was the first time in her life that she was actually making money doing something that she both wanted to do and enjoyed.

Steve, meanwhile, was enjoying himself refitting *Dancer*. After years of pinching pennies while equipping the boat in Florida, searching for parts and used equipment in secondhand marine stores, flea markets, and trash bins, it was a treat to be able just to go out and buy what he needed, when he needed it. He was looking forward to the security of a brand new engine, plus the convenience of having a refrigerator and watermaker. As the weeks passed and things slowly came together, he and Irene began to get excited about going sailing again.


Then, one day they were off. It was the middle of December, and the winter trade winds were beginning to fill in. *Dancer* bounded along on a broad reach on her way to the Dominican Republic, Haiti, and, hopefully, Cuba. Steve and Irene were looking forward to new ports, new adventures, and the chance to make use of all the improvements Steve had made to their boat. Irene had lain in a stock of paints, a pile of T-shirts, and had several new ideas she planned to try out. Judy was adamant in encouraging Irene to keep painting. She said that the T-shirts were one of the bestselling items in her boutique.

The winter, rich with promise, stretched out ahead of the two young sailors. As the sun began to set on their first night at sea, Steve looked at Irene, next to him in the cockpit, and for no particular reason, reached over and held her tight.

Meanwhile, 1,200 miles to the west, in Costa Rica, John and Paula sat down to dinner amid the incessant insect din of a tropical forest. With them were Peter and Lucy, their hosts and the owners of the Jungle Inn. Low watt bulbs cast a pleasant yellow light over the open-air dining room. John raised his beer and proposed a toast.

"To a great season this year!"

"Amen to that! We sure need it." said Peter.

Three weeks ago Paula and John dropped anchor in Golfito, a sleepy little town at the head of a deep bay on the west coast of Costa Rica. Once they stumbled across the Jungle Inn on the outskirts of town, it did not take them long to get to know Peter and his wife Lucy. Now every two or three days John and Paula would come for dinner at the resort, and inevitably, the discussion turned to business, or rather the lack of it. The resort had been open for a year, but so far Peter and Lucy were not even breaking even.

"I don't understand it," Peter said to John. "We've got this beautiful location, our prices are more than fair, we've been open for a year, and we're still not getting any business. What are we doing wrong?"

John didn't have an answer. As he talked more with Peter, however, an idea began to form. Peter told John that they relied on two travel agents in the United States for all their bookings.

"How well do you know these guys?" John asked Peter over dinner. "I mean, if they're not actively promoting the Jungle Inn, you're dead in the water. And why list with only two travel agents? Why not ten, or twenty? A lot of people in the States don't even know where Costa Rica is. You've got to really get the Jungle Inn name noticed if you want people to go to the trouble of coming to a backwater like this."

"Yeah, I know you're right, John," Peter said.

"The thing is, Lucy and I got into this business to avoid all that hassle. We wanted a low-key life out here in the jungle. But we have to get some business soon, or we're not going to be able to hang on."

John's idea was beginning to coalesce. Over the next several nights he convinced Peter to let him give it a try. Next week he was flying back to Los Angeles anyway to sort out some problems with the couple renting his house. John's idea was to give some of his old contacts a call, and maybe generate a little publicity for Peter's resort. After all, that *was* what he used to do for a living, though that seemed like another life now.

It was now a year and a half since John and Paula had left Los Angeles. The previous winter they dawdled their way down the Baja peninsula in the company of George and Sheila. When spring came, however, George said he wanted to head north. He and Sheila wanted to see Oregon and maybe get as far as Seattle, waters they had not yet explored. John and Paula were hooked on the tropics and wanted to continue south. The two boats separated, vowing to stay in touch via SSB radio.

During the course of the summer *Drifter* worked her way down the Mexican coast. After the tranquility of many of the nearly deserted bays in Baja, the hectic tourist resorts of mainland Mexico were a shock. Though they enjoyed some of the smaller communities, John and Paula did not care to linger in Mexico. They had heard good reports of Costa Rica from northbound cruisers and were anxious to see the country for themselves. Also, Paula wanted a secure and pro-tected anchorage where they could stop for a while, and she could indulge herself in a new hobby.

During the lazy Baja winter, Paula found herself once again taking up an old interest: sewing. Before they left, she and John had equipped the boat with a heavy-duty sewing machine, as they had read accounts of sailors repairing sails underway and doing their own canvas work. They thought that they should be equipped to do the same. Paula figured she should be able to get the knack of it fairly quickly, since years ago she had done a fair bit of sewing, making dresses for herself and sewing the curtains for her first house. After her career took off though, Paula found herself with less and less time for non work-re-lated activities, and the sewing machine was packed off to the attic.

In Baja, Paula once again found herself enjoying being creative. The first project she tackled was an awning. Even in the winter, the sun in Baja was intense, and she and John quickly realized they needed some sort of shade on their boat. Another boater had some surplus marine canvas, which Paula bought, and soon she had made *Drifter* a large awning. As well as shade for the boat, she and John soon realized that they needed some sort of sun protection for themselves. They noticed that most of the boaters they met had some sort of floppy sun hats. They did not see anything in the local stores that they liked though, and the Mexican straw hats they bought soon disintegrated. With her sewing machine still warm from the awning project, Paula decided to try her hand at a couple hats. She found some coarse white canvas in a little shop ashore and sat down to see what she could do.

It took her a few attempts to work out the pattern, but eventually, she produced a pair of very serviceable floppy hats. Paula sat back from her machine, rather pleased with herself. There! Not only had she made something useful, she had worked out her own pattern that she could use in the future. She realized that she was enjoying herself and resolved to tackle more sewing projects.

Now, in Golfito, Paula had what she would later think of as a brainstorm. While John was away in the States, she passed her time on the boat making several more hats. Rather than leave them white, however, she painted designs on them. In some of the Mexican tourist towns, Paula had seen hand-painted T-shirts, and the prices charged for them. She wondered, why not do the same with hats? Now she had the time to experiment, and soon she came up with a couple of interesting designs. One was a green and black approximation of tropical foliage, another a black and white zebra pattern. In a third she used small sponges and pastel colors to create an abstract montage. She had to admit, she was pleased with the way the hats looked.

When she showed Lucy the hats the next day, Lucy urged her to make more. "I'll put these in my boutique," Lucy said. "I bet our guests will snap them up. I've never seen anything like them myself. Great idea Paula!"

Even the other boaters in the anchorage were impressed by Paula's designs. Within a week she received orders for six more hats from other yachties. She realized she had stumbled onto a great idea.

Meanwhile, in Los Angles, John was getting back in the swing of things. He called up an old friend at the *Los Angeles Times* and arranged to have the paper run a piece on Costa Rica in the travel section. His friend, the travel editor, agreed that Peter and Lucy's resort would receive favorable mention. John also spent three days on the phone with travel agents throughout the country. Faxes flew back and forth and deals were made. At the end of the third day, John sat back, satisfied. Before the winter was over, Peter would play host to some fifteen different agents, virtually all of whom would leave impressed with both Peter and his resort.

Now the ball was rolling. John was confident that within months Peter would see a dramatic upswing in his business. Without further ado, John sorted things out with the renters, bought himself a new depth sounder and GPS to replace the broken ones on *Drifter*, and grabbed a flight back to Costa Rica. When he told Peter what he had accomplished back in the States, Peter was thrilled.

"That's fantastic, John," Peter said. "Listen I really appreciate all the trouble you went through. I can't afford to pay you for your time, but what if I give you a one percent commission on my business this year? If things pick up, you could make out pretty good."

"You don't have to do that Peter," John said. "But, if you want to, I guess I won't say no. Thanks, that's a nice thought on your part."

Sometimes, in the tropics, a secure anchorage and congenial companions will conspire to keep a boat in one spot for months. That was what happened to *Drifter* that winter. John and Paula settled into the Golfito community and didn't see any reason to leave. They stayed fast friends with Peter and Lucy and ate regularly at the resort. Business did indeed begin to improve dramatically. And Paula was actually hard-pressed to keep up with the demand for her hats. Days turned into weeks and weeks into months. Then one day, John looked at the calender and realized it was already the end of March. And that was it. He was ready to move on. Paula agreed and once again it was time for good-byes.

When Peter heard John and Paula were actually leaving, he disappeared into his office. Ten minutes later he reemerged and handed John a check. John looked at the amount and handed it back to Peter.

"C'mon Peter, this is too much. You must have made some mistake with the figures. You better go back and check again."

"No mistake John," Peter grinned. "That's one percent of our gross for this winter. If we have another season like this, we'll be sitting pretty come next year. And it's thanks to you. So go ahead. Take it. It's the least I can do. But Lucy and I want to see you folks around here again. Do you think you're going to be coming back up the coast?"

"Don't know, Pete. But if we do, we'll stop in for sure."

*Payday in paradise.*

"You'd better," Lucy said. "I'm going to need another bunch of those hats from Paula for next winter. The guests love them."

The next morning *Drifter* weighed anchor and pointed her bow south. Paula and John relaxed in the cockpit as the windvane guided the boat. Once again they savored the bittersweet feeling of leave-taking that is both a cruising sailor's joy and curse.

Steve and Irene's winter cruise was all that they had hoped. They danced the merengue until dawn in Santo Domingo and watched a voodoo priest kill a chicken in Haiti. In Cuba they drank beer from a tank truck and toured Santiago in a miraculously well-maintained 1957 Buick. Irene was inspired by some of the artwork she had found in Haiti, and her new batch of hand-painted T-shirts bore the unmistakable influence of the Haitian *naif* style. Even the beat back to the east was not too bad in July's waning trade winds.

Now they were back in the Virgin Islands ready to wait out another hurricane season. Her confidence bolstered by Judy's enthusiasm, Irene went around to a handful of other boutiques in St. Thomas and St. John. Most of the owners were equally enthusiastic about carrying Irene's shirts, especially when she agreed to place them on a commission basis rather than sell them to the shops outright. Irene realized she would have her work cut out for her that summer, if she wanted to keep up with the demand from all the stores and also stockpile shirts for the winter.

For his part, Steve was thinking of what he could do to stay busy through the long, hot summer months. While he was refitting *Dancer*, Steve had met several of the men working in the marine trades on St. Thomas. Three in particular, John a carpenter; Harry, another carpenter; and Charley, a diesel mechanic, had been talking about opening up a shop together. Steve wondered what had happened to the idea and one day walked down to the boatyard by the lagoon to see what was up.

The boatyard manager knew who Steve was talking about. "John and Harry? They moved over to St. John. I hear they've got a little business in Coral Bay. I haven't been over there myself."

Steve thanked him and the next day *Dancer* sailed across Pillsbury Sound and dropped anchor in Coral Bay. Ashore, Steve quickly found the shop. John, Harry, and Charley had rented a small shack on the waterfront. They expanded it, building a large covered work space in front and another small room in the back. There were a couple of boats tied in front, obviously being worked on.

Over the next week, Steve talked with the three tradesmen about their business. Evidently it was a casual cooperative arrangement with everyone pitching in when they got a big job, or, individuals working on smaller jobs by themselves. The two carpenters and mechanic were aware of Steve's electrical skills and were soon pressing him to join their business.

"I'd like to guys," Steve said, "but I'm afraid I can't commit to being around full-time. There is a lot Irene and I haven't seen yet, and we're not about to stop sailing."

"No, none of us are," John replied. "That's why this business is so informal. If somebody wants to take off to go sailing for a while they can. All we ask is that you finish whatever jobs you're working on and don't leave us holding the bag. I mean, come on, this is the V.I.! People are just happy to get the work done, and done well, without getting ripped off. They can't expect us to be around all the time can they?"

Feeling he had nothing to lose, Steve joined up with John, Harry, and Charley. Defying all expectations, the business actually hung together. As the group gained a reputation for good work, honest prices, and dependability, they acquired a steady client base. And, strangely enough, people didn't mind that occasionally one or two of the group would be off cruising for a while. John was right, in the Virgin Islands you could get away with a lot!

## WORKING FROM YOUR OWN BOAT

In the last four chapters we have examined many different kinds of jobs that cruising sailors can take advantage of. However, they have all entailed either working on someone else's boat or working onshore. In this chapter we will focus on ways you can generate income and/or explore your interests using your own boat as a base.

### CRAFT WORK ONBOARD

Paula and Irene both stumbled upon what can be both a rewarding and lucrative sideline for a cruising sailor, namely doing craft work on board. Incidentally, Paula's idea with the hats was truly a brainstorm. After Costa Rica, she sold her hats to other boaters in Panama and to both boaters and tourists in Guatemala. As she kept experimenting, she kept coming up with more and more interesting ideas and some of her creations were truly unique. I even bought one of her hats myself. Also, the last time we cruised through the Virgin Islands, Irene and another woman had formed a partnership and opened a boutique on St. John. The boutique was doing well, and amazingly enough, the only thing they sold were hand-painted T-shirts. So obviously craft work can be more than merely a way to stay busy.

There is one aspect of craft work that makes it especially attractive to the cruising sailor. This is the fact that many of the best markets are to be found in some of the most popular and attractive cruising grounds. The Caribbean, the Mediterranean, and the islands of the South Pacific—all are rife with tourist resorts sporting boutiques that sell everything from hats to hammocks. While much of the tourist-oriented craft market has become dominated by cheap knock-offs from the Third World, there is always a niche in these stores for unique and well-produced items.

Two things are indispensable for a sailor thinking of getting into craft work: one is to know the markets and the other is to know his or her skills. Knowing the markets means finding out ahead of time what can be sold in a given area. Remember that since you can not compete with cheap, Third World labor, you need to find a niche that is not already saturated by low-priced assembly line products. As Paula and Irene found out, uniqueness and creativity are the tickets to marketability. Look at tourist boutiques wherever you cruise with an eye to finding a niche. You will probably start to see that they all carry many of the same items. Your task is to think of something different.

As well as knowing the market, you need to know your own skills. Go back to the Skills Questionnaire in Chapter One, and look at how you responded. Do you have artistic talents? Are you good with your hands? Like Paula, did you once have a hobby that you have let go by the wayside? Any of these may point you in the direction of some type of craft work.

Here's another example of a cruiser's creative ideas for craft work. Pieter, had always enjoyed working with his hands, and had worked as a carpenter in his native Holland for years before going sailing. While in Morocco he was struck by the abundance of local leatherwork items and the cheapness of the raw materials. He set out to teach himself the basics of the craft, buying a set of tools at one of the many tradesmen's shops. When he decided to leave the country, he bought twenty square meters of good-quality cured leather. Pieter's money was getting low, so he sailed for the Canary Islands with the idea of selling some type of leather crafts in the tourist shops.

After he had been in the islands a few weeks looking around, Pieter noticed that although the shops carried a variety of plastic sandals, none of them were very high quality. He came up with a design for a pair of attractive and comfortable woven leather sandals. Pieter figured that while his sandals were more expensive than others on the market, the quality and unique design would appeal to tourists looking for casual, yet durable vacation wear.

After Pieter completed a few pairs of his sandals, he arranged to have them displayed in the boutique of a fancy resort. The boutique's owner suggested pric-

*Off to market!*

ing the sandals at $35 and agreed to pay Pieter two-thirds of that as a commission on each sale. Within the first week the boutique sold five pairs of Pieter's sandals and the owner requested a dozen more. After two months of steady sales, Pieter was able to sell the boutique three dozen pairs of sandals outright. Figuring he was onto a good thing, Pieter hoisted his sails and headed off to try his luck on another island.

Pieter's story illustrates two important points. First, it is always a good idea to target the high end of the market. Given the time investment necessary for most craft work, it only makes sense to invest a little bit extra to produce a high-quality product. Paula's $40 custom-painted hats certainly did not compete with $8 Chinese factory-made cotton sun hats, nor were they an alternative to the $5 Mexican sombreros. But by coming up with products that were high-quality and unique, both Paula and Pieter were able to establish a niche market.

A second lesson to be learned from Pieter's story is that although a boutique owner might be reluctant to buy your products outright, he may be willing to carry them on a commission basis. You can also usually get a larger percentage of the retail price by selling on commission. The average tourist boutique marks their products up at least one hundred percent. However, if an item is sold on a commission basis, the shop does not take any risk or have money tied up in inventory. You should be able to negotiate at least a 70/30 split.

Of course the downside of selling on commission is that you have to be around to monitor sales and collect the money. If you're going to be in an area for a while, however, it is a good idea at least to start by selling on commission. If the store's owner sees that your product is a winner, he will later be willing to make an outright purchase.

We've talked about painting T-shirts and hats as well as working with leather. What are some other types of craft work that are suitable for cruisers? If you don't have artistic talents, but do enjoy sewing, you may want to consider making some sort of clothing. Again, the only way you'll ever be competitive is *not to have* any competition. One couple we met in the Lesser Antilles sold shorts and lightweight shirts that they made out of some amazing, surrealistically patterned fabric they had found in Brazil. Though their prices were higher than those of the cheap printed beach clothes in the boutiques, no one had ever seen anything like their designs, so they sold well.

Our good friend Suzy and her husband spent many years cruising the coasts of Belize and Honduras in their 40-foot ferro-cement schooner. Suzy added to their small pension with her sales of custom clothing. Occasionally she would sew an item herself, if she had a unique design, but more often she would buy bulk quantities of T-shirts and other items at very low prices. What made her clothing unique was her creative method of tie-dying. She used wild colors and special patterns that she had developed to produce styles that were simply not available anywhere else. As she and her husband sailed the coast, she would stop in at the various small resorts and replenish the stock in their boutiques.

If you have woodworking skills you may want to consider something in that area. Although tourist shops the world over are full of cheap wooden carvings, Balinese painted animals and the like, Carl, a Frenchman we met in the Bahamas, was able to consistently sell his handmade wooden birds to shops up and down the islands. His birds were unique in that not only did each contain an ingeniously hidden compartment (Carl's design), they were also painted in a special French antique style (again of Carl's devising). They were so clearly different from anything else available that the shop owners snapped them up.

Also, if you are good with your hands, consider the field of jewelry design and fabrication. This is a craft that can be as simple as twisting some silver wire or as complex as goldsmithing and lapidary design. Jewelrymaking can be a high-value added trade if you buy your materials, particularly gemstones, in producer countries where the prices can be quite low. If you intend to make high-end jewelry, you'll need to know what you're doing and it is well worth the investment to take a course in this specialized field. More basic jewelry work does not require a large investment in materials and it is certainly possible to teach yourself, possibly with the aid of one of the many books on the subject (see Appendix E).

Obviously these are not the only crafts you can make on board. Take a careful look around any tourist boutique and you will probably see something that will make you think, gee, I could make that. The critical thing to remember, however, is that whatever you make, be certain it's unique. The only way you can be sure there isn't any competition is to research the markets. I cannot stress this strongly enough. If you do not research your market, you could find that you can't sell what you make or that you have to sell it for such a low price that it is not worthwhile. So, look around, see what's out there, then use your imagination!

Another point to consider when thinking about craft work on board is how you can take advantage of cost-of-living differentials. Of course you will get the most money for your products by selling them in high-priced boutiques. Unfortunately these are often located in high-priced areas, like the French Riviera or the U.S. Virgin Islands. The cost of living and the price of raw materials in both locations are very high. As a cruising sailor working from your own boat, however, you can exploit the benefits of nearby low-cost countries: Venezuela (for the Virgin Islands) or Turkey (for the French Riviera). Buying your materials in low-cost countries and selling your products in high-cost ones greatly increases the value added to your work.

In Appendix E, I have listed several resources for anyone interested in exploring craft work on boats. These include books on the subject, suppliers of materials, and a few sources of training in jewelry design and fabrication. In addition, for training in other types of craft work, consider evening courses offered at local high schools and universities.

Let us, then, summarize the pluses and minuses of craft work on board:

**PLUSES**

> Wide variety of skills can be accommodated

> You work for yourself, at your own pace, on board your own boat

> You can buy materials in low-cost countries and sell your products where prices are high

> For someone with the right skills, craft work can be very rewarding

**MINUSES**

> Competition from cheap Third World products is intense

> Having to sell on commission may require you to stay in one area longer than you would like

> Some crafts, like jewelrymaking, may require a sizable investment up front

> Finding room on board your boat for equipment and supplies may be difficult

## MAKING MONEY THROUGH TRADING

Another type of entrepreneurial work particularly suited to cruisers is the buying and selling of goods between countries, otherwise known as "trading." The great days of trading under sail may be gone, and the East India Company and clipper ships are only memories, but even today, it is possible for a sailor to make money exploiting price differentials between countries. It's possible, but is it likely? Let's take a closer look.

What do I mean by "trading" as practiced by the average cruising sailor? Certainly not a large scale commercial operation. Probably not even an ongoing business. Most cruisers make money trading because they are making the trip anyway and know of something that can be bought at a low price on one end and sold for a high price on the other. A sailor who knows both markets can, by taking a calculated risk, sometimes make a significant profit.

The key to the equation is knowing the markets. A potential trader must know that there is a demand for his product in the target country, or he risks either having to take a loss or being stuck somewhere for months trying to unload his merchandise. But how can a sailor know what the markets are in a given country until he gets there?

One answer is that a cruiser may find himself going back and forth between two counties repeatedly. In the Eastern Caribbean many sailors spend summers in Venezuela and winters in the Virgin Islands. In the Mediterranean, boats sometimes winter in Turkey and summer in France. In fact, one of our first encounters with the opportunities in trading was with a sailor who was exploiting just such an opportunity.

Kurt was a German cruiser we met in Honduras. He told us this was his fifth visit to that country. Kurt was always on the move, sailing from village to village on the island of Roatan. He seemed to have dozens of friends among the local people. When we accompanied him, he was always getting invited into someone's house. After we got to know him better, we found that these were not just social calls. In fact, it turned out that Kurt was a mobile electronics store! He was selling everything from SSB radios to Sony Walkmans.

Every winter when he was in Miami, Kurt would buy a stock of VHF and SSB radios, boomboxes, watches, Walkmans, and other electronic goodies to bring back to Roatan. He knew both the market and the people there very well, and he seldom had difficulty in doubling his investment. The business was made possible by the fact that most of the items he sold were simply not available in the stores on Roatan, plus the economy was thriving, which gave the islanders enough money to buy Kurt's products.

If you find yourself shunting between two countries or regions repeatedly, stop and think. Is there something that can be shipped from one to the other and sold for a profit? Remember that not only must there be a price differential, there must also be a good demand in the target country. A cruising sailor is not a land-based store, and few people want to have money tied up in inventory, not to mention losing ever-precious space on a boat.

Another type of trading is one-shot deals. In such a case a sailor researches the target market ahead of time, invests in a product, sells it on arrival, then moves on. How can you find out about a market ahead of time? It's not easy, but there are some resources available.

One resource is cruisers coming from the other direction. If you think there might be an opportunity for trading, ask the boats you meet. Find out what conditions are like up ahead. What's expensive or diffi-cult to find where you're going? Another option is high-frequency (HF) radio nets. These informal cruising networks, either on the Ham or marine SSB frequencies, can be a gold mine of information about what things are like up ahead. Another possibility is cruising newslet-ters. These are often full of specific information on the current situa-tion in many countries. One excellent, worldwide newsletter is the Seven Seas Cruising Association's monthly bulletin. Finally, some sailor's Web sites now give detailed information on specific countries (see Appendix E).

Be careful with these onetime trades though. If you're on a sched-ule, or your sailing is dictated by the weather, the last thing you want is to be stuck trying to unload merchandise when you need to be leaving. And if what you're carrying takes up a lot of space, it can certainly be inconvenient to be stuck for weeks or months trying to unload it.

In fact, this is exactly what happened once to Maggie and myself. During a cruise along the Brazilian coast, we met a French cruiser who told us about a great trade he'd made. Before leaving Brazil for the Caribbean two years earlier, he had purchased about fifty exquis-itely-made Brazilian hammocks. Within days of arriving at the Carib-bean island of Grenada he sold the whole lot to one store and more than tripled his investment. He even gave us the name of the store he had sold to.

This sounded like an opportunity we couldn't pass up. Here we had firsthand information from someone who had recently done the deal. How could we go wrong? So thinking, we loaded our boat with forty hammocks (which was as many as we could cram on board) and sailed north. When we reached the Caribbean, however, it was June, the beginning of the off-season and nobody wanted anything to do with our hammocks! In the end, we sailed with forty hammocks, and al-most no living space, for another eight months before we were finally able to sell them in the Virgin Islands. It was a good lesson in the dangers of relying on someone else's information.

Purely as a matter of interest, here are some of the trading situations that we've seen work around the world. Remember, these were good deals in the past. I don't guarantee that they still are. Don't neglect your research!

➤ Selling Guatemalan crafts in the United States

➤ Selling Venezuelan anti-fouling paint in the Virgin Islands

➤ Buying Japanese outboard engines in Venezuela and selling them in the Netherlands Antilles

➤ Buying SSB radios and laptop computers in the United States and selling them in Europe

➤ Buying Scotch whiskey in Europe and selling it in Brazil

➤ Buying Brazilian hammocks and selling them in the Caribbean

➤ Buying Brazilian bikinis and selling them in Miami

➤ Buying electronics in the United States and selling them in Honduras

➤ Buying semiprecious gemstones in Brazil and selling them in the United States

➤ Buying emeralds in Colombia and selling them just about anywhere

I'd like to just comment on the last two examples, because they involve gemstones. We have, occasionally, met sailors who were making money trading in gemstones. At one time this seemed to us like a tempting business. The stones are small, easy to transport, and if you buy at a good price, you should be able to sell them almost anywhere. The caveat to this business, and it's a large one, is that unless you know *exactly* what you are doing, it is all too easy to be swindled. This is a game for professionals, with more than its share of shysters. Make sure you've got the expertise to know what you're getting into before you plunk down your money.

Any discussion of trading while cruising would not be complete without touching on the subject of transporting illegal drugs. My advice in one word? DON'T! It's true that years ago it was not at all uncommon for the adventurous cruising sailor to make a bundle smuggling some "square grouper" (marijuana bales). Those days are long gone however, and nowadays the game is played by cutthroat professionals. Many of the top smuggling gangs keep the police off their backs by turning in naive amateurs who have been set up. If you're reading a book like this, you have no reason to get involved in the drug game, there are far safer ways to make a buck sailing.

To return to our original question, "Is it likely that a cruising sailor can make money trading?" The answer would have to be a qualified "Yes." Qualified, because although it is certainly possible to pick up some extra money now and again by buying in one place and selling in another, the logistics and timing are such that trading is unlikely to ever be a reliable source of income. Instead, it should be thought of as a windfall, which now and again you can benefit from, provided you are willing to do some research and take a calculated risk.

Let's now sum up the pluses and minuses of making money trading:

**PLUSES**

➤ Depending on your initial investment, it may be possible to make a good amount of money in a short time

➤ Can be an interesting way to meet local people

**MINUSES**

➤ There's always a risk that you may not be able to sell your merchandise or that it may take a long time to sell

➤ For people who don't like "selling" it may be hard to market your merchandise

## BUYING AND SELLING YACHTS

There is another way that sailors can make money with their boats, namely, by selling them! You probably know, or have heard of, people onshore who build up equity by buying undervalued houses, fixing them up while they're living in them, and selling them for a profit. For people who are good with their hands, and have the time to invest in renovation, this can be a good way to build fairly large sums of capital.

As a cruising sailor, you can do the same thing with boats. If you know your way around the boating world and can spot a good deal, consider cruising on a boat while renovating it, and at some point, selling it for a profit. Our friends Forrest and Suzy have managed to do just that, and not just once, but twice.

When we met them, Forrest and Suzy were living on a 27-foot wooden ketch. Forrest was working in Miami as a marine mechanic, and Suzy had a job in a sail loft. They were very much in love, and before too long their family had expanded to four. With a bit of money in the bank, they were planning on heading south, toward the Virgins and perhaps beyond. The only stumbling block was that their living conditions were already cramped, and as the children grew Suzy feared the cruising life would prove too stressful in their tiny boat. A bigger boat was well beyond their means, and even if they could afford the down payment, the purchase would set their cruising plans back years.

Then hurricane Hugo hit the Virgin islands. What was disaster for many, was pure luck for Forrest and Suzy. Wrecked boats began to appear in the Miami boatyards, as insurance companies arranged to have scores of damaged yachts shipped back to the States to evaluate the cost-effectiveness of repairs. The ones that were deemed a "total loss" were sold off for a fixed price of $10,000. Forrest and Suzy had a bit more than that in the bank and Forrest decided to take a gamble. He arranged to buy a Whitby 42, in reasonable condition, except for a large hole in one side.

Forrest had good fiberglass skills and within a month *Dulcinea* was afloat. While Forrest was repairing the hole in the hull, Suzy spent weeks cleaning the interior. She bought all new foam and sewed new cushion covers and upholstery throughout the boat. By the time *Dulcinea* was launched, the family was ready to move aboard. Forrest sold their old boat to a friend for the fire-sale price of $10,000, and they were even with the game. After another month of rebuilding the engine and checking out the sails and rigging, Forrest and Suzy took off. The boat still needed a lot of work, but Forrest was confident he could handle the repairs as they cruised.

Over the next three years the family cruised throughout the Eastern Caribbean. Forrest worked on and off in the Virgin Islands, and devoted a lot of energy to fixing up *Dulcinea*. Eventually, after much sweat, the boat that had arrived in Miami, looking ready for the wrecker's yard, ended up well-equipped and looking like new.

Forrest and Suzy had just tucked *Dulcinea* into the mangroves of St. John's Hurricane Hole, when they heard the news of hurricane

Andrew's devastating strike on the Miami area. From what Forrest could gather, a good part of Miami's Dinner Key Marina was destroyed. He saw the hand of fate at work again and wasted no time jumping on a plane to Florida. As the dust settled, and the wreckage of hundreds of boats was cleaned up, Forrest again made contact with an insurance company. Once again, boats were being sold off for ridiculously low prices. Forrest borrowed some money from a friend and for the second time found himself the owner of a "wreck."

To cut a long story short, Forrest and Suzy sailed back to Miami, moved aboard the new boat, and sold *Dulcinea* for three times what they had invested in her. Forrest paid his friend back and began the work of renovating *Crystal*, the new boat. Forrest and Suzy were beginning the cycle again, although this time they had a good amount of money in the bank.

This story may sound too good to be true. Surely, you might say, it can't be that simple to make money fixing up boats? Why doesn't everybody do it? The answer is threefold. Besides having the ability and the time to do all the work yourself, renovating boats for a profit requires knowing a good bit about valuing boats, and being in the right place at the right time. In all honesty, Forrest was quite lucky to pick up both his boats at "hurricane prices." Most people are not so fortunate.

Nonetheless, for somebody with good skills, fixing up a boat as you cruise, can indeed combine business with pleasure. The first thing you need to do is to find the right boat at the right price. As we saw with Forrest, hurricanes can provide windfalls for sailors willing to make an investment. I hate to advocate what could be construed as being an "ambulance chaser," but if you are looking for deals, going to the site of a recent hurricane can be one of the best ways to find them.

And how does one tell an undervalued boat, that looks like a wreck, from a legitimate wreck, that can never be economically renovated? Well, as they say, if you have to ask the question, you won't understand the answer. In fact, if you don't know how to tell a good deal from a bad one, you should not get involved in this business. Stick with buying a good boat and concentrate on other ways to make money. However, if you have the background to recognize a good deal when you see it, here are a few pointers on the ins and outs of renovating and selling boats for a profit.

Probably the lowest yacht prices in the world are to be found in south Florida. For many years the supply of boats has exceeded the demand. For anybody looking for good deals, this is the best place to start. It never hurts to go through several boat brokers and see what they have available. But remember, the best deals are not usually listed with brokers. People selling their boats for low prices already do not want to pay a broker a ten percent commission. So go around and do some leg work. Look on the bulletin boards at marinas, boating stores, and boatyards.

Another good resource are magazines dedicated to listing second-hand boats. A popular paper in south Florida is called *The Boat Trader*. Several online listings of used boats are also helpful (see Appendix E). Cull through the listings to get a feel for the current market. Then come up with a "short list" and go see the boats in person.

When looking at used boats, it pays to keep the following points in mind:

➤ Treat steel and wood hulled boats with extreme caution. A low-priced steel or wood hull will likely have structural problems, which may be difficult or expensive to repair. Fiberglass hulls are almost always a better value for the money.

➤ Look for boats that have been outfitted for a cruise. Anyone who has ever outfitted their own boat for cruising knows how much all the necessary "bits and pieces" cost, and how little they add to the resale price.

➤ Look for boats that are laid-up, with absentee owners. At the end of a cruise, the boat's owner may need to return to shoreside life before the boat can be sold. In such a case you can often strike a very good deal.

➤ Finally, consider shopping for a boat in countries with under-valued currencies or economies in turmoil. There were fantastic buys on boats in Argentina in the days of hyperinflation and in New Zealand and Australia soon after several Asian currencies collapsed. Think about how economic conditions can affect the price of boats.

The last consideration to think about, is where you are going to sell the boat. Bear in mind that the places with the best markets for buying, of course, also have the worst markets for selling. However, sometimes you can plan to terminate a cruise in an advantageous location.

John, an American we met in Gibraltar, explained to us how he combined sailing pleasure with business. He said he would scour the market in south Florida for good deals. When he found an undervalued boat, he would buy it, spruce it up, and sail it across the Atlantic. Prices in European markets were much higher than those in Florida, and so far he had brought three boats across, making a good profit on each. Terry, an Irish friend of ours, bought his boat in England, sailed it for three years and 20,000 miles to Japan, and sold it there for enough of a profit to pay for his whole cruise.

There are, in short, no hard and fast rules for where to buy a boat or where to sell it, or even what to buy. There is no substitute, in this case, for experience and research. I would hesitate to recommend that a novice try to "wheel and deal" in boats. The boat market is much more unstable than the real estate market and the lack of regulation means that disreputable operators can function almost with impunity. Nevertheless, as we saw from the examples above, buying and selling boats can be integrated into a cruising life and can, under the right circumstances, provide a reasonable income.

Let's just summarize the pluses and minuses:

**PLUSES**

➤ Allows you to build up "sweat equity" as you cruise

➤ It's possible to luck out and get a super deal

**MINUSES**

➤ You must know both the value of used boats and the current markets

➤ Cruising with a "work in progress" may prove stressful or discouraging

➤ There's always the risk that the project will end up being much more expensive or complex than initially thought

## WRITING ONBOARD

Like the job of chartering that we talked about in Chapter Three, writing is a job that many aspiring cruisers think of as a natural adjunct to the cruising lifestyle. After all, the cruising sailor has plenty of adventures and plenty of time. What could be more natural than to become a writer? However, like the charter business, it is important to separate the "business" of writing from the "pleasure." There is a big difference between jotting down your adventures or deep thoughts, for your own or your friends' entertainment, and making a living as a professional writer.

The first thing to realize is that if you're not a professional writer now, breaking into the business is a challenge under the best of conditions. There are many, many, more people who want to make money writing than there are opportunities that pay. Also, the major sailing magazines, though they would seem a natural market for a cruising sailor, are extremely tough to break into. One well-known sailing magazine receives over 140 submissions a month, of which they usually publish only a couple!

Furthermore, it is actually more difficult to make a living as a writer while cruising than when based onshore. For one thing, you're often out of touch, and establishing and maintaining contact with editors and publishers can be difficult. People in the professional writing world value the convenience of being able to pick up the phone and reach you. Often this is not possible on board a boat.

Another factor to consider are the many ways that the cruising life can make it difficult to write steadily. Living onshore, you can be reasonably certain of what your schedule will be like each day. You can set aside a specific block of time for writing and know that you will always have it available. Anyone who has cruised in a sailboat, however, knows that all kinds of things crop up that can make it impossible to write.

For one thing, it's nearly impossible to write seriously while underway, there are simply too many things that need to be attended to. And, even when not sailing, a cruising sailor often finds that unavoidable boat maintenance and repairs can make it impossible to allocate time for writing. Finally, when you arrive in a new country, it's only logical that you will want to get out and explore it. After all, what's the point of sailing to new places only to spend your time down below on your boat pounding away at a word processor? All these factors combine to create an environment where it may be very difficult to find time to write seriously.

I remember Tim, a friend of ours in the Virgin Islands, telling me about how he got his start as an author. The bug had bit him, and Tim was convinced that he had a great sailing book just waiting to be written. Recognizing that the distractions of domestic life on board would make it impossible for him to maintain his concentration, Tim rented a cheap room onshore. He resolved to sit and write in that room every day until he finished his manuscript. Weeks turned into months, and Tim's wife and young daughter were itching to move on, but Tim stubbornly persisted. Every day at 9:00 a.m., Tim's wife would bring him to shore, and every day at 4:00 p.m., she would pick him up. In between he would sit at his desk and write. Some days he wrote well, other days not so well, but he kept at it every single day. Finally, after three months, he was done. He packed up his typewriter, stuffed the pages of his manuscript into a box, and closed the door of his "office" for the last time.

Tim's book was a success and his career as a freelance writer launched, but, as he told me later, he was convinced he would never have even finished the manuscript unless he had allocated the time specifically for writing.

Assuming you're willing to make the necessary time commitment and you can work it into your cruising plans, the next thing you need to do is target your market. In other words, who will you sell to? As a writer, you can sell to three distinct markets: newspapers, magazines, and book publishers. The approach varies with each, so let's briefly look at how you can get started.

## FREELANCE WRITING FOR NEWSPAPERS

Many writers just starting out overlook the newspaper market. While it's true small newspapers do not generally pay a lot, there are many of them. For a writer willing to invest a little time and postage, soliciting several small newspapers may prove rewarding.

Newspapers may buy a single article (such as a piece for their Travel Section), or they may contract with you to write a regular column. As a new writer, you will have the best chances of selling single articles by submitting them "on spec," that is, already written. As you become established, you can approach newspapers with an idea first, and get their go-ahead before writing the article. Remember that photos will always improve an article's chance of acceptance, especially for travel pieces. Editors at both newspapers and magazines greatly favor color slides over prints, so if possible, shoot in this format.

A regular column can be about almost anything, but make sure that the subject is something you have expertise in. Individual newspapers do not pay much for each column, so you will have to syndicate to several newspapers to make it worthwhile. Small local papers are easier to break into than big-city dailies because they are usually short-staffed and must rely on freelancers for their articles. Local papers also do not consider newspapers from other areas competitors, so they don't mind if you sell your column to them as well.

When you have come up with an idea for a column, get the names and addresses of several newspapers (see Appendix E for where to find these) and send out "queries." Typically a query contains a cover letter, some sample columns, and "clips." The cover letter is a general outline of the nature of the column and a description of why you're qualified to write it. Along with the cover letter, include at least five or six sample columns already written to show what you can do. If you have already been published, send along photocopies of your published work (called "clips" in the business). Much more information on writing for newspapers can be found in the books listed in Appendix E.

## Pluses and Minuses of Writing for Newspapers

### PLUSES

➤ Small newspapers may provide relatively accessible markets

➤ A short column written weekly will not dominate your life

➤ Being published in newspapers is a way to establish credibility as a professional writer

### MINUSES

➤ May require a large mailing to find enough papers interested in your idea

➤ Small papers generally pay very little

➤ A weekly deadline may prove tiresome or difficult to fulfill in a cruising lifestyle

## FREELANCE WRITING FOR MAGAZINES

Writing for magazines can be relatively lucrative for the time invested, particularly if you can crack the markets of the larger publications. Most magazines with a substantial circulation will pay anywhere from fifty cents to a dollar per word. Smaller magazines, while they may not pay well, can provide an accessible market for the beginning writer to get published.

If you are thinking of submitting to magazines, get a reference source, such as *Writer's Market* (listed in Appendix E), then target several publications. Go out and buy several copies of each magazine. Read them thoroughly. This is very important! In order to sell to a magazine, you must understand the tone, style, and content of the publication. You can only do this by carefully studying several issues. The biggest complaint I hear from magazine editors is that they receive too many submissions that don't suit their format. Also get a copy of each magazine's writer's guidelines. These will give you specific guidelines as to what a magazine wants in terms of length, style, and content. The majority of magazines now have their writer's guidelines available online (see Appendix E).

Once you have targeted a few magazines and know what their requirements are, write several articles for each magazine, send them out, and hope. Don't be deterred by rejections, remember that if, in the beginning, you sell one article for every ten you write, you'll be doing well. If you want to crack the magazine markets, you must produce good work in quantity.

When I first started writing for magazines I felt like I was sending off messages in bottles. I knew the odds were very slim that any one article would end up at the right magazine at the right time, so I figured my only hope was to send out plenty. As I started to have magazines accept my work, I saw that indeed, getting published is not only about writing well, it's about sending the right work to the right publications, and being persistent.

## PLUSES AND MINUSES OF WRITING FOR MAGAZINES

### PLUSES

➤ The great variety of magazines gives you tremendous freedom in choosing subjects to write about

➤ Writing for the larger magazines can be lucrative relative to the time invested

➤ Regular publication in magazines goes a long way toward building credibility

**MINUSES**

➤ Most magazine markets are highly competitive

➤ Sending out many articles "on spec" can become discouraging after repeated rejections

## WRITING A BOOK

Now we come to the book market. Are there any cruising sailors out there who *don't* dream of someday writing a book? Judging from all the sailors I've talked to over the years, if there are any, there are not many! Something about the cruising life seems to inspire people with the conviction that their travels and adventures are of burning interest to the rest of the world. And who knows, they might well be right. But there is much more to writing a book than just having a good story to tell.

If you are planning to write a novel, go ahead and follow your muse. Get it completed and then go shop for an agent. There are very few agents who will consider a fiction idea without seeing a completed manuscript, and there are very few publishers who will consider a manuscript unless it's submitted by an agent. Much practical information on finding an agent can be gleaned from *Writer's Market* (see Appendix E).

On the other hand, if you have a great idea for a nonfiction book, do some research before you start writing. Find out whether there is a market for your idea. Find out how many other books have addressed your topic. Think about how you will sell the idea to a publisher. The publisher will want to know what sets your book apart from anything else on the shelves. He will also want to know who will buy your book, and why. Once you have refined your idea to a unique, marketable concept, put together a proper proposal. Excellent advice on how to do this can be found in *Writer's Market*. Now you're ready to try to sell your proposal to an agent or publisher.

The business of book writing, including finding an agent and a publisher and going through the whole long, drawn-out process of getting a book into print, is the subject for a book in itself. In fact, there are many good books on the subject. If you think you might have it in you to write a novel or a nonfiction book, I advise you to read one or more of the very informative guides listed in Appendix E.

## PLUSES AND MINUSES OF WRITING A BOOK

### PLUSES

- ➤ Can be a very rewarding process
- ➤ Gives you an excellent reference for future writing projects
- ➤ It's possible (though not likely), that a book may provide substantial royalties

### MINUSES

- ➤ Very difficult to break into the market (most publishers accept two- to three-percent of the manuscripts they receive)
- ➤ Generally the pay is very low for the amount of time invested
- ➤ Can monopolize your life for months at a time

## COMMUNICATIONS FOR THE WRITER

Over the last several years the rapid development of the Telecommunications and Information Technology sectors has given a tremendous boost to cruising sailors who wish to write. Working on board with a laptop computer and a sophisticated word processing program then transmitting your work via e-mail over the Internet is now well within the capabilities of most sailors.

We will discuss the whole Telecommunications Revolution and its impact on cruising sailors in more detail in the following section, but there is one point I'd like to make here. This is, that while e-mail is fast and convenient for cruisers, it still has a bad reputation in much of the publishing industry. Most agents, publishers, magazines, and newspapers *do not* want to be contacted initially via e-mail. The proliferation of "spam" (unsolicited junk e-mail) has turned most people off to the idea of receiving e-mail from anyone they don't know. The best way to make the first contact with anyone in the publishing industry is still the old-fashioned way, through the printed page and by regular "snail" mail. That being said, once you establish a relationship, many magazine and book publishers are quite happy to correspond via e-mail.

In short, then, writing can indeed be a viable career for the cruising sailor. The point to remember is that, like any other career, it will require a substantial investment of time and energy, particularly at the outset. Also, it would be foolish for any aspiring writer to expect to make much of a living in the beginning. But for people hankering to express themselves in print, but who have not had the time to devote to it in a land-based lifestyle, combining writing with sailing may be the perfect solution.

## THE TELECOMMUNICATIONS REVOLUTION AND WORKING ONBOARD

There are two converging trends that will, over the next several years, have a tremendous impact on the opportunities available for cruising sailors who wish to work from their boats. The first is the revolution in telecommunications technology. The second is the changing nature of the onshore workplace and the increasing trend towards outsourcing, contract work and telecommuting. Let's take a look at each in turn.

The last ten years have seen unprecedented change in worldwide telecommunications. As recently as the late 1980s, I can remember the extreme difficulties in placing a long distance call from Third World countries. In Venezuela, I would wait in line for an hour to make a call to the United States from the offices of the phone company. When I finally got an outside line, the charges were so prohibitive that I had to restrict my call to a couple of minutes.

Nowadays, for many cruisers, making a call is simply a matter of picking up an onboard cellular phone. At worst, you only need to go to shore, find a pay phone, and make a call with a credit card. Worldwide rates have come down significantly and are continuing to fall. However, while improvements in voice communications are certainly convenient, the most significant development for cruisers, who wish to work from on board, is the ability to send and receive data on the boat (i.e. linking a personal computer to the Internet).

A few years ago the only way to send and receive data from the boat was either through a physical land line (which meant being in a marina), through an analog cellular phone, which was often unreliable and/or expensive, or through a satellite phone, which was exorbitantly expensive and slow. By the time this book is in print however, the cruising sailor will be able to avail himself of any of at least three options.

The first, which is already on the market, is to use a digital cellular phone. These phones, with built-in e-mail capability and complete PC compatibility are available in much of the world right now. There are excellent networks in Europe, the Americas, and Australia that allow easy and economical service. For the sailor venturing further afield, out of reach of land-based cellular networks, there is a new network of satellites, and an integrated portable phone, that will provide global coverage and reliable data transfer at a very reasonable cost. Another option is wireless data networks, similar to wireless voice (cellular) networks, but vastly less expensive for data (i.e. Internet) usage. More details on these new hardware options can be found in Appendix E.

What this means for the cruising sailor is that flexible, low-cost communications over the Internet will finally be a practical reality. E-mail, fax, and even voice communications will all be able to be handled through an on board computer from anywhere in the world.

At the same time as communications become easier and cheaper, another revolution is occurring in shoreside job markets. Telecommuting, telecontracting, outsourcing, and freelancing, call it what you will, the acceptance of, and the demand for, short-term contract workers operating from a remote location is growing by leaps and bounds

According to a 1998 survey conducted by the consulting group, CyberDialogue, in 1990, there were 3.4 million telecommuters in the United States. By 1994, the figure had risen to 9.1 million, and in 1998, it was 15.7 million! By 2003 it is estimated that fully a third of the United States work force will be telecommuting in some fashion, and that worldwide there will be approximately 130 million teleworkers. The numbers speak for themselves. Obviously this is one of the fastest growing sectors of the workforce.

How does this impact you as a cruising sailor? What jobs will be available, and how desirable will it be for you to pursue them? Good questions.

To answer them, let's look at the telecommuting market as two sectors. The first involves telecommuters who are still *employees* of a company.

In almost all cases these workers were hired as full-time employees then evolved into telecommuters. They often have a mixed schedule, working at home a few days a week, then in the office for a few days. Occasionally they are highly valued employees who have moved away from the company, but still maintain a relationship over the phone lines.

Our friend Larry is a perfect example of the latter. Larry was a successful securities analyst for Merrill Lynch in New York in the late 1980s. In fact, he was so successful that one day he decided that there was no reason to stay in New York. Rather than fight the commute from New Jersey everyday, Larry moved to Miami and bought a sailboat. Even in the early 1990s, since he was living in a marina and had a telephone line, he was able to stay in contact with his office via the Internet. He could access the same securities data that he had in New York, via a secure Internet link, and office communications were handled by regular phone. He continued to produce for Merrill, earning a lot of money for himself and for the company, and he never saw Manhattan again.

If you are currently employed in a land-based job and are thinking of chucking it and going sailing, consider the possibility of becoming a remote worker. More and more companies are seeing the benefits of having employees who work away from the office. Study after study has shown that workers' productivity and job satisfaction almost invariably rises in a telecommuting situation. And, the company saves money through lower overhead (reduced need for office space), less time lost on sick days, and more flexible scheduling.

So if you're hearing the rumblings of the telecommuting revolution in your office, consider whether you could perform your job remotely, and if so try, to convince your management to give it a go. There are even books that provide you with arguments you can use to bolster your case (see Appendix E). Bear in mind, however, that unless you have a very flexible schedule, maintaining a regular job as a telecommuter will probably restrict your actual sailing as much as a traditional office job. While, like Larry, you will have the convenience of working from your home, and you may be able to move the boat around the States during vacation times, it is unlikely that you will ever be able to pursue a real cruising life while still an employee.

If you do want a full-time cruising life, there's another option to consider, that of working as a "telecontractor." More and more businesses worldwide are hiring remote workers as independent contractors working on short, fixed-length contracts. Here is just a partial listing of jobs that are currently being outsourced to remote contract workers:

➤ Writers, copy editors, indexers

➤ Graphic artists and illustrators

➤ Public relations and marketing consultants

➤ Engineers

➤ Accountants

➤ Programmers

In the United States many small firms now prefer to use remote personnel to work on different phases of a project. This reduces office overhead and start-up expenses, plus talent can be recruited from anywhere. Small publishing houses, engineering firms, software development houses, and even accounting firms are all seeing the benefits of hiring remote contract workers on a job-by-job basis.

How telecontracting can benefit the owner of a small business was shown to me by my friend John. After 22 years of working as an engineer with Boeing, John decided to set off on his own. He intended to start a business as an engineering consultant, providing technical assistance to small aerospace companies. The only problem was that his very limited budget did not allow him to hire any employees. Rather than take the traditional route of seeking outside funding to provide seed money to start his business, John figured he'd try the new "flexible" model.

Using the Internet and an online placement agency, John recruited two qualified engineers who were willing to work on a contract basis. Interestingly, each was a woman who had left her traditional engineering job to raise her children. They were both, however, more than happy to work as telecommuters from their homes. John was in Seattle, one woman lived in Philadelphia, and the other in Houston. When John got his first consulting contract, he employed the two women, with the understanding that it was a short-term situation with no guarantees after the end of the contract. There is no reason, given the technology currently available, why either of the two engineers John hired couldn't have been cruising sailors, telecommuting from their boats!

For a cruising sailor the best kind of contract work is something that requires delivery of a fixed quantity of information all at once, rather than a job that requires constant back and forth interactions. Consider, for instance, the example of a freelance copy editor. She receives the complete text of a new book via e-mail from a publisher. Over the next week she sits on her boat in the Mediterranean and does the editing, then e-mails the book back to the publisher. Any questions are resolved via e-mail, and when the publisher is satisfied, payment is deposited to her Stateside bank account. For people who are expert in their fields, opportunities for this kind of contract work are growing exponentially every year.

Another example of the modern telecontractor was our friend Peter. Peter had been working as a freelance programmer in England for several years when he decided to escape the cold and sail south. He notified his placement agency he was listed with and told them to place his file on inactive status. He would call them again, he said, when he next wanted to be considered for a job.

Six months later he was in the Canary Islands. It was September, and he was relaxing into the rhythm of the cruising life. There was no point in rushing across the Atlantic, he thought. He would stick around and spend the winter in the Canaries. Thinking it couldn't hurt, he gave his old agency a call. He told them he would be available for work for the next couple months, if something came up.

When his cell phone rang a week later, Peter was surprised, but not shocked, that his agency had found a two-month Y2K debugging job for him. Peter checked his boat into a marina, got his laptop hooked up to the Internet, and began downloading files. He worked on the project at his leisure, sometimes working late into the night during a binge of productivity, sometimes taking several days off to go diving. He knew that as long as he met his deadline everyone would be happy. Two months later his contract was finished and Peter unplugged his computer, cast off his docklines, and set sail for the Cape Verde islands. His agency was happy with his work, he'd had the chance to use his skills again, and his bank account had received a nice shot in the arm.

Anyone interested in short-term remote contract work should take a look at the placement services on the Internet (see Appendix E). If you have skills that are in demand, particularly if you are conversant with the Web and data communications, you should not have too much difficulty in locating an agency that caters to your specialty. Also consider contacting professional and trade organizations for your specialty, they will often be able to advise you on where to look for the best opportunities.

A word of warning, though. Be very cautious with employment agencies on the Web. If an outfit asks for money up front before they even find you a job, be very suspicious. Most of the reputable agencies do not charge contractors anything. All fees are paid by the employer. Also be very skeptical of any schemes claiming that you can make a bundle without any specialized skills. Most employers who hire freelance telecontractors are looking for highly-skilled, well-qualified people. Although there are telecommuting jobs that cater to low-skilled workers, direct marketing being one example, these are usually both unrewarding and underpaid. Anyone offering a "once in a lifetime" chance to get rich is probably just one of the many scammers that populate the Web.

Also consider the opportunities to work as a freelance telecontractor on an informal basis for employers outside the United States. The opportunity that John had to promote the Jungle Inn would have been a perfect example, if the technology had been available to him at the time. John could have made contact with his friends at the *Los Angeles Times* and travel agents throughout the country all without leaving his boat. Someone with contacts in America, and the ability to access them abroad, can often find themselves very marketable.

If you think you have skills that would be marketable as a telecontractor, take a look at the resources in Appendix E. Make contact with agencies, professional organizations, and possibly some of the experts in the field of telecommuting. If it seems that you have reasonable prospects of finding work, look into what hardware is available to get you hooked up on board. Things are changing very fast in this regard, and finding the right hardware will be a matter of matching current technology to your needs.

Even if you are not interested in telecontracting now, or don't feel you have the skills that are in demand, keep an eye on this sector for the future. No one knows yet how the remote job market is going to develop. Like so many other things relating to the IT revolution, telecommuting is still in its infancy. It is virtually impossible to predict which types of work will be available to cruisers even a few years from now.

As far as cruising sailors are concerned, the concept of telecommuting from on board your boat is one of the most exciting developments of the Information Technology Revolution. If you are able to put together a package that works for you, you may find that it gives you the ability to pursue a lucrative and rewarding career from literally anywhere in the world, something that was undreamed of even a few years ago.

# CHAPTER SEVEN

# NOT NECESSARILY FOR PROFIT:

## VOLUNTEER WORK AND ENTREPRENEURIAL POSSIBILITIES FOR CRUISING SAILORS

Kent leaned back in his chair on the veranda of the Morrocoy Yacht Club, and watched the show overhead. Flying in pairs, clouds of scarlet ibises momentarily dominated the evening sky, turning the golden sunset red. Then, a few minutes after the ibises departed, hundreds of pairs of bright green parrots, squawking and screeching, also settled in the mangroves. Soon, Kent knew, the graceful and majestic great white herons would pass overhead as well. The yacht club was located in the national wildlife refuge of Morrocoy, an area unusually rich in bird life, and as he relaxed beneath the avian clamor, Kent thought to himself how lucky he was.

Two days ago he and Jan had received news of a destructive hurricane strike in the Virgin Islands. Scores of boats had been destroyed, and electricity and water were still out. Kent thought thankfully of *Osprey's* secure anchorage, deep in the mangrove-lined channels of the park. Not only was the anchorage safe, but the likelihood of a full hurricane hitting the Venezuelan coast was minimal. But it was not just the fact that his boat was safe that made Kent feel lucky. Nor was it even that he and Jan had the good fortune to be sharing a tropical evening of rare beauty with their good friends Andre, and his wife Luciana. No, it was more than all that.

Kent had never been particularly introspective. He preferred to act on his impulses and trust his energy and intellect to sort things out. However, as he relaxed in the tropical twilight, the ex-executive began to put things together.

For most of his life Kent had always believed that happiness came through accomplishing goals. He had continually set goals for himself, and had been singularly good at achieving them. Pushing through an important business deal, getting his kids through college, learning to sail and going cruising, all these were goals he had accomplished. When he got an idea in his head, he pursued it doggedly, to the exclusion of everything else, because he found that that's what it took to succeed. He had no time for distractions, and no interest in anything but achieving his goal.

However, for the last year, things had been different. For the first time in his life he was not pursuing one goal monomaniacally—he was balancing several different parts of his life at once. He was maintaining the boat, and doing much of the cooking, while Jan was busy with her teaching. He was still studying Spanish. He was sailing, exploring, and diving with Jan whenever they had the chance, and he was also working on his business venture with Andre. In addition, he was relaxing into the Latin pace of life. Two hour lunches were now the norm and three day weekends, why not? Not that he felt lazy, far from it. In some ways Kent thought that he had never been more productive. But for the first time in his life Kent was taking a little bit from many plates rather than a lot from one. And, he realized, that was what had given him his contentment.

"So what do you think Kent, are we ready to get our first shipment in next week?" Andre's voice brought Kent back to the present. Like Kent, Jan, and Luciana, Andre too had been mesmerized by the birds overhead, but now he fixed his attention on his partner.

"Yeah, I think so," Kent replied. "We've got everything set up. The water quality looks good. Pedro and Juan seem to understand what they need to do. So sure, let's bring the critters down." They were speaking in Spanish, at Kent's insistence. He still felt he had a lot to learn, though both Jan and Andre thought his conversational ability was more than adequate.

"You guys are excited about this aren't you?" Jan asked Kent. "You sound like a couple of kids planning a caper." Several months ago, when she had learned what Kent and Andre were up to, Jan was at first puzzled

"I've seen the future . . . and it's in crawfish!"

and then amused. Kent, however, was both serious and excited about his project.

"Look, Jan," he had said, "it's just what this coast needs. The fisherman can't keep taking lobsters from the reef the way they have been. Their catch is already going down every year. Pretty soon they're not going to have enough income and they're going to start taking smaller and smaller animals. That'll be the end of lobstering round here. If my idea works, it'll give them another way to make a living. Plus I think it's going to be the wave of the future."

"But crayfish?" Jan looked at Kent wryly, "Those itty-bitty little things that my brother used to catch in the creek? I don't know Kent. I just don't know." Jan laughed at the serious expression on Kent's face.

Crayfish were indeed the "secret project" that Kent and Andre were working on. Despite Jan's patronizing remarks, Kent thought that they were onto a good thing. Research he'd done back in the States showed him that there was a small but growing trend among restaurants to buy farm-raised fresh water crayfish. They were being marketed as the new trendy gourmet item. And the ones Kent had seen on an aquaculture project in Belize were hardly "itty-bitty," measuring some eight- to ten-inches from head to tail.

He and Andre planned on starting a small pilot project on their own, with just two workers and a half dozen small tanks. If everything went according to plan, next year they would seek funding from an international development organization. If they could demonstrate the feasibility of their project, Kent was sure they could secure a grant.

Their plan was to then expand the program to involve fishermen's cooperatives up and down the coast. Although he knew the income from the crayfish could never entirely replace the income the fishermen derived from lobstering, Kent hoped that it would at least prop them up enough that they would not overfish the reefs. If they could stabilize the lobster population where it was now, Kent and Andre would consider their program a success.

Jan, Luciana, and Fiona loved to poke fun at the "boys'" seriousness. Nevertheless, Jan gave Kent credit for trying something new. She believed that the project stood at least a fighting chance of success, although she wasn't about to admit it to Kent. And she agreed that something had to be done soon to stop the rapid depletion of the off-shore reefs.

Jan was still teaching with Fiona and, as the oldest teacher at the school, was something of a fixture. She had made several good friends among the other teachers, most of whom were in their mid-to late-twenties. It was fun to hang out with a young crowd, especially after the predominantly over-50 set she and Kent had been socializing with in Trinidad. Nevertheless, she had told Fiona last winter that next year she only wanted to teach two out of the four terms. She and Kent had decided that although they were enjoying their life in Venezuela, they wanted to get out and spend some time cruising too.

"What about Curacao and Aruba? We've never been to those islands," Kent had said.

"Yeah, and the south coasts of the Dominican Republic, Cuba, most of Puerto Rico, there are all kinds of places to visit in the northern Caribbean," replied Jan.

"If you get your crayfish project rolling this summer, let's bail out and take six months next winter to just play."

"Sounds good to me. I'll be ready for a break by November."

At the yacht club, the sun sank below the mangroves, and Andre lit a couple mosquito coils. All around them the two couples heard the screeching, squawking, and clacking of thousands of birds getting ready for sleep. Kent came out from the bar carrying a round of drinks, and as he passed them, he grinned at his wife and two friends. Then, with a contented sigh, Kent collapsed into his deck chair, put his feet on the railing, and listened absently as Luciana and Jan planned the evening meal.

While *Osprey* was securely tucked away in Venezuela, John and Paula were exploring the magical archipelago of Panama's San Blas islands.

Although they had a hard time coming to the decision, in the end they had decided that it was better to carry on through the Panama Canal rather than return to Costa Rica. The two sailors would have loved to see Peter and Lucy again, but the draw of the unknown was stronger.

After a couple weeks in the San Blas islands they were glad they had come. The hurricane season passed in a pleasant blur of fishing, diving, trading with the Cuna Indians, and sailing from one tiny reef-fringed island to the next. One day Paula surprised herself with the realization that since they had left Costa Rica, not once had she thought about their financial situation. That night over cocktails in the cockpit, she remarked on this to John.

"You know," Paula said, "it's not like we're actually any better off financially than when we left Los Angeles, at least not on paper. But over the last two years we've managed to keep from using our savings, plus we've figured out different ways we can make money. I've got the feeling now that wherever we go we'll be able to work at something. I'm even thinking that maybe we should stay out cruising longer than the five years we'd planned. What do you think?"

John tilted his head back and looked at Paula over his beer and chuckled. "You want to know what I think? I think that I've got one smart cookie for a wife."

The following winter John and Paula explored the Bay Islands of Honduras. Paula found four different boutiques who were happy to carry her hats, and she continued to sell to other yachties as well. As they moved around the islands diving, sailing and socializing, they kept hearing about Guatemala's Rio Dulce. When May arrived, and *Drifter* had been in the Bay Islands for almost six months, John and Paula decided it was time to head west and see what all the hype was about.

Three days later *Drifter* was winding her way between the vertical, vine-strewn walls of the six-mile long canyon that is the entrance to the Rio Dulce. As they proceeded upstream, John and Paula gazed around, amazed at the violent fecundity of the jungle. Near-naked Indians paddled silently by in tiny dugout canoes, and Lilliputian reed shacks poked out from the leafy greenness. As *Drifter* reached the end of the canyon and entered a small lake, they saw a sailboat anchored near shore, where a few primitive buildings seemed to be under construction. Curious, John motored over to the other boat.

A figure appeared on deck. "Hey there! How y'all doin'? Do you think you could stop and give me a hand?"

"Sure, what do you need?" asked John. "Is something broken on your boat?"

"Nah, I need someone to help me onshore. Why don't you folks stop and anchor, and I'll tell you all about it. Come on over to my boat for drinks and dinner once you get yourselves situated."

John looked at Paula. She nodded her head, tacitly agreeing to stop, and John brought *Drifter's* bow to the current, dropping anchor about fifty feet from the other boat. After getting things stowed away and changing into clean clothes, John and Paula got in their dinghy and went over to talk to this outgoing sailor.

It turned out his name was Wally, and he was originally from Texas. He told John that he used to be a singlehander, and he had been coming and going to the Rio Dulce for years. A year ago he had fallen in love with a lovely local woman, Juanita, who was also a dynamic activist for Indian rights.

Juanita had convinced Wally to direct his considerable energies into helping her start the first school and clinic that would cater specifically to the Indians living on the remote reaches of the lower Rio Dulce. She had a parcel of land that had been donated by a rich Canadian yachtie, and had scraped together funding to cover the cost of construction materials. Wally said that right now he was directing a construction crew of some eighteen Indian volunteers and pushing to get the project completed before the summer rains set in.

This was all explained to John and Paula over dinner on Wally's boat. John took a liking to Wally, though his bluntness was a bit disconcerting at first. Wally quickly came to the point—he needed help with the construction. Of course, he couldn't afford to pay them, but would John and Paula be interested in volunteering for a few weeks? John had been nonplused at first, startled by the suddenness of the request, but as the evening wore on, it began to seem like a better and better idea. By the time everyone had finished dinner and were sitting around having drinks in the cockpit, John was even enthusiastic enough to propose a toast to the success of the project.

The next month brought back memories of the construction job in Morro Bay for John. He was working alongside a crew of eight Indians and directing them in the completion of the school. Paula was working with Juanita, supervising the digging of latrines and the construction of sleeping quarters. Wally was handling the completion of the largest building: the clinic.

Wally and Juanita were vivacious and enthusiastic, and the enthusiasm was contagious. Soon John and Wally were engaged in a good natured competition to see who could get the most concrete poured or galvanized roofing laid in a day. Many evenings the two couples shared dinner, either on *Drifter* or on *Tuppence*, Wally and Juanita's boat.

John and Paula found the weeks flying by, and often in the evenings they compared their impressions. Back in Los Angeles neither of them had given much thought to charities or volunteerism. Sure they "gave at the office," but the idea of actually volunteering time and labor? Even if they had the inclination, there was simply no time. Now here they were, sweaty and dirty in a tropical jungle, supervising crews of Indians whose language was incomprehensible, and having a ball. Who would have thought?

After six weeks, the buildings were finally completed, and Wally gave John and Paula their "walking papers."

"I know you folks want to see the rest of the river, and of course I don't blame you. It's lovely up there. But remember, whenever you come by this way, stop in and say Hi. Watch out though, Juanita might just put you to work again! And guys?"

John and Paula looked at Wally.

"Thanks for everything. You really made a difference."

As John weighed *Drifter's* anchor and Paula directed the boat back into the mainstream of the river, that phrase echoed in his mind, again and again. "You really made a difference."


Two weeks later *Drifter* was anchored amidst the steaming virgin rain forest in the middle reaches of the Rio Dulce. John and Paula felt that they had discovered a little slice of paradise. Surprisingly, given all the talk they had heard in advance, there were only about fifteen boats anchored on the river. The couple soon fell into the congenial social scene, which revolved around the bar at the Tres Amigos Marina.

John learned that Tres Amigos had been started four years earlier by Clint, a sailor who had come up the river one day and never left. Clint could usually be found behind the bar at Tres Amigos, and one night he and John got to talking about *Drifter's* plans. When Clint asked John how long he and Paula were going to be on the river, John heard something in Clint's voice that told him it was more than an idle question.

"We're not sure, Clint," John replied. "We don't have any fixed plans. Paula tends to get bored after a while if we're just staying in one place. But if we could find something to do here, we might spend some time."

"That's just why I was asking you, John. I like you both, and it sounds like you've had experience in the tropics. I'd like to make a proposition to you, so tell me how this sounds. I'm getting tired of running this place all by myself. After all, I came down here to get away from having a lot of responsibilities. Now they seem to be following me. Anyway, what I wanted to know is, would you and Paula be interested in taking over the running of Tres Amigos for six months? That would give me a chance to take a breather. I'd like to go up in the mountains for a while and hang out."

And so, as simply as that, John and Paula found themselves managing a tiny tropical marina and bar. The "marina" was really nothing more than a dock with space for about six boats to tie stern-to. Currently there were only three boats there, but Clint said in the hurricane season he was usually filled up. For two weeks Clint stayed to help the couple get the hang of the place. Then, with a promise to be back in a month or so, he took off into the mountains of the interior.

Although on the surface it looked like there was not much work to running Tres Amigos, at first John and Paula were kept busy almost full-time. To begin with, there was no electricity or running water, so John needed to monitor the diesel genset and water pump to insure the supply of these necessities. Also, without access to a road, all supplies had to be brought in by boat. John quickly realized that he needed to think ahead to make sure the staff delivered what was needed, when it was needed. Paula, for her part, was kept busy monitoring the unattended boats at the dock and supervising the myriad details of running the bar.

As cruisers, John and Paula had experienced the slowness and inefficiency common to the tropics. However, when trying to run a business, even one as small as Tres Amigos, the "mañana attitude" quickly went from being funny to being infuriating. One night, after the third attempt to get one of their workers to bring five cases of beer from town, John blew up.

"I just can't believe it!" he said to Paula that night back on their boat. "I mean, damn it, what does it take to get through to these people. I know my Spanish isn't the greatest but come on. 'Cinco cajas de cerveza!' I mean that's pretty clear, right? And not once, not twice, but three bloody times Pedro goes to town and forgets to bring them back!"

"Calm down, dear." Paula passed him a beer. "Look, we wanted the experience of running a business, now we're getting it. And don't take everything so seriously. You've got to lighten up, relax, have the attitude that everybody else has around here. You know, 'Mañana, mañana.'"

"Easy for you to say. I've seen you lose your cool too."

Gradually John and Paula learned the ropes. They learned how to accomplish things with a minimum of stress, and they learned which things they could let slide.

Thanks to their hard work, in a couple months Tres Amigos was doing more business than ever. After she became comfortable with the business, Paula decided to hire a cook and add a simple menu to the bar. She only served burgers, fried chicken, and hot dogs, all things that could be kept in the freezer if there wasn't much demand. By adding food to the bar, Paula found that she allowed the boaters to stay and continue the cocktail hour into the dinner hour. The concept was a success, and before long the bar business was booming.

Of course the bar and restaurant also provided a perfect venue from which Paula could market her hats. During the course of the summer, she maintained a small but steady business selling them to boaters coming through.

John soon noticed that the majority of boaters who left their boats at the Tres Amigos dock did so in order to fly back to the States. Why not, he thought, incorporate a second row of boats behind the first? After all, nearly all boats are unoccupied, so nobody needs immediate access to the dock. This is what he did, and the second row filled up in a few weeks.

John and Paula were happy. They were enjoying the activity and the challenge of keeping everything working. It was a big change from their last lazy summer in Panama, but they had no complaints. Also, it was pleasant to find themselves considered "locals" by the boaters passing through. They enjoyed being able to help people find things they needed and get things done.

Then too, they were actually managing to put a reasonable amount of money in the bank. Clint had told them that, while he couldn't afford to pay them a salary, he was perfectly willing to let them keep whatever profits the bar and marina made in his absence. He said not to expect too much, however. If they cleared enough money from the bar to cover their personal expenses, they'd be doing well. In fact, now with the increased bar business, plus twice the number of boats at the dock, Tres Amigos was generating a decent profit.

Clint stopped by a couple of times and was impressed with the changes brought to his business. When the six months was up, Clint pressed John and Paula to stay on.

"Hey," he said, "I don't need the money from this place. I just started it as a lark and as a place to park my boat and have friends over for drinks. But I'm having a good time up in the mountains now. Why don't you folks stay on for another six months?"

"Thanks Clint, but no." John declined the offer. "We're ready to move on. Seven months on this river is enough for us. We might be back though, you never know. If we do come back, we'll look you up and more than likely take you up on your offer."

It was now late December and John and Paula were anxious to sail to Belize and spend the winter exploring and diving on its huge barrier reef. Once again, *Drifter* was bound for new horizons.

## ENTREPRENEURIAL OPPORTUNITIES FOR CRUISERS

In the last chapter we looked at ways cruising sailors could make money using their boat as a base. Some opportunities entailed setting up what was basically a business operating from the boat. But what about starting a business ashore? Is it feasible, worthwhile, or desirable for cruisers to try to start a business in a foreign country, especially if they want to continue cruising? In this chapter we'll examine the various options available.

The focus will be mainly on starting a business in a foreign, usually developing, country. From my experience these are the places that cruising entrepreneurs are most likely to be interested in. The challenges and sense of adventure entailed in starting a business in a foreign country are often the main attraction to a former businessman. Many of the precepts illustrated here, however, apply equally to businesses started in the sailor's home country.

Let's first look at Kent's business in Morrocoy as an example. It contains several elements that contribute to a successful business start-up abroad.

First, Kent started out in partnership with a local person, and even better, with one who had influence with the authorities. The law in some countries stipulates that only citizens of that country can own a majority share in a local business. In other countries, although laws may not preclude you from owning a business, it is still a good policy to go into partnership with a local. In many, if not most, developing countries, business is run very much by the "old boy" network. In order to get anything done, whether it's buying supplies, arranging advertising, or sorting out government permits, it's very much the case of "who" you know rather than "what" you know. A local partner, especially a well connected one, is invaluable in sorting out the innuendo, intrigue, and outright lies to which a foreigner is often subjected when trying to set up a business.

Another thing Kent did right was to start a business for which there was no competition. There is no surer way to stir up ill feelings and sow the seeds for future problems than for a foreigner to start a business which competes directly with established local businesses.

Our friends Jorge and Francesca made this mistake several years ago in Brazil, and I don't think they'll ever forget it. Jorge and Francesca were Argentine sailors who left their country during the "dirty war" of the late 70s. Since leaving Argentina their family had grown to include three children, all living aboard their 44-foot ketch. In Brazil it was not easy for locals to make money, let alone foreigners, and Jorge, although he had been living there for years, was still considered a foreigner. So when the established Brazilian charter boat operators saw Jorge try to start a day-charter business in the resort town of Porto Seguro they were furious.

If Jorge had retained a Brazilian partner he may have smoothed some ruffled feathers, but as it was he and his family soon had the ire of the whole community directed against them. His docklines were cut at night, his charterers were harassed as they boarded his boat, and finally he began to receive anonymous threats. Enough was enough for Jorge and Francesca, and one day they made the inevitable decision to move on and try to set up somewhere else.

This scenario can apply to any type of business, so do your research before making an investment. Be sure that you will not be stepping on anybody's toes. And remember, even if you're legally in the right (as in fact Jorge was in Brazil) this may not make any difference to local feelings. Remember that you're a guest in someone else's country, and what might be acceptable business practice in America, is not necessarily thought to be so elsewhere.

The final thing that guaranteed that Kent's success as an entrepreneur was that he did not set out with the intention of making a lot of money, or actually in his case, even of making a profit. As anyone who has run a business in the Third World can attest, it is significantly more difficult to make money there than in more advanced countries. It's not simply a matter of being able to speak the language or even of knowing the local customs. An advanced economic system simply has more potential for growth and the creation of wealth. In developing countries, where a substantial part of the population lives at the subsistence level, there is simply less money to go around, and it's much harder to get hold of. There's a saying that the easiest way to make a small fortune in a developing country is to start out with a large one!

What this means, for anyone thinking of setting up a business abroad, is that unless you happen to be very lucky, you will always receive less for your investment of time and money than you would in your home country. If you are a cruising sailor, who wants to set up a business abroad, it should be for reasons other than just making money.

To sum up then, the three rules for a sailor who wants to start a business abroad are:

➤ Retain a local partner

➤ Make sure there is no direct local competition

➤ Don't expect to make a lot of money

## REASONS TO START A BUSINESS

So what *are* the reasons to start a business abroad? One perfectly valid reason is, that like Kent, you simply can't get "business" out of your system. Like a doctor who can't stay away from doctoring or a teacher who needs to teach, as a businessman who has "dropped out" and gone sailing, you may not have lost your taste for running a business. An enjoyment of the challenge of competition is often the main motivator for pursuing a business career in the first place. I have met many people who placed more importance on successfully competing in the business world than on merely making money. It would be irrational to think that such a strong drive disappears just because one buys a sailboat.

A second reason to start a business abroad can be the desire to make a positive change in people's lives. Whether it's starting a boatyard so the local people can learn marketable carpentry and fiberglass skills, or opening a canning plant to allow fisherman to sell their catch at fair prices, direct investment by foreigners can be used to bring positive change to backward parts of the world. The backwater ports that sailors find themselves in, in fact those which they actually seek out, are far from principal cities and are often forgotten by larger development organizations. An energetic and committed cruiser can make a surprising difference in such places.

As we saw in Kent's case, the two reasons—love of business *per se* and the desire to help improve local living conditions—need not be mutually exclusive. Kent was enjoying the challenge of researching a new field, finding out how to go about setting up his crayfish farm, and figuring out how to market and ship his product. But he also felt that his project would benefit Venezuela in a larger sense. His idea of franchising the business to fishing co-ops had the potential to significantly impact the ecology of the area. This scenario is exactly the kind of win-win situation that motivated cruisers can create.

Another attraction for cruisers who have run businesses in Europe or America is the unfettered nature of most Third World economies. While you won't find the wealth or diversity of markets that more developed countries offer, neither will you be stifled by government regulations and taxes. Bureaucracy and red tape are not impenetrable barriers in most developing countries. They are more in the nature of challenge to one's creativity.

As a Mexican friend of mine once said when I complained about his country's Byzantine system of licensing, "You've got to understand. That's why we have corruption. It's the only way we get things done!" Again, knowledge and connections that a local partner can provide will open many doors.

Here's an example of a sailor who found better opportunities abroad than at home. Wilhelm was a Dutch boatwright who for thirteen years ran a small business in Rotterdam building sailing dinghies. Year-by-year he felt more and more strangled by government regulations: environmental regulations, worker's compensation schemes, insurance requirements, all seemed to be conspiring to drive him out of business. When one year he made less money than any of his employees, despite record sales, Wilhelm decided to get out. He resolved to cruise the Mediterranean in his sailboat and work casually on other boats as he went along.

Upon reaching Turkey, the Dutch sailor became friends with Mehmet, a Turkish carpenter. Wilhelm was impressed by the skill level he saw among the Turks, and, encouraged by Mehmet, he started another boat building business. In Turkey there was a very low tax rate, almost no environmental regulation, and very few insurance requirements. This was the way Wilhelm wanted to do business. After three years, he had built up a good client base and was building two- to three-custom boats every year. He and Mehmet shared the responsibilities for overseeing the eight employees, and during the summer, Wilhelm could get out and sail the spectacular Turkish coast.

## POTENTIAL PITFALLS

So far we have painted a very rosy picture. But there must be downsides to starting an overseas business. What does a cruiser who is interested in this option need to look out for? First, of course, is the fact that in many parts of the developing world, foreigners are seen simply as "walking wallets." Anyone who is thinking of making an investment in a Third World country needs to be very sure that he is not being swindled.

As I said before, it is important to have a local partner. Selecting this partner, however, can be one of the biggest hurdles facing a foreign investor. Kent was lucky. He found someone whom he could trust and who was easy to get along with. It isn't always that easy, however. When you enter a new country, you cannot be in a hurry. You need to spend time getting a feel for the culture and making local contacts.

It may be advantageous to check with the local Rotary or Kiwanis clubs. If these have chapters where you happen to be, this can be a good first step toward meeting the local business people who matter. See if there is a local chamber of commerce, also, and speak with them. Remember that the more serious business people that you can speak to before you make a commitment, the better.

A second point, is that starting a new business can end up dominating your life. Many times the very reason that a business person goes sailing is to get away from the all-consuming, workaholic way of life. Unfortunately, the very characteristics that contribute to being a successful entrepreneur can tend to lead someone back down that road again. Here again, a partner can help to alleviate the stress. This is what Kent found with Andre, and what Clint was hoping to arrange with Tres Amigos. While "all things in moderation" is a precept more easily quoted than followed, maintaining the balance between work and pleasure is a key point to keep in mind.

One more thing to remember is that while starting a business in a new country can be rewarding and interesting, it also has the potential to turn into a nightmare. Bureaucracy, corruption, and plain obstructionism can waylay the best laid plans. Before going in, make sure you have an escape route, a way to bail out if all goes bad. Figure out ahead of time how you will get your investment out, if you can. Otherwise don't invest more than you can afford to lose. Remember that the whole reason you got involved in sailing was to get more out of life. If your new business venture isn't giving you that, dump it.

Having covered the pros and cons of starting a new business abroad, let's look at the types of businesses that are best for cruisers. Obviously, marine-oriented businesses are a natural. We have seen many people, like Clint in Guatemala, who arrive in a port and fall in love with the area. With the decision to stay, often comes the idea of starting a small business. Starting a marina, for instance, requires a minimal investment, usually the purchase of a building on the water with a dock. Running a small marina, sometimes with a bar/restaurant sometimes without, appeals to many cruisers who want an active social life and a base in the country.

Other cruiser-oriented businesses that I have seen started successfully include:

➤ Marine repair businesses

➤ Restaurants

➤ Mail handling and message taking service

➤ Laundry services

➤ Customs expediting (arranging to get spares, replacement parts, etc.)

➤ Internet café

Besides catering to cruisers, the sailing entrepreneur may start a business that brings something new to an area or community. When it comes to securing the necessary permits and clearances from the government, being able to show that your business will bring a positive change to the area is a good bargaining chip.

Harry and Laura, two American sailors we met in Belize, were taking advantage of local conditions in what was certainly a unique way. Harry learned that Belize, like most Central American countries, receives large amounts of secondhand clothing from U.S. relief organizations. Much of this clothing was sold at rock-bottom prices in shops around the country. As he started looking at these shops, Harry got to thinking. It seemed there were many, many, more clothes than people would ever buy. What happened to all the stuff that never got sold? When he asked the question, Harry found out that the unsold clothing was simply burned!

Harry and Laura brainstormed about how they could take advantage of this "resource." Eventually they came up with a great idea. In partnership with a Belizean family, Harry and Laura set up a small plant that would produce paper from old clothes. But this was not any ordinary paper. Harry's whole concept centered on the idea of making high-priced, heavyweight paper for artists in the States.

One day he showed me some of his product. The paper was thick, off white, and rough. One piece, about two square feet, sold in the United States for twenty dollars! I thought to myself, here was a perfect example of utilizing existing conditions in a unique way. Clothes thrown away in America are donated to the Third World where cheap labor turned them into high-priced paper to be sold back in the States. Jobs were created, waste was reduced, and everyone won. Perfect!

Another selling point when it comes to securing permits is being able to show that your business will employ a good number of local people. Remember that it is your job to convince the powers that be, that it is in their interests to have your business in their community. In much of the Third World, job creation is often as desirable as profitability. The attitude in many poor countries is that it's better to have twenty people working for low wages than ten people making a decent living. This is the reality, whether or not you agree with it as an economic policy. The more workers you plan to employ the better.

Over the years, we have seen many cruiser-started businesses that exploit existing opportunities in a new way. Here are a few of them:

> Converting an existing, but unused, shrimp packing plant to the processing of shark meat

> Using a Free-Trade Zone to assemble furniture with imported wood, using graduates from a local vocational school

> Employing many local people in a project to build local fishing boats out of fiberglass instead of wood, then selling the boats to the local fishermen

> Raising alligators in captivity on a boggy, unprofitable cattle ranch

*Ideas for entreprenurial possibilities abound!*

Each of these businesses opened a market that would probably never have been tapped by the locals themselves. As a foreigner, with a different perspective, the cruising sailor can often bring new ideas into a community.

## TOURISTIC DEVELOPMENT

Another area of business that almost always finds favor among the locals is tourism. In many developing countries tourism is seen, rightly or wrongly, as a "free ride" to wealth. The feeling is that if wealthy foreigners will pay handsomely to see your country, why not let them? Unfortunately, it is often the local people who facilitate some of the worst forms of exploitative, unsustainable tourism. In the last decade there has been a lot of attention paid to eco-tourism and low-impact adventure tours. If you do consider getting into the tourism business, I urge you to consider both the ecological and cultural implications of your venture.

Will it really benefit local Indians to have groups of camera-toting tourists wandering around their village? What will be the effect of running jeep safaris over fragile jungle roads? How will the increased use of outboard-powered boats affect the fragile ecology of a mountain lake? I am not saying that all tourism businesses are bad or exploitative. I am only making the point that as a relatively well-educated cruiser, it is your responsibility to research and assess the implications of your plans before you implement them.

Daniel, a Swiss sailor on the Rio Dulce, decided that he wanted to do more than just start the usual bar/restaurant/marina. After a year in Guatemala, he had become fast friends with Raul, a local businessman and yachtsman. Together the two of them bought a large section of nearly virgin jungle and the remains of a disused rubber plantation. The concept that they came up with for their resort was an interesting example of creative marketing.

Initially Raul had the idea of just opening up a jungle lodge. They would build several small buildings, nestled in the trees, connected with walkways over the sensitive jungle floor. It would be a very low-impact development and would take advantage of the growing eco-tourism movement. Daniel agreed with Raul's idea but expanded on it. What if, in addition to the lodge, they brought the rubber trees back into production. They would process the rubber in the traditional manner, over open fires, and market their lodge to tourists as not just another jungle hotel but as a working rubber plantation.

Raul objected. He claimed that the whole reason for shutting down the plantation in the first place was that it was no longer profitable to harvest rubber traditionally on a small scale. They were guaranteed to lose money. Daniel countered that whatever they lost on the rubber production, they would make up for with tourist revenues.

It turned out Daniel was right. As a marketing tool, the working plantation more than made up for the income that was lost subsidizing production. Tourists loved riding around on horseback with the rubber tappers and helping with the traditional curing process. In fact, after a European travel magazine wrote praising their concept, Daniel and Raul began to make a decent profit at the venture. They were employing many local campesinos at a decent wage and had saved a chunk of jungle from more exploitative development.

Hopefully the examples above will stimulate the imagination of any cruising sailor who may be considering starting some type of business. Over the years, what has amazed me most about the various cruiser-started businesses I have seen around the world, has been their sheer diversity. I am still fascinated by the interesting ways in which sailors contrive to utilize local conditions in unique ways. If you're one of those people who can't get business out of your blood, consider the entrepreneurial angle as a way to augment your cruising life.

## PLUSES AND MINUSES OF STARTING A BUSINESS ASHORE

### PLUSES

> Can be a rewarding and stimulating challenge for someone with "business" in their blood

> An excellent way to develop a real relationship with a local partner

> Benefitting the local community can be satisfying

### MINUSES

> Not usually very profitable for the time and effort invested

> Can end up dominating your life

> Potential for losing your investment and/or becoming ensnarled in the local bureaucracy

## WORKING AS A VOLUNTEER

What about volunteering? Instead of starting a business that may not make a profit and which might even lose money, why not just go ahead and donate your time? There are as many reasons for a cruising sailor to work as a volunteer as there are opportunities available. Let's look at a few of them.

Obviously the principle attraction of working as a volunteer is the satisfaction of knowing that you are helping people on a very immediate level. For example, when John and Paula next cruised down the Rio Dulce, they stopped in to visit Wally and Juanita. Not only were the buildings that they had worked on completely finished, they were already in use. The school was filled with some thirty-odd Indian children, and the clinic had about a dozen people waiting outside for treatment.

Wally told John that through contacts in the States he had been able to recruit doctors and nurses to come down and work in the clinic. The school was staffed by a couple of teachers Juanita had recruited from among her friends in Guatemala City. When John saw how much was being done, he was glad he'd had the chance to be part of it. Here was something that had already changed the lives of many Indians, and would continue to do so.

Besides emotional satisfaction and a feeling of accomplishment, volunteering can have other material benefits for cruising sailors. Sometimes a volunteer situation will come with "fringe benefits," like dockage for the boat or the use of shoreside facilities such as a laundry or a workshop.

Also, volunteering is a great way to meet people, both locals and other foreigners. When you volunteer, everyone is trying to make a difference, and this common bond often paves the way to friendships. Volunteering can thus allow you to make friends with local families and other non-boater travelers, which can sometimes be a pleasant change from the social circle of the boating community.

So if you do want to work as a volunteer, what is out there? What kind of organizations exist, and what are the good and bad points of each?

For the purposes of this discussion, let's break volunteer organizations into two types: formal and informal. Formal volunteering organizations tend to be large and often recruit volunteers in advance from their home countries. Informal organizations offer the type of work Paula and John found with Wally and Juanita.

There are many, many of these tiny volunteer operations scattered around the Third World. Most are too small to advertise or recruit people from afar. These organizations rely on word-of-mouth and personal contacts to attract volunteers. The advantages of these informal positions are that usually you do not have to commit to a fixed length of time, and you can work directly with the people running the operation.

The best way to find these positions is to ask around. Other boaters who have lived in the area a while, as well as locals, will usually be able to direct you to anyone looking for help. Skills in high demand include everything from construction experience to teaching, medical services, basic accounting and business management, public relations, legal advice, secretarial work, and much more. From what we have seen, these tiny grassroots operations are usually desperate for any help they can get and will welcome the average yachtie with his wide range of practical skills.

Another way in which you can help small volunteer organizations as a sailor is by providing transportation. We once worked with an orphanage in Brazil that was so strapped for cash that they couldn't afford fuel for their outboard. As a result, even though one of the shop owners in the nearby town had donated a 50 kilo bag of beans and another of flour, the orphanage had no way of getting the supplies and was actually beginning to run short of basic foodstuffs.

When we offered to ferry the food downriver from town, Jean, the woman in charge, was ecstatic. From then on we were treated like visiting royalty at the orphanage and became friends with several of the volunteers there. Small things like this not only give you a feeling of helping out, they also contribute to building a community spirit and help to create a reputation for cruising sailors as being more than just tourists.

If you want to find out about volunteer opportunities in a region before you arrive, research worldwide listings of aid organizations (some of which can be found in Appendix F). These organizations run the full gamut from religious missionary groups to international trade organizations to disaster relief funds. Once you determine which specific organizations fit your interests, write, e-mail, or telephone them to learn whether they require your skills and whether they expect a commitment from you. If you find an organization that is interested in your skills, see if you can leave things open-ended until you arrive in the country. You should be able to work out an arrangement that pre-

*Honey, I know we're trying to help, but the chickens gotta go!*

cludes you from being pinned down in such a way that your sailing plans are constrained.

Also, find out exactly what the organization does for the local people. There are some "volunteer" organizations that require you to pay a stipend for the privilege of donating your time and skills. To me, these outfits are really selling low-cost "adventure travel" under the title of volunteerism. Since you will be taking care of your own transportation and lodging, I would be very skeptical of any group that requires you to commit money as well.

Whether you contact a large formal aid organization or a small locally-based one, be sure you understand up front what you are committing to. Find out just what is expected of you and for how long. Are

you committing to a fixed period of time, or to the completion of a specified project? What if you have to leave early because of weather or other commitments? Are there any legal or immigration issues that you should be aware of? It is a good idea to have the answers to all these questions before making a commitment of time and energy to any volunteer organization.

You do not, of course, have to work for any established organization. If you are motivated and a self-starter, you can implement your own program and make changes in the country you visit. Mimi, a friend of ours for many years (and the illustrator of this book), showed us just what is possible when a sailor decides to "take the bull by the horns."

After single-handing her classic wooden sloop around the Bahamas for a couple years, Mimi made an interesting discovery. On the island of Great Abaco there were several groups of wild horses living in the outback. No one knew exactly how many there were, where they came from, or even what type of horse they were. Intrigued, Mimi began to study them herself. When she found that the horses on Abaco were both a possibly unique breed and were under threat from man, she decided to do something.

With characteristic energy Mimi set about establishing a nonprofit foundation to study and protect the horses. She worked with interested local people in the Bahamas, and in the States she set up a newsletter and a Web site to promote the foundation. Contributions began to come in from horse lovers, and Mimi used the money for medicines, advertising, and the myriad of supplies necessary to keep her in the field. In the space of a few years Mimi went a long way toward furthering both the understanding and the protection of the wild horses.

Mimi continues to cruise the Bahamas regularly and enjoys the tranquility of being a singlehander out on the cays. However, by starting and maintaining the Wild Horse Foundation, she has given her cruising a new dimension, and she finds that her work on Great Abaco serves as a welcome anchor to her nomadic wandering.

For the cruising sailor who is looking to make a difference, or who perhaps just wants to experience something different, volunteering can be a worthwhile avenue to explore. Remember that it does not take much to make a big difference and that you, as a volunteer, will benefit as much or more than those you help.

## PLUSES AND MINUSES OF WORKING AS A VOLUNTEER

### PLUSES

➤ Usually rewarding in that you see immediate changes and results as a result of your labors

➤ Often you can work out a flexible schedule that allows you sailing/personal time when you want it

➤ Many times positions come with "fringe benefits"

### MINUSES

➤ Not a way to make money!

➤ Conditions may be primitive and/or uncomfortable

➤ Some larger organizations may require a long-term commitment

# CHAPTER EIGHT

# CONCLUSIONS, SUMMING THINGS UP, AND LOOKING TO THE FUTURE

Perhaps you wonder, after following them this far, what our three pairs of friends—Steve and Irene, Jan and Kent, and John and Paula, are doing now. How have things worked out for them after several more years of sailing?

Steve and Irene are still in the Virgin Islands. Steve is working with his boat repair co-op, and Irene is still painting T-shirts. Although we have not seen them for a few years now, we still receive Christmas cards regularly. A couple of years ago they wrote to us that they had sold *Dancer* and bought another, larger boat. They are very happy on St. John and have settled into the small community of Coral Bay on the east end of the island. They still manage to take a cruise every year, sometimes for only a couple months, sometimes for the better part of a year. The last we heard from them, they were talking about possibly taking a break from the Caribbean for a couple years and sailing trans-Atlantic.

John and Paula moved on from the Western Caribbean after spending another year in Belize and the Bay Islands. Encouraged by their experience at Tres Amigos, the two sailors began looking around the Eastern Caribbean for another resort management position. Eventually they found just what they were looking for, in a small hotel/restaurant on the island of Vieques. After working there for a couple of months, John and Paula were struck by the scarcity of customers for a resort of obvious charm. John thought about his success with the Jungle Inn in Costa Rica and spoke with the resort's owner.

"Go ahead," John, the owner said, "If you think you can boost my business, go to it. I'll be happy to give you a commission on any more business we get. Why not?"

This time, since they were still in a U.S. Territory (Vieques being part of the Commonwealth of Puerto Rico), John was able to make a lot of his contacts by phone from the resort. After laying the ground-work, he flew to Miami and met with contacts at several newspapers and a number of large travel agencies.

Once again, he was successful. Business increased steadily over the winter, and the grateful owner happily paid John his commission. John began to think that maybe he could actually work as a P.R. man as they cruised. Hey, he thought, why not?

Once again, Paula's hats were a success at the resort. As she evolved the current generation, however, she was glad that she had decided to sell them only part-time. Paula resolved that when they were actually cruising she would not bother marketing the hats. She would only sell them if they stopped for a while to work. This relieved her of the need to be constantly working on new hats, thus avoiding the irony of be-coming a slave to what was supposed to be fun.

After a year on Vieques, John and Paula were ready to leave. The last we heard from them, they had crossed the Atlantic to the Mediter-ranean and were thinking about continuing east on a circumnaviga-tion.

Kent and Jan settled in Morrocoy. They bought a car and a small house on the water, close to the yacht club where they kept *Osprey*. Kent's aquaculture business was neither a failure nor as big a success as he had hoped. Even with Andre's contacts and backing, the two partners had a difficult time convincing the local fisherman to tend the crayfish.

The fishermen accepted the equipment, the training, and the baby crayfish, but more often than not, they neglected the crucial filtering and monitoring of water quality. As a result, many of the co-ops experienced disappointing or nonexistent yields. Some are producing, though, and Kent and Andre still hope that as the news spreads that it is possible to actually make money at the scheme, more fishermen will take it seriously.

Jan is still teaching part-time with Fiona. Fiona's instincts were right, and despite the uncertain economic times in Venezuela, her school is a success. She and Jan still play piano together, and Jan wrote recently that she has even given a few casual concerts at the school.

In the meantime, Kent and Jan still manage to sail for six months each year. They find Morrocoy to be a perfect base for exploring the Caribbean and have traveled as far afield as Guatemala, Panama, and Colombia. We last heard from them a year ago, and they sounded quite content.

## SUMMING THINGS UP

Now that we have covered, rather exhaustively, the options open to cruisers who wish to work underway, let's stop and review some of the lessons that have been illustrated. For no matter what specific type of work you wish to pursue, in the cruising world, certain constants always apply. First...

## DON'T EXPECT ONE JOB TO DO IT ALL

Time and again we have seen that diversity is the key to financial freedom for sailors who have successfully married work and cruising. In all probability, it will be several talents, not just one, that allow you to support your cruising lifestyle. A portfolio of skills and a wide range of experience will give you the best chances of securing work wherever you go. As a cruiser, however, you do have several things working in your favor when it comes to exploring different alternatives.

First, you should have the time, space, and freedom to look at yourself and decide what you want. Buying a boat and setting sail may have its drawbacks. It may at times be uncomfortable, even dangerous. It may be cold, wet, and miserable, and more hard work than you envisioned. But one thing you will gain when you step off the land is the space and freedom of the sea. This freedom is both mental as well as physical. Night watches and time spent alone are invaluable assets for someone who wants to learn more about himself or herself. Anyone who uses this time creatively will find that it can provide the opportunity for significant personal growth.

Second, as a member of the sailing community, you have a tremendous amount of psychological liberty to indulge your interests. There simply is not a "career mentality" among sailors. This is what John and Paula found in their very first jobs in northern California. The lack of societal or peer pressure was a liberating and refreshing change. The sailing community, by its very nature, freely accepts eccentrics, free thinkers, and "square pegs."

Third, and perhaps most important, as you cruise you will learn very quickly that you, and you alone, have control over, and responsibility for, your actions and their consequences. Few lifestyles give you such control. As a nomadic, cruising sailor you control everything from how you make electricity to what laws you live under. You determine your own budget—whether it be lavish, miserly, or in between. You decide which boat and gear are best for you. Should you go high tech or low tech? Should you put comfort or cost as your top priority? Where will you cruise, how long will you stay, what will you do in your new location?

The very nature of a modern shoreside life, with its technological interconnectedness and necessary dependence on the "system," tends to deprive people of many of these options. Although as a cruising sailor, you will still be dependent on technology and modern infrastructure, you have many more options to choose as to when, where, and how much you make use of it.

These three things—the freedom and space to examine your desires, the lack of expectations or pressures from your peers, and the power and responsibility to take control of your life—give you, the cruising sailor, the opportunity to construct the best possible synthesis of earning money, helping others, and having a good time. So don't limit yourself to just one or two options. Be creative and explore! Use those long night watches and lazy tropical days to daydream and ponder, to come up with not just one or two but many ways to enjoy your freedom.

## START PLANNING AHEAD

Hopefully amidst the myriad of real-life examples I have presented throughout this book, you have found a few that pique your interest. If you have not yet taken the jump and gone cruising, think about how you can prepare yourself to exploit these possibilities. Make planning your new working life an integral part of your preparations before beginning your cruise.

Too often I have seen would-be cruisers intent only on escaping their current jobs and work situations. They focus all their energies on getting their boat ready and getting away. If they do think that they might need to work along the way, like Steve and Irene did, they usually try to put the idea out of their minds. They think of it as distasteful and somehow at odds with the cruising dream. They figure it will be a bridge they'll cross if and when they come to it.

Don't let this be you. Instead, take a proactive approach. Establish some work options you are interested in, and prepare for them before you leave. Maybe you have an interest in cooking, so you take a course in restaurant culinary skills. Or maybe working as a professional crew turns you on, so you get certified in that. Or perhaps you decide to research the latest opportunities in telecommuting. Whatever. The idea is that, at the same time you're learning to navigate, buying charts, and reading books on boat gear, also start planning how you will work underway, for fun, for profit, or both. Also, if you know where you will be sailing, research work opportunities in the countries you'll be visiting.

Whether you're just planning your cruise or are already sailing, you can also take advantage of information from other sailors. Ask questions about their experiences with different types of work. As you start networking you will probably find that there are many more opportunities than I have covered in this book. What I have tried to do here is simply whet your appetite, point you in the right directions, and give you some tools and resources to explore your interests. There are also many sides to every story, and while I have tried to portray the pluses and minuses of each job as objectively as I can, there is no substitute for other opinions.

Also remember, while you're cruising always keep an eye open for work opportunities and options that you might not normally consider. These serendipitous experiences are one of the great joys of cruising. I'm sure Paula had never expected to work as a waitress. Jan had never even thought of teaching English. And John certainly had not intended to be supervising a crew of Indians in the jungle. All of these opportunities occurred because the cruisers were willing to take a chance and try something different. This is also what I mean by "financial freedom" that is, the freedom to explore new ideas and challenges when you want, how you want, and where you want. Again, the cruising sailor is uniquely privileged in this regard.

## IT'S GOOD, AND GOOD FOR YOU

As I hope you have seen in the case histories used in this book, and especially in the stories of the three couples whom we have followed, sailors who integrate working and sailing will reap benefits that go far beyond the monetary. All three couples met people and made friends they never would have made otherwise, had they not been working while cruising. All three couples found that, far from distracting or detracting from the cruising life, working while underway actually added a whole new dimension to their experience. And two of the couples at least, John and Paula and Kent and Jan, would probably have given up the cruising life if they had not pursued some kind of work.

These are not Pollyanna fables or stories concocted to make a point. These stories, and all the others in this book, are true and actually happened to people we know. I hope that by sharing some of the experiences my wife and I have had, I have been able to dispel some of the preconceptions and fears shared by many people contemplating a long-term cruising life.

Perhaps you have also noticed that many of the people in this book have enjoyed themselves and benefitted from situations where they did not make a lot of money. Having the freedom to volunteer, if you want, or to work at a low-paying job that you might never consider onshore, are real advantages offered by the cruising life. Again, you may find yourself meeting people and moving in directions that you never would have planned.

One common thought we have heard from many people who have figured out how to integrate work into their cruising lifestyle is, "Wow, I wish I had known before I set out what I know now. It sure would have made everything easier." Well since you have bought and read this book, now you know.

## REAL SECURITY IN LIFE

Finally, let me address a point some people have raised in the past with my wife and myself. "Okay," they have said, "There may be a lot of possibilities for supporting myself while cruising. But you say yourself, there's no one magic solution, and things are always changing in a cruising life. I've got a steady job now. Maybe it's not the greatest, but it's a job. I'd like to go cruising, but I don't want to give up the security of this stable life until I've salted away enough to live on. If I went sailing, how would I deal with the constant insecurity of not knowing how I would support myself from one year to the next? It all sounds like a prescription for ulcers to me!"

Let's take a look at some of the fallacies inherent in these assumptions. The first assumption is that a steady shoreside job, or career, provides you with security. This may have been true years ago when people could be reasonably sure of a lifetime job with one company. (Although I question if trading your most productive years for a pension and a gold watch was ever really that good a deal!) Nowadays, however, I don't think even the most naive employee is under any illusions about a company's loyalty to its workers. The wave of downsizing, outsourcing, and laying off of employees, perhaps to re-hire them as independent contractors, that has occurred during the last fifteen years has shown the transient nature of the modern workplace.

The second fallacy is that because you have a stable life, you can predict what will happen next year, or the year after. The ability to extrapolate the future from the past is a convenience that people have evolved to allow themselves an "illusion" of security. In truth we *don't* know what the future will bring. You may be hit by a car tomorrow, a loved one may die, or your house may burn down. There's no telling what changes might occur in your life next week, or next month, let alone next year. In fact, the only things you can be certain of about next year are that you will have aged a year, and that you won't be able to get it back.

Finally, where does this assumption that a sailing life is inherently less secure than a stable shoreside one come from? If one looks at real security, that is, having control over what will happen to you in the short- and medium-term future, there are few lifestyles more secure than that of a self-sufficient, cruising sailor. The keyword here is self-sufficient.

For a sailor to have real security, he or she must be self-sufficient in three ways. He must be a competent seaman, able to navigate his boat safely wherever he sails. He must be able to maintain the boat in seaworthy condition at all times. And he must be financially self-sufficient, able to support his lifestyle anywhere. Hopefully, with the aid of this book, you will be able to find ways to achieve this last. As you do, you will find, like Paula did in Panama, that soon you will have confidence in yourself and your ability to support yourself anywhere, anytime. This is real security.

If you are reading this book, obviously you are interested in a long-term cruising life. If so, ask yourself this—is it just money and security issues that are tying you to your present life? If you could be guaranteed financial security, would you opt to try cruising? If the answer is yes, consider this.

Over the years, my wife and I have met literally hundreds of cruising sailors in dozens of countries around the world who were managing to support their lifestyle as they went along. Although their methods and solutions were as diverse as those seen throughout this book, there was one common thread. Everyone, once they evolved their own personal approach, was surprised at not only how easy, but how enjoyable it was to combine working and cruising. Many times what had begun as a "break" from shoreside life ended up as a whole new and unexpected lifestyle.

## THE BOTTOM LINE

Hopefully, by showing how accessible a cruising life is to all sailors, regardless of age, experience, or income level, I will have spurred someone who might otherwise not have "made the break." Perhaps, too, some sailors who are planning on going cruising, or who are already "out there," will find suggestions that allow them to extend their long-term plans. And perhaps a few experienced cruisers who are looking for something more out of their cruise, but who haven't been sure of what it is, will find some ideas that motivate them to move in new directions.

The worldwide cruising community continues to grow. Each year I see more and more boats traveling longer and longer distances. Some experienced sailors today bemoan the difficulty of finding an uncrowded anchorage. Others rail against the proliferation of modern technology on many yachts. Some feel that the inherent "magic" is going out of cruising. I beg to differ.

The magic is still there, and though you may have to look a little harder to find a deserted anchorage, there are still plenty out there. What the increase in cruising boats means, however, is a concomitant increase in opportunities for the long-term sailor to find work. Whether it's doing repair work, crewing, or working at a shoreside business, more jobs are available now than ever before. Also, as we have seen in this book, the advances in modern technology have opened up work possibilities that never existed ten years ago. For the IT professional, telecommuter, or writer, the communications revolution is a godsend. In short, for the sailor who wants to work underway, things have never been better.

The danger, as the world's harbors are filled with increasing numbers of cruising boats, is that cruisers themselves will have only a "vacation" mentality. Like the hordes of tourists coming off a cruise ship, or the piles of pale bodies on a Club Med beach, sailors who only think of themselves as tourists deprive both themselves and their hosts of valuable interactions. By marrying work and cruising, a sailor can transcend this tourist role and can interact more with other sailors and the people of the countries he visits. Broadening the cruising experience in this way becomes a win-win situation for all concerned and is, at the bottom line, what this book is all about.

*Port St. Louis du Rhone, France - Fethiye, Turkey*
*October 1998 - May 1999.*

## APPENDIX: A

# RESOURCES FOR THE MARINE TRADES

## RESOURCES FOR SAILMAKING AND CANVASWORK

### TRAINING

Custom Marine Canvas Training Workshops
828 E. Main Street
Marblehead, OH 43440
Phone: 800-798-7627
Fax: 419-798-5290
e-mail: canvastr@dcache.net

These folks offer short workshops where you learn the basics not only of how to work with marine canvas but also information on pricing, contracts, and suppliers. They also sell a series of videos (ten in all) covering everything from "sewing tips and techniques" to "estimates" to "industrial sewing machine maintenance and repairs."

Delta College
University Center, MI 48710
Phone: 517-686-9000
Web site: www.delta.edu

Offers occasional one-day workshops with Jim and Connie Grant, the founders of Sailrite. They cover the basics of both marine canvaswork and sailmaking.

Sailrite
305 West Van Buren Street
P.O. Box 987
Columbia City, IN 46725
Phone: 800-348-2769
Fax: 219-244-4184
Web site: http://www.sailrite.com

Offers home-study courses in canvaswork and sailmaking.

The Arques School
P.O. Box 2010
Sausalito, CA 94966
Phone and Fax: 415-331-7134
Web site: http://www.arqueschl.com

Offers a one-day "Introduction to Sailmaking Skills" course, and a four-day "Sailmaking Skills" course.

## BOOKS

Casey, Don. *Canvaswork and Sail Repair.* Camden, ME: International Marine, 1996. A good beginning text. Covers sails, sail covers, cushion covers, awnings and biminis, and more. Illustrated.

Grant, Jim. *The Complete Canvasworker's Guide,* 2nd ed. Camden ME: International Marine, 1993. Guide on how to fabricate dozens of useful items for your boat including such things as flags, bosun's chairs, and spinnaker socks. Large format, illustrated with appendix of suppliers.

Harvey, Derek. *Sails: The Way They Work and How to Make Them.* Dobbs Ferry, NY: Sheridan House, 1997. A good introduction, covering both the theory and practice of sailmaking.

Lipe, Karen. *The Big Book of Boat Canvas: A Complete Guide to Fabric Work on Boats.* Camden, ME: Seven Seas Press, 1988. A good selection of projects covering virtually everything you would want to make out of canvas for your boat.

Marino, Emiliano. *The Sailmaker's Apprentice: A Guide for the Self-Reliant Sailor.* Camden ME: International Marine, 1994. An excellent introduction to the essential skills of sailmaking and sail repair. Used as a textbook at the Arques School.

## MATERIALS AND SUPPLIES

Sailrite
305 West Van Buren Street
P.O. Box 987
Columbia City, IN 46725
Phone: 800-348-2769
Fax: 219-244-4184
Web site: http://www.sailrite.com

The first and probably still the best mail order house catering to the nonprofessional or semiprofessional canvasworker or sailmaker. Besides fabrics and hardware they also offer books, sewing machines, and expert advice.

Vaughan Brothers
P.O. Box 14158
Portland, OR 97214
Phone: 503-233-1771
Fax: 503-233-1557
(Wholesale Only)

Offers a wide variety of specialty marine canvaswork products, including foam and stainless and aluminum tubing. "Small orders and cut yardage are our specialty" they say.

# RESOURCES FOR MARINE WOODWORKING

## TRAINING

Maine Technology Center
16 Deep Cove Road
Eastport, ME 04631-9618
Phone: 207-853-2518
Fax: 207-853-0940
Web site: http://www.by-the-sea.com/mtc.html

Offers short courses and certificate, diploma, and A.A.S. (Associate of Applied Science) courses in wooden boat construction, small craft design, and composite boatbuilding technology.

The Arques School
P.O. Box 2010
Sausalito, CA 94966
Phone and Fax: 415-331-7134
Web site: http://www.arqueschl.com

Offers several courses in wooden boat building and design, and even courses in such esoterica as lumber harvesting, drying and applications, and even tool making.

Seattle Maritime Academy
4455 Shilsole Avenue NW
Seattle, WA 98107-4645
Phone: 206-782-2647
Fax: 206-782-2821
Web site: http://www.scattlecentral.org/maritime

Offers certificate courses in marine carpentry and boatbuilding.

The Wooden Boat School
P.O. Box 78
Naskeag Road
Brooklin, ME 04616
Phone: 207-359-4651
Fax: 207-359-8920
Web site: http://www.woodenboat.com

Arguably the best non-certificate marine school around. Offers a wide range of two-week, hands-on courses in areas as diverse as marine electrics, blacksmithing, and celestial navigation. An excellent array of woodworking courses.

## BOOKS

MacIntosh, David C. (Bud). *How to Build a Wooden Boat.* Brooklin, ME: WoodenBoat Publications, 1987. A well-illustrated and humorously written book by a Harvard-educated boatbuilder who has done it all.

Saunders, Mike. *Yacht Joinery and Fitting.* (Out of print.) The emphasis is on interior yacht joinerwork.

Smith, Hervey Garrett. *Boat Carpentry: Repairs, Alterations and Construction*, 2nd ed. New York: Prentice Hall Press, 1986. Another excellent book that covers interior joinerwork as well as hull construction.

Stewart, Robert M. *Boatbuilding Manual*, 4th ed. Camden, ME: International Marine, 1994. One of the classics in the field. Written by an "old school" boatbuilder, this book is used as a textbook in many schools.

Vaitses, Allen. *Fiberglass Boat Repair Manual*. Camden, ME: International Marine, 1988. An excellent introduction to both cosmetic and structural fiberglass work.

## RESOURCES FOR MARINE MECHANICS, ELECTRICIANS, AND REFRIGERATION TECHNICIANS

### TRAINING

California Maritime at California State University
P.O. Box 1392
Vallejo, CA 94590-1000
Phone: 707-654-1000
e-mail: Enroll@csum.edu
Web site: http://www.csum.edu/center.html

Offers courses of 40- to 80-hours in small, boat-engine maintenance, diesel engine operations and maintenance, marine electrical troubleshooting, and much more.

Delta College
University Center, MI 48710
Phone: 517-686-9000
Web site: http://www.delta.edu

Offers short, non-certificate courses in diesel engine repair.

Key Power Institute
613 NW 7th St.
Miami, FL 33309
Phone: 305-371-5555
Fax: 305-371-7572

Offers short courses and certificate courses in marine diesel mechanics.

Marine Mechanics Institute
Phone: 800-342-9253
Fax: 407-240-1318
e-mail: admin@uticorp.com
Web site: http://www.uticorp.com/techtraining/mmi

Offers certificate programs in marine technician training for either diesel inboard or outboard/sterndrive. Located in Orlando, Florida.

Pacific Maritime Institute
Phone: 707-279-4329
e-mail: bellhaven@bellhaven.com
Web site: http://www.bellhaven.com/pacificmarinjeinst.html

Offers short non-certificate courses in: marine engines, basic and advanced electricity, marine refrigeration and marine engine, as well as mechanical surveying.

PTEC
6100 154th Avenue North
Clearwater, FL 33760
Phone: 727-538-7167
e-mail: bylander@popmail.firn.edu
Web site: http://www.ptecclw.pinellas.k12.fl.us/marine.htm

Offers 1,800-hour (60-credit) certificate courses in marine mechanics technology and air conditioning technology.

## BOOKS

Block, Leo. *Diesel Engines: A Boatowner's Guides to Operation and Maintenance.* Centerville, MD: Cornell Maritime Press, 1991. Covers the basic concepts of marine diesels and their maintenance. Not a "how-to" repair manual. Also covers stern gear and transmissions.

Calder, Nigel. *Boatowner's Mechanical and Electrical Manual.* Camden, ME: International Marine, 1996. An encyclopedic treatment of virtually every mechanical and electrical system found on small- to mid-sized yachts.

Calder, Nigel. *Marine Diesel Engines.* Camden, ME: International Marine, 1992. A step-by-step guide covering everything from basic maintenance to a full rebuild.

Calder, Nigel. *Refrigeration for Pleasureboats.* Camden, ME: International Marine, 1991. A thorough though somewhat basic manual for sailboat refrigeration.

Stocker, Hugh. *Marine Engines for Recreational Boats: Characteristics, Comparisons, Maintenance and Troubleshooting.* Graham, WA: Systems Co., 1990. An excellent overview of marine engines.

Tanenbaum, David. *Air Conditioning and Refrigeration Toolbox.* New York: Arco: Distributed by Prentice Hall Trade Sales, 1990. A book written "to help apprentice and journeyman cooling system technicians do their work safely and more efficiently." Called "the perfect on the job reference book."

Yates, James. *Boat Electrics.* Ramsbury, Marlborough, Witlshire: Helmsman Books, 1992. Basic overview of electrical systems found on smaller pleasure boats.

# RESOURCES FOR WORK IN THE MARINE INDUSTRY

## WORKING AS A CHARTER CAPTAIN OR MATE

### TRAINING TO GET A CAPTAIN'S LICENSE

Sea School
5905 SE 4th Street
St. Petersburg, FL 33703-4147
Phone: 800-435-3393 or 800-237-8663
Web site: http://www.seaschool.com

> Large and well-established training and licensing school. Offers training and testing for the six-pack (OUPV), Master, Launch Operator, and more. Offers classes in all Eastern Seaboard States from Alabama to New York.

Chapman School of Seamanship
4343 SE St. Lucie Blvd.
Stuart, FL 34997
Phone: 800-225-2841
Fax: 561-283-2019
Web site: http://www.chapman.org

> Offers a twelve-week, 369-hour course in Professional Mariner Training "designed for people seeking a career in the marine industry." Offers a job placement service after graduation.

Charter Captains Courses
C/O R&D Boat Supply
22 Washington St.
Cambridge, MD 21613
Phone: 410-228-0674
Fax: 410-221-0425
Web site: http://www.shorenet.net/r&dboat/captains.htm
   Offers courses for six-pack and Master's licenses.

Captain Roy's, Inc.
P.O. Box 57313
Webster, TX 77598
Phone: 281-335-4635 (also receives incoming faxes.)
e-mail: marinertw@ev1.net
Web site: http://www.capt-roys.com
   Offers home study courses for six-pack and Master's licenses.

Houston Marine Training Services
Examco Inc.
5728 Jefferson Highway
New Orleans, LA 70123-5113
Phone: 800-947-7737 or 504-733-8400
e-mail: marsales@examco.com
Web site:  http://www.houstonmarine.com
   Courses for six-pack and Master's licenses, including home study.

## BOOKS ON SEAMANSHIP AND PROFESSIONAL LICENSING

Gonder, Bud. *The Coast Guard License: Six-Pac to Master-100 Tons: Sail and Power,* 14th ed. Summerland, CA: Charters West, 1993. A basic overview of what is needed for these two licenses.

Hayler, William B., Editor. *American Merchant Seaman's Manual.* Centreville, MD: Cornell Maritime Press, 1981. Covers "every phase of good seamanship and all navigation necessary for the U.S. Coast Guard License." Used as a textbook at the U.S. Merchant Marine Academy.

Hubbard, Richard K. *Boater's Bowditch: The Small Craft American Practical Navigator.* Camden, ME: International Marine, 1998. An up-to-date and comprehensive version of the classic navigation reference geared towards pleasure boaters and commercial operators of small craft.

*Jobs Afloat: A Guide to Finding Work on Cruise Ships and Yachts.* A very comprehensive publication on all aspects of working on boats. Lists over 250 companies who hire crew, and discusses how to go about looking for a job on a yacht or with a charter company.
Available from:
Travelmate Contact & Publishing Services
52 York Place
Bournemouth
BH7 6JN
United Kingdom
Phone: 44-012-02 43-1520
Fax: 44-012-02 43-1520
e-mail: ian@hantsweb.co.uk
Web site: http://www.dorsetweb.co.uk/leisure/travelmate

Wing, Charles. *Get Your Captain's License.* Camden, ME: International Marine/McGraw-Hill, 2000. A home-study guide to prepare for the six-pack and Master's exams. Updated every two years.

# WORKING AS A PROFESSIONAL CAPTAIN OR CREW

## CREW TRAINING SCHOOLS

Chapman School of Seamanship
4343 SE St. Lucie Blvd.
Stuart, FL 34997
Phone: 800-225-2841
Fax: 561-283-2091
Web site: http;//www.chapman.org

Offers training for stewards/stewardesses, mates, and engineer positions.

American Yacht Institute
1003 SE 17th Street
Ft. Lauderdale, FL 33316
Phone: 800-759-0743
Web site: http://www.americanyachtinstitute.com

Offers training for entry-level steward/stewardess positions.

The Art Institute of Fort Lauderdale
1799 SE 17th Street
Fort Lauderdale, FL 33316-3000
Phone: 954-522-1044

Offers courses and a degree program in culinary training.

The Culinary Institute of America
433 Albany Post Road
Hyde Park, NY 12538-1499
Phone: 914-452-9600
Web site: http://www.ciachef.edu

Offers extensive courses in the culinary arts; both short courses and degree programs.

## CREW PLACEMENT AGENCIES

Crewfinders International, Inc.
404 & 408 SE 17th Street
Ft. Lauderdale, FL 33316
Phone: 800-438-2739
Fax: 954-761-7700
Web site: http://www.crewfinders.com

Established in 1982, Crewfinders is the oldest crew placement agency in the U.S. Annually places thousands of crew on yachts around the world.

Action Marine: Professional Maritime Crew Placement
P.O. Box 3466
Princeville, Kauai, HI 96722
Phone: 808-826-9038
Fax: 808-826-7269
e-mail: captd80@hotmail.com
Web site: http://www.kilohana.com/jurassic/marine

Places crew worldwide for: charter yachts, private yachts, vessel deliveries, sportfishing yachts, and film productions.

HasselFree, Inc.
404 & 408 SE 17th St.
Ft. Lauderdale, FL 33316
Phone: 954-522-2739 or 800-438-2739
Fax: 954-761-7700
Web site: http://www.hasselfree.com/marineindustry.html

Places professional captains, mates stewards/esses, chefs and engineers on domestic and international vessels of all types and sizes.

The Crew Data Bank: The Office
Antibes, France
Phone: 33-493-340-996
e-mail: ays@imen.com
Web site: http://www.gscom.fr/ays

Data-bank of crew CV's worldwide.

Absolute Yachting
RI-INVEST SL
Federico Garcia Lorca 8,
L5 07014 Palma de Mallorca
Spain
Phone: 34-971-738-427
Fax: 34-971-780-251
Web site: http://www.webcom.es/crew.htm

An online placement service based in Palma, Mallorca.

Drakes of London
7 Leeward House, Square Rigger Row
Plantation Wharf, York Road, Battersea
London SW11 3TX
UK
Phone: 44-171-801-0130
Fax: 44-171-801-0131
e-mail: team@drakesoflondon.com
Web site: http://www.drakesoflondon.com

A large, well-established, and reputable placement agency based in London.

## BOOKS AND RESOURCES FOR CHARTERING YOUR OWN BOAT OR DOING DELIVERIES

Edwards, Fred. *Making Money with Boats*. Centreville, MD: Carnell Maritime Press, 1996. A "must-read" for anyone contemplating the operation of a charter business, and has much of value for those already involved in charters.

Gibbons, Rod. *No Cost Boating: How to Own Your Dream Boat for Less...or for Nothing at All*. (Out of print.) Covers the basics of self-chartering and also many other ways to make money with your boat.

Kimball, Mike; Smith, Roger A.; Lee, Karen S. *Tax Guide for the Business Use of Yachts*. Seattle: Outdoor Empire Pub., 1992. A short but very detailed treatment by three certified public accountants of U.S. tax regulations as they apply to yachts.

Rains, John and Miller, Patricia. *Passagemaking Handbook: A Guide for Delivery Skippers and Boat Owners.* Camden, ME: Seven Seas Press, 1989. A good treatment of what to expect if you start your own delivery business. Written by an experienced delivery skipper.

Rogers, Larry V. *Boatowner's Legal and Financial Advisor.* Camden, ME: International Marine, 1994. A comprehensive look at legal issues that affect boaters including "chartering issues, commercial arrangements, economics, taxes, and regulations." Sample legal agreements, and a list of State and U.S. Coast Guard offices.

## USEFUL WEB SITES FOR LOCATING CHARTER COMPANIES

http://www.travelsource.com/yachts
A huge index of charter operations worldwide.

http://www.charterlink.com
Another large index site.

http://www.duhe.com
World Wide Sail. Yet another large worldwide listing.

http://www.yacht-charters.com
Worldwide listing of over 750 charter yachts, and links to brokers in New York, Palm Beach, Sausalito, London, Hong Kong, Acapulco, and Sweden.

http://www.floatplan.com/skippers.htm
A site with ads for captains and delivery skippers.

http://www.floatplan.com/charters.htm
A listing of charter companies and boats for hire.

http://www.floatplan.com/crew.htm
Ads from boats looking for crew.

http://www.crewplusboats.tw.odessa.ua
Another site with boats looking for crew.

# RESOURCES FOR RESTAURANT, RESORT, AND TRADE WORK ON SHORE

## RESOURCES FOR RESTAURANT, BAR, AND RESORT WORK

### TRAINING FOR BARTENDING AND COOKING POSITIONS

American Professional Bartending School
Phone: 800-532-9222

> Thirteen locations nationwide, in New York, New Jersey, Illinois, and California.

Professional Bartending Schools of America
Phone: 888-4-BARKIT
e-mail: info@pbsa.com
Web site: http://www.pbsa.com

> Nineteen locations nationwide.

Academy of Culinary Arts–Atlantic Community College
5100 Black Horse Pike
Mays Landing, NJ 08330-2699
Phone: 609-343-5000 or 800-645-CHEF
Fax: 609-343-4920
e-mail: accadmit@atlantic.edu
Web site: http://www.atlantic.edu/~bordonar/aca.html

> Offers a two-year A.A.S. degree, as well as many shorter courses.

San Francisco State University College of Extended Learning
1600 Holloway Avenue
San Francisco, CA 94132
Phone: 415-338-1533
e-mail: maryp@sfsu.edu

Offers six-week certificate courses in commercial cooking.

Let's Get Cookin'
4643 Lakeview Canyon Road
Westlake Village, CA 91361
Phone: 818-991-3940
Fax: 805-495-2554
e-mail: lgcookin@aol.com
Web site: http://www.letsgetcookin.com

Offers six-week certificate courses, as well as shorter courses in professional cooking.

Southeastern Academy
233 Academy Drive, Box 421768
Kissimmee, FL 34744
Phone: 800-765-4732
Fax: 407-847-8793
e-mail: admissions@southeasternacademy.org
Web site: http://www.southeasternacademy.org

Offers a thirty-week diploma course.

http://www.shawguides.com/index

This search engine/database lists over 400 culinary schools worldwide, and can be searched by region, course length, price, etc.

## PLACEMENT SERVICES FOR RESTAURANT AND RESORT WORK

http://www.hospitalityonline.com

A "career resource for the hospitality industry." A worldwide placement agency for work in hotels, resorts, restaurants, etc. Listings of thousands of jobs with hundreds of employers. No fee.

http://www.escoffier.com

Not an employment agency but rather "the largest collection of foodservices employment resources on the Web."

## USEFUL BOOKS ON RESORT MANAGEMENT

Gee, Chuck Y. *Resort Development and Management*. East Lansing: Educational Institute of the American Hotel & Motel Association, 1996.

Hotton, Georgia. *Introduction to Resort Management*. Chicago: Nelson-Hall Inc., 1982.

## USEFUL BOOKS FOR SHORT-TERM/CASUAL WORK ON SHORE

Bell, Arthur H. *Great Jobs Abroad*. New York: McGraw-Hill, 1997.

Griffith, Susan. *Work Your Way Around the World*, 9th ed. Oxford: Vacation Work, Princeton, NJ. Distributed in the U.S. by Peterson's Guides.

Hubbs, Clayton A, (Editor). *Work Abroad: The Complete Guide to Finding a Job Overseas*, 2nd ed. Amherst, MA: Transitions Abroad, 1999.

Kocher, Eric. *International Jobs: Where They Are and How to Get Them*, 5th ed. Reading, MA: Perseus Books, 1998.

Landes, Michael. *The Back Door Guide to Short-Term Job Adventures*. Berkeley, CA: Ten Speed Press, 1997.

Lay, David Caldwell and Leerburger, Benedict A. *Jobs Worldwide*. Manassas Park, VA: Impact Publications, 1996.

Zink, Richard. *Resumés for Overseas and Stateside Jobs*. Zinks International Career Guidance, 1994.

*Casual Work on the Mediterranean and Canary Islands. Jobs teaching English. Work in bars, restaurants, and night clubs*. All the opportunities plus advice and essential information on health and travel. Available from Overseas Jobs Express.

Web site: http://www.overseasjobs.com

## DIVE-ORIENTED WEB SITES AND LINKS

http://www.siesystems.com/sharky/cert.htm

The home of "Sharky's Dive Certification Agencies Links," a group of dive-related links including PADI's Web site and a worldwide listing of certification agencies.

http://www.diverlink.com

A large listing of dive-related sites, including dive resorts worldwide, and where to get training and certification.

NAUI Worldwide
9942 Currie Davis Drive, Ste. H
Tampa, FL 33619-2667
Phone: 800-553-6284
Fax: 813-628-8253
e-mail: nauihq@nauiww.org
Web site: http://www.naui.org

A large international diver's organization. The Web site has a large (737 k) downloadable list of affiliated agencies throughout the world. For specific questions about training, e-mail: training@nauiww.org.

# RESOURCES FOR PROFESSIONAL WORK ON SHORE

## RESOURCES FOR JOBS IN THE MEDICAL PROFESSIONS

### JOB PLACEMENT SERVICES

Médecins Sans Frontières/Doctors Without Borders (MSF)
Rue de la Tourrelle, 39
Brussells, Belgium 1040
Phone: 32-2-280-1881
e-mail: msfcan@passport.ca
Web site: http://www.msf.org

> The international MSF sends over 2,000 volunteers per year to work in over 70 countries. Their Web site includes information on how to volunteer.

MedHunters
Phone: 800-664-0278
Fax: 416-977-2869
e-mail: jobs@medhunters.com
Web site: http://www.medhunters.com

> MH was founded in 1996 to provide worldwide recruitment services on the Internet for healthcare employers and professionals. MH claims to be "at the forefront of healthcare recruitment on the net, has developed unique and advanced job-matching technology." Their Web site has an electronic resumé database and internationally-oriented medical news.

Project Concern International
3550 Afton Road
San Diego, CA 92123
Phone: 858-279-9690
Fax:858-694-0294
e-mail: contactus@projectconcern.org
Web site: http://www.projectconcern.org
OPTIONS is a nonprofit, nonsectarian, volunteer healthcare placement service of Project Concern International. They refer experienced
healthcare professionals who wish to volunteer in hospitals, community
clinics, and medical facilities in critically, under-serviced areas in the
U.S., Asia, Africa, and Latin America. Placements are on a volunteer
basis and range in duration from a few months to a few years.

Global Medical Staffing Inc.
6915 South 900 East
Salt Lake City, UT 84047
Phone: 800-760-3174
Fax: 801-561-9864
e-mail: doctors@gmedical.com
Web site: http://www.gmedical.com
This is a service that specializes in placing Medical Doctors from the
United States in rural communities in Australia and New Zealand.

## WEB SITES OF INTEREST

International Red Cross
Web site: http://www.icrc.org

UNICEF
Web site: http://www.unicef.org

United Nations
Web site: http://www.un.org

World Health Organization
Web site: http://www.who.int

The Village Doctor
Web site: http://www.villagedoctor.com

This is a nonprofit agency which places physicians in small, needy communities around the world.

Nurse and Doctor Jobs in International Health and Humanitarian Relief
Web site: http://www.imc-la.com/imcempl3.htm

## BOOKS AND PUBLICATIONS RELEVANT TO OVERSEAS MEDICAL WORK

*Directory of U.S. Based Agencies Involved in International Health Assistance*, NCIH, 1997
Available from:
National Council for International Health
1701 K Street N.W.
Washington, DC 20006
Phone: 202-833-5900
Fax: 202-833-0075

Provides comprehensive information about U.S.-based international organizations, including areas of expertise and contact persons. Lists a wide range of positions in international health fields.

*Golden Opportunities: A Volunteer Guide for Americans Over 50*; Andrew Carroll, 1994
Available from:
Peterson's Guides, Nelson Canada
1120 Birchmount Road
Scarborough, Ontario M1K 5G4
Phone: 800-268-2222
Fax: 800-430-4445

Detailed information for older adults who want to offer their services abroad. The book also mentions special opportunities for doctors and healthcare professionals, and recommends resources.

# RESOURCES FOR ACADEMIC TEACHING ABROAD

## JOB PLACEMENT SERVICES AND JOB FAIRS

International Schools Services
15 Roszel Road
P.O. Box 5910
Princeton, NJ 08543
Phone: 609-452-0990
Fax: 609-452-2690
e-mail: iss@iss.edu
Web site: http://www.iss.edu

> An independent, nonprofit job placement service placing over 700 teachers a year. Also holds job fairs in Boston, San Francisco, and Winter Park, Florida.

Ed-U-Link Services, Inc.
Post Office Box 2076
Prescott, AZ 86302
Phone: 520-778-5581
Fax: 520-776-0611
e-mail: info@edulink.com
Web site: http://www.edulink.com

> A new online placement service.

Friends of World Teaching
P.O. Box 84480
San Diego, CA 92138-4480
Phone: 800-503-7436
Fax: 619-224-5363
e-mail: fowt@fowt.com
Web site: http://www.fotw.com

> Another large placement service.

## USEFUL WEB SITES FOR OVERSEAS TEACHING

http://www.uni.edu/placemnt/overseas

University of Northern Iowa Job Fair - The oldest and largest international recruiting fair in the United States.

http://www.joyjobs.com

A large and comprehensive site with many resources for anyone interested in teaching abroad. Contains a listing of addresses of International Schools.

http://www.odedodea.edu

The listing for Department of Defense schools for U.S. Service dependents. Operating schools in 14 countries.

## BOOKS AND PUBLICATIONS RELATED TO TEACHING ABROAD

*Comprehensive Guide to Teaching in International Schools*
A CD-ROM available from the Web site at http://www.joyjobs.com/tips

*International Educator Newspaper, The*
P.O. Box 513
Cummaquid, MA 02637
Phone: 508-362-1414
Fax: 508-362-1411
e-mail: tie@capecod.net
Web site: http://www.tieonline.com

The global newsletter of the international teaching community. Published quarterly. Each issue has advertisements for between 60 and 140 International Schools seeking teachers.

Muckle, James. *How to Find Jobs Teaching Overseas*, 2nd ed. Sebastopol, CA: K S J Publishing Company, 1992.

# RESOURCES FOR EFL TEACHING POSITIONS

## COURSES FOR THE RSA/CELTA CERTIFICATE IN THE UNITED STATES

**The Center for English Studies (CES)**
Web site: http://www.cescorp.com
This is the only organization in the U.S. offering the RSA/CELTA. They currently franchise the course through the following three schools:

CES New York
330 Seventh Avenue, 6th Floor
New York, NY 10001
Phone: 212-629-7300
Fax: 212-736-7950
e-mail: cesnewyork@cescorp.com
Mr. Bruce Sharpe, Teacher Training Director

CES San Francisco
450 Sansome Street, 8th Floor
San Francisco, CA 94111
Phone: 415-986-0898
Fax: 415-986-0985
e-mail: cessanfrancisco@cescorp.com
Mr. Ira Cohen, Center Director

CES Fort Lauderdale
301 East Las Olas Boulevard
Fort Lauderdale, FL 33301
Phone: 954-522-8810
Fax: 954-522-6955
e-mail: cesfortlauderdale@cescorp.com
Mr. Steve Cunningham, Center Director

## EFL JOB PLACEMENT SERVICES

Agora Employment
Web site: http://www.agoralang.com/agora/employment.html

Employment listings for the language workplace. Many listings not only for teachers, but also for directors positions and other languages.

Chat4Job
Web site: http://www.chat4job.com

A real-time online chat page designed to put possible ESL, EFL, TESOL or TEFL employers and teachers in touch.

Web site: http://www.eslcafe.com/search/Jobs (web address seems to be case sensitive on Jobs.)

Probably the most complete and up-to-date listing of available ESL/ EFL teaching positions from around the world.

Europa-pages
Web site: http://www.europa-pages.co.uk/jobs

Post a free job wanted announcement and/or view the list of ELT job offers from around the world. Employers can also post their vacancies for free.

TEFL.net
Web site: http://www.tefl.net/jobs/index.htm

TEFL Teaching resources including jobs offered, classroom resources, teaching forums, an e-zine and a guide section on teaching in various countries.

TESL Job Opportunities
Web site: http://www.linguistic-funland.com/tesljob.html

Another great teacher's wanted listing.

Lora's Board
Web site: http://www.loras.com

> Lora's Board offers a completely free service, and provides visitors with approximately 80 of the latest vacancies each week.

## ANOTHER USEFUL WEB SITE FOR TEACHING EFL

International House, Central Department
106 Piccadilly
London W1V 9FL
England
Tony Duff, Director General
Elaine Smith, Director, Central Department
Phone: 44-171-491-2598.
Fax: 44-171-499-3708
e-mail: central.dept@ihlondon.co.uk
Web site: http://www.international-house.org

> The central department of an extremely well-run group, with affiliated schools in over 30 countries throughout the world. Works closely with Cambridge University and the British Council to uphold high standards of teaching. A job with one International House school will often allow you to move laterally throughout the network around the world.

## BOOKS AND PUBLICATIONS OF INTEREST TO EFL TEACHERS

Griffith, Susan. *Teaching English Abroad,* 2nd ed. Oxford: Vacation Work, 1994. Distributed in the U.S. by Peterson's Guides. The definitive guide to short- and long-term opportunities for both trained and untrained teachers of English as a second language. Covers country-by-country opportunities, salaries, and even potential red tape.

O'Sullivan, Jerry. *Teaching English: Japan,* 2nd ed. Lincolnwood, IL: Passport Books, 1996. Everything that you ever needed to know about teaching English in Japan.

Snow, Donald B. *More than a Native Speaker: An Introduction for Volunteers Teaching English Abroad.* Alexandria, VA: Teachers of English to Speakers of Other Languages, Inc., 1996.

# RESOURCES FOR IT PROFESSIONALS

## JOB PLACEMENT SERVICES

Optima Partners
1250 Executive Place, Ste. 404
Geneva, IL 60134
Phone: 630-232-7800
Fax: 630-232-7808
Web site: http://www.optima-partners.com

Atkinson Search & Placement (ASAP)
Arthur Atkinson, President
P.O. Box 493
Fairfield, IA 52556
Phone: 515-472-3666, 800-888-9248
Fax: 515-472-7270
e-mail: asap@aatkinson.com
Web site: http://www.aatkinson.com

Conexis Resource Partners, Inc.
290 Turnike Road, Ste. 202
Westboro, MA 01581
Phone: 800-665-7779
e-mail: info@conexisinc.com
Web site: http://www.conexisinc.com

Master Team
Phone: 408-626-7905 or 877-627-8373
Fax: 408-626-7906
e-mail: jobs@masterteam.com
Web site: http://www.masterteam.com

Software Developers Net
Web site: http://www.developers.net

A resource net for software developers including a job finding service
with a searchable database of over 10,000 jobs and an e-mail service
which can advise you of new openings.

Jobs for Programmers
Web site: http://www.prgjobs.com

 Free site listing telecommute programming jobs.


## MCSE PROFESSIONAL CERTIFICATION COURSES

These companies offer self-study courses (with exams) for the MCSE certification, as well as others. Courses range from $1,500 to $3,000 and take from one- to six-months to complete.

Bad Dog Computer's Training Planet
10606 Pekolee Drive
Grass Valley, CA 95949
Phone: 888-932-8881
Fax:917-464-8083
e-mail: sales@trainingplanet.com
Web site: http://www.baddogcomputer.com

Business Training Library
745 Craig Road, Suite 210
St. Louis, MO 63141
Phone: 888-432-3077
Fax: 314-567-4783
e-mail: info@bizlibrary.com
Web site: http://www.bizlibrary.com

CDi Communications, Inc.
10 Mayer Drive
Suffern, NY 10901
Phone: 800-617-5586
Fax: 914-368-2472
e-mail: sales@cdicomp.com
Web site: http://www.netwind.com

# GENERAL RESOURCES ON WORKING OVERSEAS

## WEB SITES OF INTEREST

Expat Exchange
Web site: http://www.expatexchange.com
> Provides career information and resumé database services to job candidates, employers, and recruitment firms.

The Escape Artist
Web site: http://www.escapeartist.com
> Large site with all kinds of resources for anyone thinking of living abroad. Highly recommended.

## BOOKS AND PUBLICATIONS

Camenson, Blythe. *Opportunities in Overseas Careers.* Lincolnwood, IL: VGM Career Horizons, 1998. Full of valuable tips on defining and targeting the overseas job of choice, plus an examination of the range of lifestyles readers may encounter overseas, and more.

Krannich, Ronald. *Complete Guide to International Jobs and Careers, Your Passport to a World of Exciting and Exotic Employment.* Manassas Park, VA: Impact Publications, 1992.

Krannich, Ronald L. and Krannich, Caryl R. *International Jobs Directory,* 3rd ed. Manassas Park, VA: Impact Publications, 1998. The third edition of this popular guide outlines today's international job market and provides detailed information on over 1,000 major international employers.

Leppard, David. *The Directory of Work and Study in Developing Countries,* 4th ed. Oxford: Vacation Work, 1986. Fourth edition of the authoritative guide to employment, voluntary work, and academic opportunities in the Third World. Thousands of short- and long-term opportunities for work and study with over 400 organizations in Africa, the Middle East, Asia, Far East, Pacific, Latin America, and the Caribbean. Available from Overseas Jobs Express, at http://www.overseasjobs.com.

## GENERAL OVERSEAS JOB PLACEMENT SERVICES

Overseas Jobs Express
Premier House
Shoreham Airport
Sussex BN43 5FF
United Kingdom
Phone: 44 (0)1273 440220
Fax: 44 (0)1273 440229
e-mail: editor@overseasjobs.com
Web site: http://www.overseasjobs.com

> A placement service that also sells books about finding work abroad, sells addresses of employers offering work abroad, and more.

## SOME RESOURCES FOR RESEARCHING IMMIGRATION POLICIES

Escape Artist Embassy Resources
Web site: http://www.escapeartist.com/embassy1/embassy1.htm

> This site lists the only "official" sources of immigration policy information: national embassy and consular Web sites.

BCL Immigration Services
Web site: http://www.visa-free.com

> This company provides services to those seeking admittance to the U.K., United States, New Zealand, Canada, and Australia.

The Center for Immigration Studies
Web site: http://mail.cis.org/guest/RemoteListSummary/CISNEWS

> The Center for Immigration Studies in Washington, D.C., operates CISNEWS, a free e-mail distribution list on immigration policy for "academics, policymakers, journalists, attorneys, activists, and others." The service covers developments both in the United States and abroad. CISNEWS is a moderated list for announcements, news items, reviews, queries, etc.

Dual Citizenship FAQ
Web site: http://www.webcom.com/richw/dualcit/

*Dual Nationality and United States Law;* by Rich Wales is an extensive Web site on the issue of Dual Citizenship.

Wilson White
Web site: http://www.wilsonwhite.co.nz/immig.htm

A site by a New Zealand job placement firm with a very clear, concise synopsis of New Zealand Immigration requirements. Very useful for anyone thinking of working in that country.

# RESOURCES FOR WORKING FROM YOUR BOAT

## RESOURCES FOR CRAFT WORK

### BOOKS ON LEATHERWORK

Gattis, L.S.,III. *Basic Leathercraft: Stamping and Designs.* Cheetah Pub, 1998. A basic introduction into decorative leatherwork.

West, Geoffrey. *Leatherwork.* Crowood Pr, 1998. A comprehensive, introductory guide to leather craft, with advice on tools, step by step techniques, and a variety of fully instructed projects.

### BOOKS ON JEWELRYMAKING

Fitch, Janet. *The Art and Craft of Jewelry.* Chronicle Books, 1994. A book containing instructions for numerous types of projects and color photos of pieces made from a variety of materials by various artisans.

McGrath, Jinks. *The Encyclopedia of Jewelry-Making Techniques: A Comprehensive Visual Guide to Traditional and Contemporary Techniques.* Running Press, 1995. This book includes a wide variety of jewelrymaking techniques primarily dealing with metalsmithing. Simple wire projects, and more advanced techniques such as inlaying are shown and described.

Schumann, Walter. *Gemstones of the World.* New York: Sterling Publications, 1997. A very well-done, comprehensive reference source for anyone thinking of buying gemstones.

223

Von Neumann, Robert. *The Design and Creation of Jewelry*. Chilton Book Co, 1989. Extensive reference resource for all aspects of jewelrymaking.

Woodward, Christine. *Gemstones*. New York: Sterling Publications, 1988. A compact guide to gemstones around the world. Excellent photography.

## COURSES IN JEWELRYMAKING

The California Institute of Jewelry Training
5800 Winding Way
Carmichael, CA 95608
Phone: 800-731-1122
e-mail: cijt@jewelrytraining.com
Web site: http:/www.jewelrytraining.com

Florida Jewelry and Watch Academy
115 East Palmetto Park Road
Boca Raton, FL 33432
Phone: 800-630-4844
Web site: http://www.jewelryacademy.com

Paris Junior College
2400 Clarksville Street
Paris, TX 75460
Phone: 903-782-0380
Fax: 903-782-0452
e-mail: tshannon@paris.cc.tx.us
Web site: http://www.paris.cc.tx.us

Stewart's International School for Jewelers
651 W. Indiantown Road
Jupiter, FL 33458
Phone: 800-843-3409
Fax: 561-746-7586
e-mail: JewelSch@aol.com

## WEB SITES FOR JEWELRYMAKING

FDJ/On Time
1180 Solana Avenue
Winter Park, FL 32789
Phone: 800-323-6091
Fax: 800-634-1070
e-mail: info@fdjtool.com
Web site: http://www.fdjtool.com

> A large source for all kinds of jewelry supplies, equipment, books, etc. Highly recommended.

The Jewelry Mall
Web site: http://www.jewelrymall.com

> A source for links to jewelry supply houses, magazines, etc.

Ganoksin Jewelry
Web site: http://www.ganoksin.com/index.htm

> Another large selection of links, and many interesting articles and papers on the art and craft of jewelrymaking.

## RESOURCES FOR WRITERS

### ONLINE JOB LISTINGS

An Avalanche of Jobs
Web site: http://www.sunoasis.com/online.html

> Not exactly an avalanche, but a fair selection of Internet-oriented writing jobs.

The Manuscript Depot
Web site: http://www.manuscriptdepot.com

> Not a job service but a relatively low-cost way to post a manuscript or clips, and hope that someone likes it.

The Write Edge
Web site: http://www.writeedge.com/forms/careers.asp

> Jobs for freelance writers, researchers, copy editors and proofreaders.

## WEB SITES OF INTEREST

Authorlink
Web site: http://www.authorlink.com

An information and news service for editors, agents, and writers. Features interviews, news, and links.

Bookwire
Web site: http://www.bookwire.com

A large site with all kinds of information about the writing and publishing worlds.

Editor and Publisher
Web site: http://www.mediainfo.com

A huge resource site for professionals. Features several industry news magazines, lists of media, and a searchable database. Highly recommended for researching specific topics.

Web site: http://www.seaworthy.com

Seaworthy Publications, Inc., is a nautical book publisher that specializes in cruising guides and boating how-to books.

## LIST OF NEWSMEDIA

Web site: http://www.n-net.com

An easily-accessed list of newspapers throughout the United States. An excellent and comprehensive site for anyone thinking of submitting to newspapers.

## ONLINE WRITER'S GUIDELINES

Web site: http://www.writersdatabase.com

A great list of magazine writer's guidelines. A must for anyone thinking of writing for magazines.

## BOOKS ON WRITING

Goodman, Alan. *The World on a String: How to Become a Freelance Foreign Correspondent.* Henry Holt, 1997. A guide to what you need to know to become a freelance foreign correspondent.

Holm, Kirsten C., (Editor). *The Writer's Market.* Cincinnati: Writer's Digest Books, 1999. The "Bible." Contains listings of over 1,500 consumer magazines, 400 trade magazines, 1,100 book publishers and much more. An indispensable resource for anyone serious about writing professionally.

Writer's Digest Books
1507 Dana Avenue
Cincinnati, OH 45207
Web site: http://www.writersdigest.com
A large selection of books covering virtually every aspect of writing. Highly recommended. Some Books Published by Writers Digest Books are:

*30 Steps to Becoming a Writer, and Getting Published;* by Scott Edelstein. A step-by-step guide to what it takes.

*Beginning Writer's Answer Book;* by the editors of Writer's Digest. Answers questions of writers at all stages of their careers.

*Writer's Digest Handbook of Making Money Freelance Writing;* by the editors of Writer's Digest. A collection of over forty articles from the magazine.

*How to Write a Book Proposal;* by Michael Larsen. The basics of constructing a proposal, the essential first step for anyone who wants to write a nonfiction book.

*Travel Writing: A Guide to Research, Writing and Selling;* by L. Peat O'Neil. All the ins and outs of travel writing from the former travel editor of the Washington Post.

*Magazine Writing That Sells;* by Don McKinnery. A practical guide to how to break into the magazine market.

## MAGAZINES FOR WRITERS

### PRINT MAGAZINES

Publisher's Weekly
Bowker Magazine Group, Cahner's Publishing Company
245 W. 17th Street
New York, NY 10011
Phone: 212-645-0067

> The industry trade magazine. The latest news for publishing professionals.

The Writer
120 Boylston Street
Boston, MA 02116
Phone: 617-423-3157

> A monthly magazine for writers.

Writer's Digest
1507 Dana Avenue
Cincinnati, OH 45207
Phone: 513-531-2690

> Another monthly writer's magazine.

### ONLINE MAGAZINES

The Painted Rock
Web site: http://www.paintedrock.com

> This site includes a free weekly newsletter, a free research service, and an online library.

Freelance Success
801 NE 70th St.
Miami, FL 33138
e-mail: freelance-success@usa.net
Web site: http://www.freelancesuccess.com

> Newsletter gives nonfiction writers the tools to earn a full-time living. Detailed market information and online writing classes. Send a SASE or e-mail.

The Inkspot
122 St. Patrick Street, Box 123
Toronto, Ontario, Canada M5T 2X8
Web site: http://www.inkspot.com

> A very interesting site with information on workshops, market information, resources, publishers, associations, and much more. Offers a free online magazine.

Publisher's Weekly Online
Web site: http://www.bookwire.com/pw/pw.html

> The industry standard, on the Internet.

## RESOURCES FOR TELECOMMUTING

### SOURCES OF HARDWARE AND SOFTWARE FOR TELECOMMUTING

Road Warrior International
9393 Gateway
Reno, NV 89511
Phone: 800-274-4277
Fax: 714-850-9490
Web site: http://www.roadwarrior.com

> Offers a wide range of products for mobile computing.

Globalstar
3200 Zanker Road
P.O. Box 640670
San Jose, CA 95164-0670
Phone: 408-933-4000
Fax: 408-933-4100
Web site: http://www.globalstar.com

> Offers worldwide portable phone coverage through a combination of satellites and existing cellular networks.

Modern Living, USA
916 Plaza del Gado
Sierra Vista, AZ 85365-4440
Phone: 888-298-0521
Fax: 520-417-9736
e-mail: sales@mod-usa.com
Web site: http://www.mod-usa.com

They provide a wide range of products for mobile computing.

Wireless Solutions
Phone: 800-214-4488
Web site: http://www.wirelesssolutions.com

Another company offering a large selection of products for the mobile computer user without a land line.

The Escape Artist
Web site: http://www.escapeartist.com/internet/telephone.htm

Web page offering numerous links to hardware suppliers specializing in "offshore Internet communications solutions."

## JOB PLACEMENT SERVICES

Telecommuting Jobs Web Page
Web site: http://www.tjobs.com

A large non-profit online service specializing in telecommuting positions.

DICE
Web site: http://www.dice.com

A no-fee career center for high-tech jobs online.

International Telejobs Network
Web site: http://www.telejobs.net

Lists telecommuting jobs worldwide.

TELEMAN Nutancao
Web site: http://www.teleman.pt

An international company, based in Portugal, that hires telecommuters worldwide to perform a variety of services, including, desk top publishing, direct marketing, and accounting.

Will Work 4 Food
Web site: http://www.2020tech.com/ww4f/index.html

An online job placement service that describes itself as being, "the very first telecommuting employment page devoted solely to telecommuting employment. This page is designed to connect the cyber employer and the telecommuter."

## WEB SITES

http://www.telecommute.org/index.html

This site is maintained by the Telecommuting Advisory Council, dedicated to promoting the benefits of telecommuting.

http://www.gilgordon.com/publications.html

Gil Gordon Associates maintains a list of books, articles and journals relating to mobile computing and telecommuting.

http://www.langhoff.com

Site sponsored by June Langhoff, a nationally-recognized authority on telecommuting. Contains a wide range of tips, links, and of course June's books. Recommended.

## BOOKS AND PUBLICATIONS ADDRESSING TELECOMMUTING

Bredin, Alice. *The Virtual Office Survival Handbook: What Telecommuters and Entrepreneurs Need to Succeed in Today's Nontraditional Workplace.* New York: John Wiley & Sons, 1996. The telecommuter and the entrepreneur's practical manual to starting, managing, and thriving in a virtual office. Expert advice on working in all types of virtual offices, including the home office, satellite work center, time-shared workspace, and mobile office.

Langhoff, June. *The Telecommuter's Advisor: Working in the Fast Lane.* Newport, RI: Aegis Publishing Group, 1999. June Langhoff's book is derived from a long, successful career in telecommuting and extensive research on the current art of telecommuting. It gives you the lowdown on using the latest communication tools in simple, non-technical language. From handling e-mail to setting up your boat office to desktop conferencing. Available from http://www.tjobs.com/tadvisr.htm

Langhoff, June. *Telecom Made Easy.* Newport, RI: Aegis Publishing Group, 1996. Over 40,000 people turn to this easy-to-grasp June Langhoff book to help determine the best communication system for their businesses— from basic wiring options, phone systems and services, cellular phones, answering devices, paging, modems, faxes, and networked systems to ISDN and going online. Available from http://www.tjobs.com/tadvisr.htm

Leonhard, Woody. *The Underground Guide to Telecommuting: Slightly Askew Advice on Leaving the Rat Race Behind.* Reading, MA: Addison Wesley Longman, Inc., 1995. This book offers no-nonsense advice on what hardware and software to buy, what hot new technology will pay for itself, and which gizmos are a waste of your time and money. Find out the difference between ISDN, ATM, and ESPN, and what's best for you.

Schepp, Debra and Schepp, Brad. *The Telecommuter's Handbook: How to Earn a Living Without Going to the Office,* 2nd ed. New York: McGraw-Hill, 1995. The top 50 jobs for telecommuters, the 100 U.S. companies that currently offer this option to their employees, and much more. Essential reading for would-be telecommuters, as well as the millions already telecommuting.

## ONLINE NEWSLETTERS

*The Road News*
Web site: http://www.roadnews.com

A fascinating, free, online newsletter that invites queries from readers, and answers from same. Addresses a wide range of concerns relevant to anyone connecting to the Internet overseas and/or from a mobile location.

*Road Warrior News*
Web site: http://www.warrior.com/library/periodicals.html

A free quarterly online newsletter covering topics of interest to mobile computer users.

*Telecommuter's Digest*
Web site: http://www.tdigest.com

A monthly newsletter that lists companies that have telecommuting positions available.

# RESOURCES FOR ENTREPRENEURS AND VOLUNTEERS

## RESOURCES FOR STARTING YOUR OWN BUSINESS

### BOOKS AND PUBLICATIONS

While there are literally thousands of "how to start a business" books, I have just selected a few whose ideas and philosophy are particularly in tune with those found in *Financial Freedom aFloat*. Hopefully, more than specific tools, they will provide ideas for a new approach to running your own business.

Ludden, Laverne L. *Be Your Own Business!: The Definitive Guide to Entrepreneurial Success*. Indianapolis: Park Avenue, 1998. A look at entrepreneurship in general and a guide to how to get started.

Schwerin, David. *Conscious Capitalism*. Boston: Butterworth-Heinemann, 1998. Not a business guide but an insightful analysis of ethics and their role in modern business. Schwerin's ideas echo many of those found in this book.

Winter, Barbara. *Making a Living Without a Job*; New York: Bantam Doubleday Dell, 1993. This is an excellent primer on discovering a new approach to "work" in general. The author's approach dovetails with many of the ideas found in *Financial Freedom aFloat*.

## WEB SITES OF INTEREST

Working Solo, Inc.
P.O. Box 190
New Paltz, NY 12561
Phone: 914-255-7165
Fax: 914-255-2116
e-mail: office@workingsolo.com
Web site: http://www.workingsolo.com

> A well-done resource center featuring newsletters, books, and seminars on many aspects of entreprenuership.

# RESOURCES FOR PEOPLE INTERESTED IN VOLUNTEER WORK

## BOOKS ON VOLUNTEERING

Downey, Adrienne. *Volunteer: The Comprehensive Guide to Voluntary Service in the U. S. & Abroad.* New York: The Council on International Educational Exchange, 1995. Another guide to opportunities available.

Pybus, Victoria. *The International Directory of Voluntary Work,* 6th ed. Oxford: Vacation Work, Princeton, NJ. A worldwide directory of agencies who use volunteer workers.

Raynolds, John F. *Beyond Success.* New York: MasterMedia, 1988. A useful primer for anyone thinking of getting involved in volunteer work.

## USEFUL WEB SITES

Action Without Borders
Web site: http://www.idealist.org

> A huge site that lists over 17,000 nonprofit non-governmental organizations (NGO's) in over 130 countries around the world. Also publishes *Ideas in Action,* a free monthly newsletter. All in all an excellent resource, and a good place to start in a search for volunteer opportunities.

Voluntary Work Information Service
Web site: http://www.workingabroad.com

A Swiss organization that specializes in providing personalized information about opportunities to people interested in volunteering. In addition, they publish four region-specific guides, for Asia, Latin America, The Middle East, and Europe.

A World Directory of Development Organizations and Programs
Web site: http://www.coop4coop.org

Select Nonprofit Organizations on the Internet
Web site: http://www.ai.mit.edu/people/ellens/non.html

Development Links
Web site: http://europa.eu.int/comm/development/index.htm

How to apply for volunteer jobs overseas
Web site: http://www.oneworld.org/vso/volunt/apply.htm

# INDEX

# FINANCIAL FREEDOM AFLOAT ONLINE

Every book is out of date the day it is printed. For a book like this, in which much of the content is extremely topical, trying to stay up-to-date in print is a futile task. To address this, I have recently launched a Web site to complement the book. This site, http://www.freedomafloat.com, will provide a way for me to update my readers on the latest changes in working conditions around the world, technology advances of use to working cruisers, and other related devlopments.

More than just a platform for my opinions, however, http://www.freedomafloat.com will serve as a forum for cruisers who are actually out there, doing it, to share their experiences with the cruising community. Real information, from real cruisers, at close to real time; check it out.


Charles

## About the Author

Since leaving New York City in 1986, Charles Tuller has lived the lifestyle described in *Financial Freedom aFloat*. He and his wife, Maggie Purnell, have sailed their 61-year-old cutter *Fomalhaut* extensively in the Caribbean, Atlantic and Mediterranean. When not sailing or exploring ashore Tuller can be found teaching English, restoring classic yachts, and writing. He has written for numerous sailing magazines, including *Yachting Monthly*, *SAIL*, and *Cruising World*. This is his first book.

*Fomalhaut.*

## OTHER TITLES AVAILABLE FROM
## SEAWORTHY PUBLICATIONS

| | | | |
|---|---|---|---|
| ☐ | 0-9675905-0-7 | SPANISH FOR CRUISERS | $24.95 |
| ☐ | 0-9639566-7-1 | THE EXUMA GUIDE: 2nd Edition | $29.95 |
| ☐ | 0-9639566-9-8 | ON AND OFF THE BEATEN PATH, THE CENTRAL AND SOUTHERN BAHAMAS GUIDE | $34.95 |
| ☐ | 1-892399-02-4 | THE ABACO GUIDE | $29.95 |
| ☐ | 1-892399-01-6 | THE TURKS AND CAICOS GUIDE | $22.95 |
| ☐ | 0-9639566-3-9 | THE PANAMA GUIDE | $39.95 |
| ☐ | 1-892399-00-8 | CHARTRACKER TO THE ICW: NORFOLK TO JACKSONVILLE | $39.95 |
| ☐ | 1-892399-03-2 | WE FOLLOWED ODYSSEUS | $27.95 |
| ☐ | 0-9639566-4-7 | TWO ON A BIG OCEAN | $15.95 |
| ☐ | 0-9639566-5-5 | ALWAYS A DISTANT ANCHORAGE | $15.95 |
| ☐ | 0-9639566-6-3 | CHASING THE LONG RAINBOW | $15.95 |
| ☐ | 1-892399-05-9 | TWO AGAINST CAPE HORN      (VIDEO) | $22.95 |
| ☐ | 1-892399-04-0 | WHISPER'S PACIFIC VOYAGE      (VIDEO) | $22.95 |
| ☐ | 1-929006-00-4 | SAILING DESIGNS – VOLUME 1 | $14.95 |
| ☐ | 1-929006-01-2 | SAILING DESIGNS – VOLUME 2 | $18.95 |
| ☐ | 1-929006-02-0 | SAILING DESIGNS – VOLUME 3 | $24.95 |
| ☐ | 1-929006-03-9 | SAILING DESIGNS – VOLUME 4 | $29.95 |
| ☐ | 1-929006-04-7 | SAILING DESIGNS – VOLUME 5 | $39.95 |
| ☐ | 1-892399-06-7 | FINANCIAL FREEDOM aFLOAT | $19.95 |
| ☐ | 0-9639566-2-0 | THE MEATLESS GALLEY COOKBOOK | $16.95 |
| ☐ | 0-9639566-0-4 | LIGHTNING AND BOATS | $ 9.95 |

If you would like more information about any of the above titles, please call, or visit our Web site.

*Seaworthy Publications, Inc.*
507 Sunrise Drive
Port Washington, WI 53074
Phone:  262-268-9250
Fax:  262-268-9208
e-mail:  publisher@seaworthy.com
Web site:  http://www.seaworthy.com